Supply Market Intelligence for Procurement Professionals

Research, Process, and Resources

Jeanette Jones
Kelly Barner

J. ROSS PUBLISHING

ISBN-13: 978-1-60427-101-0

Printed and bound in the U.S.A. Printed on acid-free paper.

10 9 8 7 6 5 4 3 2 1

Library of Congress Cataloging-in-Publication Data

Jones, Jeanette.
Supply market intelligence for procurement professionals : research, process, and resources / by Jeanette Jones and Kelly Barner.
pages cm
Includes bibliographical references and index.
ISBN 978-1-60427-101-0 (hardcover : alk. paper) 1. Business logistics. 2. Business intelligence. I. Barner, Kelly, 1978- II. Title.
HD38.5.J664 2015
658.7'2--dc23
2014037480

Direct all inquiries to J. Ross Publishing, Inc., 300 S. Pine Island Rd., Suite 305, Plantation, FL 33324.

Phone: (954) 727-9333
Fax: (561) 892-0700
Web: www.jrosspub.com

DEDICATION

To Don, Pat, Ben, and G & G—always in my heart.

Jeanette Jones

To my Dad, who always told me that I can do anything I set my mind to, and who has never been wrong.

Kelly Barner

CONTENTS

LIST OF FIGURES AND TABLES

PREFACE

> Knowledge is of two kinds. We know a subject ourselves, or we know where we can find information upon it.
> —*Samuel Johnson, 1775*[1]

The scope of procurement's responsibilities varies widely by organization and industry. Traditional tasks include soliciting bids, negotiating contracts, and managing distributed buying activity. In addition to these responsibilities, procurement manages a number of strategic initiatives, including supply chain risk mitigation, collaboration and innovation with suppliers, regulatory compliance, and the outsourcing of non-core functions.

In many organizations, procurement has evolved from a tactical, transaction-oriented purchasing department into a strategic function responsible for establishing spend management objectives for the entire organization. While the tools they use and the skills they possess have increased overall effectiveness and efficiency, procurement's internal reputation has not evolved at the same rate. As a result, many procurement organizations struggle to reposition or rebrand themselves internally, looking to establish a value-based focus for their objectives and performance metrics.

In many cases, procurement's ability to contribute to a competitive profit margin is less bound by their talent and capacity than it is by how well they are able to market their capabilities internally. The goal is for procurement to position themselves in such a way that the rest of the organization recognizes their full potential and relevance to corporate competitiveness.

Internal perspectives of procurement cannot be changed without positive executive-level relationships. Earning the respect and consideration of the C-level requires that procurement demonstrate their relevance by delivering unique competencies. The transformation of procurement's reputation must be directly associated with their ability to generate measurable value.

Supply market intelligence creation is just such a capability for generating measurable value. It offers the ability to improve procurement's own results, as well as to contribute to other efforts in the organization, such as risk mitigation, merger and acquisition activities, and the identification of competitive threats from both expected and unexpected sources. Supply market intelligence adds an external context to the internal information procurement holds, improving their understanding and value potential simultaneously.

This book provides procurement professionals with the process, skills, and resources to develop a supply market intelligence program that will deliver value to the organization as a whole. We will clearly explain each of the concepts we introduce, and then provide the background and steps required to make their execution possible. Developing the skills required to build and use supply market intelligence has value to the organization through its positive impact on current supply management activities. It also improves executive level regard for the procurement function by demonstrating a market-driven perspective of the company.

Every company's competitiveness must be evaluated in the context of their industry, the economy, changes in supply markets, and expectations of the customer base. When procurement emphasizes their ability to track and respond to contextual forces through supply market intelligence, they simultaneously position themselves as a function with critical capabilities, and improve their performance as measured through realized savings and spend under management.

The authors of this book have decades of experience in conducting research to support procurement teams and as procurement practitioners themselves. We firmly believe that a market-driven approach to supply management presents a huge opportunity for procurement professionals and the organizations for which they manage spend.

Although procurement teams are traditionally regarded as watchdogs of the corporate bottom line, their priorities and objectives are subject to the same market forces that affect the top line. Supply availability, regulatory compliance, emerging markets, and shifts in addressable market affect a company's sales and purchasing activities simultaneously. Procurement's performance is highly contextual, whether they realize it or not. By recognizing and embracing the importance of this context, procurement can drive the decisions and priorities of the organization from a position of intelligence-based authority.

The Internet makes information available quickly and in large quantities. However, it is easy to get frustrated with search results that are either too high level or not specific enough. When information is acquired through fee for use databases or reports, the information used for critical decision making can be very expensive. Leveraging the wrong resources leads to inefficiency, and may result in procurement paying too much for information that is not on target. Doing an initial search that requires no investment of funds is the best way to satisfy intelligence needs on a budget or improve the actionability of fee-based information. Ultimately, it is the actions that result from well-crafted intelligence that create value and, therefore, quality and accuracy are key concerns.

THE STRUCTURE OF THIS BOOK

In 2013, Jeanette Jones published *Information and Research Resources for Procurement Professionals.* Her goal was to help procurement professionals find information to support strategic sourcing, supplier management, and purchasing activities. No sooner had she published the book than she realized how much more content there was to cover, and how many procurement organizations were interested in applying research and analysis techniques to their management of supply markets.

Jones made the decision to write an expanded second edition, and to bring on a co-author who could contribute additional insight into how procurement can benefit from access to improved supply market intelligence. Kelly Barner's time as a procurement practitioner and consultant have given her a clear perspective of the opportunity that exists for procurement teams as well as the process, governance, and ownership models required to sustain results. This book, *Supply Market Intelligence for Procurement Professionals: Research, Process, and Resources*, is the result of their combined efforts.

Part I: Supply Market Intelligence Program Design, outlines how to design a supply market intelligence program that meets the needs of the organization, while integrating with existing procurement team structures and processes. Building internal capabilities makes it possible to maintain the benefits of supply market intelligence, without making long-term investments in consultants with specific category expertise. If decisions are to be supply market intelligence driven, it is critical to ensure that the information gathered is accurate. Proper governance is required to continually review the veracity of sources and the recommendations made as a result of them. Part I consists of:

- **Chapter 1: Overview of Supply Market Intelligence**
  We provide a foundational explanation of supply market intelligence by breaking it down into its parts, and then exploring them in reverse: first defining *intelligence*, then considering the evolving nature of *markets*, and finally, transitioning to the many perspectives on *supply management.* Of the three terms, *intelligence* is the most ambiguous, but definitions

of markets and best practices for managing sources of supply are rapidly evolving, as well. Despite the challenges associated with capturing and articulating the relevance of supply, markets, and intelligence in their own right, the ultimate goal is for procurement to create an environment where the three intersect to their full potential.

- **Chapter 2: Supply Market Intelligence and the Procurement System**
  This chapter addresses how supply market intelligence intersects with, or advances the efforts associated with, procurement initiatives, such as strategic sourcing, category management, supplier relationship management, supplier collaboration, risk assessment and mitigation, spend analysis and opportunity assessment, and procurement transformation. The creation of supply market intelligence is not a new initiative, but rather an approach to improve all initiatives that are already underway. It also provides an opportunity for procurement to demonstrate their value potential through an understanding of the external factors that influence the organization as a whole.
- **Chapter 3: Supply Market Intelligence Creation Process**
  The process for creating supply market intelligence within a specific procurement effort, such as a sourcing project or supplier performance review, consists of four steps, plus an internal approval hurdle. The steps are:

  1. Identify and Define
  2. Research, Read, and Refine
  3. Analyze, and
  4. Document.

  Between Analyze and Document, we advocate pausing to discuss conclusions and recommendations within procurement, before finalized intelligence documentation is shared with stakeholders outside of procurement. There are a few keys to success embedded within the details of this process, including how to get started and how to structure the information collected.
- **Chapter 4: Supply Market Intelligence Research Tactics**
  Beyond the process for creating supply market intelligence, it is important for procurement to build their knowledge of research techniques, proper documentation, and special cases (private companies, and research to validate vs. to discover). It is important to note that while we refer to "tactics," this process is anything but tactical. Creating supply market

intelligence requires critical thought, as well as the desire to learn more about whatever topic is being researched.

- **Chapter 5: The Business Case for Supply Market Intelligence**
  Beyond tactics for carrying out the creation of supply market intelligence, procurement organizations need to know how to manage supporting resources, skills, executive sponsorship, communication, knowledge management, and terminology. The program needs to be laid out purposefully, and properly staffed with qualified resources. Once intelligence is created, there must be a way to keep it current and make it accessible to all interested parties.
- **Chapter 6: Quality Assurance**
  Since the information collected during supply market research forms the basis for procurement's subsequent analysis, recommendations, and conclusions, it is essential that it be thoroughly screened. We outline how to determine quality factors, such as credibility, impartiality, timeliness, and motivation. In addition, we consider the need for knowledge management, when to pay for content or research assistance, and what to do when supply market intelligence does not prevent a negative outcome.

In Part II, Supply Market Intelligence Resources, Chapters 8 through 31, are detailed listings of resources available to procurement professionals who are looking to perform research in order to create supply market intelligence. Each chapter is organized by source type and industry, and highlights the best available resources, always with an eye for value and with the understanding of the crucial role that quality information plays in decision-making processes. For professionals new to research and the discipline of creating supply market intelligence, Part II will prove to be a trusted guide to a seemingly endless pool of resources, as well as a targeted quick reference for more experienced researchers.

A NOTE ON TERMINOLOGY

There are many views on the differences between the labels "purchasing," "procurement," "supply management," and "strategic sourcing." For the purposes of this book, *procurement* is defined by using the following explanation from *PurchasingInsight.com*:

> "To define procurement broadly, 'Procurement' is the overarching function that describes the activities and processes to acquire goods and services. Importantly, and distinct from 'purchasing,' procurement involves

> the activities involved in establishing fundamental requirements, sourcing activities such as market research and vendor evaluation and negotiation of contracts. It can also include the purchasing activities required to order and receive goods."[2]

We hope readers will seize the opportunity that exists professionally and organizationally if they place supply market information at the center of all procurement's efforts. Although supply market intelligence creation is not a typical part of procurement training and professional development, it is an achievable capability, and one that can be built on an individual level or as a group effort.

Jeanette Jones
Kelly Barner

REFERENCES

1. "Knowledge Is of Two Kinds," *The Quote Yard.* Accessed June 26, 2014. http://www.quoteyard.com/knowledge-is-of-two-kinds-we-know-a-subject-ourselves-or-we-know-where-we-can-find-information-upon-it.
2. "Definition of Procurement—Procurement vs. Purchasing," *Purchasing Insight*, November 21, 2010. http://procureinsights.wordpress.com/.

A NOTE FROM THE AUTHORS

Both authors, Jeanette Jones and Kelly Barner, are affiliated with some of the resources that are included in Part II, Supply Market Intelligence Resources. Jeanette Jones is the founder and owner of Cottrill Research, which is listed in Chapter 17, Procurement Blogs. Kelly Barner is the Managing Editor of *Buyers Meeting Point*, which is listed in Chapter 12, Procurement Service Provider Directories, Chapter 15, Procurement Websites, Networks, and Communities, and whose blog "The Point" is listed in Chapter 17.

We feel confident that we have not given our affiliated resources more coverage or attention than they are due. If anything, these sources may be under-represented, as they are such a familiar part of our professional landscape that we are more focused on identifying and profiling other resources.

We would also like to point out that none of the resources, services, sites, organizations, associations, or publications listed in this book have compensated us in return, nor have they previewed or approved the content beyond the details we used from their own website descriptions. We have made every effort to be comprehensive, thorough, and objective about selecting content for this book. Any error in description or identification is either unintentional or can be attributed to the natural changes and updates that take place in such offerings and their associated URLs.

—Jeanette Jones

—Kelly Barner

ABOUT THE AUTHORS

JEANETTE JONES

Jeanette Jones has more than twenty years of experience providing corporate business and strategic sourcing research services. Jones is the founder of Cottrill Research, which is a provider of supply market intelligence research services.

Her corporate experience includes establishing libraries with research functions for Arthur Andersen and the IT Vendor Management Group at Bank One (JP Morgan Chase), and providing research services for the Strategic Sourcing Group at Wachovia. In these positions, she routinely researched and wrote about industry and market trends and events, enabling consultants and procurement professionals to make informed critical decisions.

In addition to corporate expertise, Jones has academic experience, including serving as an adjunct professor at Ohio Dominican University, where she taught a Special Libraries class for the Library and Information Sciences Department. She has also taught research and information literacy skills to students at Collin College and College of Southern Nevada. She has authored detailed research guides, covering the subject areas of business, supply chain management, hotel management, casino management, and culinary arts/food and beverage management. She maintains the Cottrill Research Blog, which provides news and analysis about the latest research and information resource offerings for procurement professionals.

Jones earned a Master of Library Science degree from Kent State University, and is a member of the Association of Independent Information Professionals, Special Libraries Association, and Institute for Supply Management.

KELLY BARNER

Kelly Barner is the Managing Editor of *Buyers Meeting Point*, an online resource for procurement and purchasing professionals. Barner has a decade of experience working in procurement and supply chain management. Her unique perspective on supply management is based on her time as a practitioner, a consultant at a solution provider, and as an independent thought leader.

Barner's introduction to procurement was in the not-for-resale (indirect) procurement organization for a global grocery retailer. While there, she developed a specialization in sourcing location-based and corporate services. After earning an MBA, she took a position on the consulting team at Emptoris, a procurement solution and services provider that was acquired by IBM in 2011. She has led projects involving members of procurement, supplier, and purchasing teams, and has practical skills in strategic sourcing program design and management, opportunity assessment, knowledge management, and custom taxonomy design.

Barner is a popular and regular guest content contributor to publications and blogs, such as Procurement Insights, the American Purchasing Society Journal, the eSourcing Forum, and the ThomasNet *IMT Procurement Journal*. Since 2011, she has delivered a weekly procurement Internet radio update, which covers the coming week's events, and a guest soundbite with editorial commentary.

Barner earned a Masters of Business Administration (MBA) degree from Babson College, a Master in Library and Information Science (MLIS) from Simmons College, and Bachelor of Arts in English and History degrees from Clark University. In 2012, 2013, and 2014, she was awarded a Provider "Pro to Know" designation by *Supply & Demand Chain Executive* magazine; and, in 2013, she was recognized as one of 28 "Top Female Supply Chain Executives."

Web Added Value™

This book has free material available for download from the Web Added Value™ resource center at *www.jrosspub.com*

Tools that enhance the learning experience and give readers an opportunity to apply what they have learned. That is why we offer ancillary materials available for download on this book and all participating Web Added Value™ publications. These online resources may include interactive versions of material that appears in the book or supplemental templates, worksheets, models, plans, case studies, proposals, spreadsheets and assessment tools, among other things. Whenever you see the WAV™ symbol in any of our publications, it means bonus materials accompany the book and are available from the Web Added Value Download Resource Center at www.jrosspub.com.

Downloads available for *Supply Market Intelligence for Procurement Professionals: Research, Process, and Resources* consist of:

- Supply Market Intelligence Process Diagrams: *Supply Market Perspectives, Supply Market Intelligence Process*, and *Information Needs by Procurement Initiative.*
- Logistics Quick View Analysis Chart: The logistics spend category is supported by a voluminous amount of statistical and regulatory data that is available from global organizations, national government agencies, professional associations, and trade literature. The areas that fall under the logistics umbrella—general logistics, trade, transportation, materials handling, warehousing and corrugated—are all represented in this chart of resources, which can be quickly viewed and used as a starting point for research. The chart lists key representative resources for each area.
- Regular updates of important new resources that are related to the chapters in Part II and have been vetted by the authors and are considered authoritative and relevant to procurement.
- Regular updates to the resource entries in Part II that reflect the anticipated changes due to the nature of the content, which can become quickly outdated. As stated in Chapter 7, it is likely that at the time of this book's publication, there will be sources listed in Part II where a website's design, content, or address will have been changed, upgraded or enhanced.

- "Business, Strategy, and Management Classics That Have Influenced the Discipline of Procurement": The classics that have strongly influenced the discipline of business management, and in turn the discipline of procurement, are listed here with commentary.
- "Books for the Procurement Professional's Bookshelf": Selected titles recommended by the authors for procurement professionals to include in their personal libraries.

PART I

SUPPLY MARKET INTELLIGENCE PROGRAM DESIGN

1

OVERVIEW OF SUPPLY MARKET INTELLIGENCE

It is important to have an actionable definition of any approach in order for it to be successfully implemented in an organization. Therefore, we start our book with this definition of supply market intelligence:

> *Supply market intelligence* is created when external information is collected and analyzed to form actionable conclusions that affect a company's ability to strategically locate, secure, and manage sources of supply.

This book is for procurement practitioners, who are the front line managers and individual contributors working to improve the use of corporate resources, as well as category managers and Chief Procurement Officers (CPOs). As a result, we will balance the book's focus between execution and management.

In this chapter, we provide a foundational explanation of supply market intelligence by breaking it down into its parts, and then exploring its terms in reverse:

1. Defining *intelligence*,
2. Considering the evolving nature of *markets*, and
3. Transitioning to the multiple perspectives on *supply* management.

Of the three terms, *intelligence* is the most ambiguous, but definitions of markets and best practices for managing sources of supply are rapidly evolving, as well. Despite the challenges associated with capturing and articulating the relevance of supply, markets, and intelligence in their own right, the ultimate goal is for procurement to create an environment where the three intersect to their full potential.

INTELLIGENCE

As stated above, intelligence is an abstract concept. The term has a different meaning in each situation where it is invoked. In the context of procurement, *intelligence* is the strategic, context-sensitive interpretation of information relevant to managing contracts, suppliers, and spend categories. Procurement professionals manage both internal and external intelligence in the regular course of their duties. Internal intelligence is based on a combination of historical spend, forward-looking budgets, and corporate strategies for growth, consolidation, and reorganization. External supply market intelligence is driven by information from outside of the organization, deemed relevant based on each company's unique perspective. The input required to create external intelligence comes from sources such as incumbent and prospective suppliers, industry analysts, databases, and news resources. When created effectively and applied appropriately, supply market intelligence represents an undeniable competitive advantage for an organization.

Nothing that creates a measurable advantage is easy to come by, and intelligence is no exception. Although source information is often easily and (over) abundantly available, crafting intelligence requires a sustained investment of time and resources. Intelligence is not big, fast, or loud. It cannot be achieved just by collecting vast amounts of data, nor are its advantages revealed quickly or obviously to the casual observer. Information does not become intelligence until it has been read, qualified, and considered. The process of converting information into intelligence is influenced by a number of inputs, and therefore, is often based on trends rather than data that represents a single point in time. This combination of information filtering and analysis takes skill and effort to complete because it is performed in pursuit of a nuanced idea that has not yet materialized in the minds of the professionals seeking it.

The combination of information and analysis that lead to intelligence are not to be taken for granted. Reliable resources and methods are required to gather the relevant, quality information that ultimately provides the spark that becomes intelligence. Information is a raw material that must be collected and processed. The quality of this raw material and procurement's interpretation of it are just as critical as they would be in any manufacturing or development process. As such, governance standards and processes should be established to ensure that only accurate, verifiable information and objective analysis are incorporated into the intelligence creation process. The pressure to become more strategic may lead procurement teams to turn their backs on tactical efforts, believing that they are less important. A choice does not need to be made between tactical and strategic; effective teams develop a long-term strategy and then outline the short-term, tactical steps required to execute it.

As desirable as intelligence is, it is not knowledge or information, and therefore, cannot be proven accurate in advance of a business decision based on it. There is inherent risk in the process of intelligence creation. There are endless examples of bad intelligence throughout history, many of which proved costly for the people and organizations that acted upon it. For example, in the late 19th century, J. P. Morgan invested heavily in Thomas Edison's direct current (DC) model for electricity. Nikola Tesla, one of Edison's former employees, invented a competing model called alternating current (AC). Morgan was a cautious investor, and he asked Edison if the competitive threat from AC was real. Edison disregarded AC as unsafe and assured Morgan that his own invention would be the prevailing technology. As a result of Edison's assurances, Morgan continued to make sizable investments in DC. Unfortunately for both men, Edison was wrong. In a series of bids where the two technologies competed head to head, including the 1893 World's Fair in Chicago and the 1895 installation of an electric power generating plant at Niagara Falls, AC was selected as the preferred form of electricity, and remains the standard to the present day.[1]

J. P. Morgan received nonobjective, inaccurate intelligence from Edison and acted on it in a series of decisions that cost him in excess of $83 million in today's dollars. The scientific details regarding how the AC and DC systems operated, along with their respective advantages and shortcomings, did not directly motivate Morgan's investments. It was Edison's interpretation of the competitive threat from AC as minimal and fleeting that served as the intelligence behind Morgan's decision to invest. Although Edison was far from objective, his expertise in the emerging technology of electricity qualified him as a source of supply market intelligence. Had there been a less involved third party available to validate the information and Edison's analysis and recommendations, Morgan might have made a different decision.

This historical example demonstrates the difference between information and intelligence. It also serves as a cautionary tale for creators of supply market intelligence and those who rely upon it. As the authors of the Wright Interface Blog summarized, "If J. P. Morgan would have listened more to his father's advice and took [sic] more time to get to know Edison's team at the time, he could have had analysts perform a third-party review that would have saved millions in J. P. Morgan investments and would have resulted in much faster profits for J. P. Morgan."[2] The perspective of the person responsible for performing the research and analysis has a direct impact on the quality of the intelligence created as a result. That person serves an important role with regard to the information that will become intelligence in the form of risks, recommendations, and trends. The professional in this position filters, analyzes, synthesizes, interprets, and defines action items. As shown later in this chapter, the importance of *perspective* creates an opportunity for procurement to amass supply market intelligence even when there is expertise elsewhere in the company.

Although this reliance on the perspective and capabilities of a person or team leaves the door open to the misinterpretation of information, there are few if any comprehensive, viable alternatives. Intelligence will always involve judgment calls, both in the analysis of information and in the execution of the resulting recommendations. The intelligence creation process cannot be automated using technology because of the subjective understanding required to conduct research and process the results. Professionals conducting research must understand the motivating business conditions, as well as the information being considered and how they intersect, in order to arrive at relevant conclusions on behalf of the organization.

Some research can be outsourced or conducted by a consulting firm or services partner, but having an understanding of the relevant nuances gives an edge to an internal resource. Budget limitations may even prevent third parties from being relied upon for ongoing research and analysis. Procurement's need for supply market intelligence does not end with the signing of a supply contract. Intelligence is regularly relied upon during the term of any agreement to manage supplier performance, evaluate new alternatives, revisit delivery timing, and optimize relationships between the buying organization and suppliers. Building the in-house capability to gather information and convert it into usable intelligence presents an opportunity for the organization as a whole, for procurement as a function, and for the individual possessing or developing the skills.

The subjective, context sensitive nature of intelligence expands the career possibilities for professionals with the skills required to conduct research and then apply critical thought to the information gathered so that it becomes usable intelligence. The internal applications for these skills are numerous. Each opportunity to leverage supply market intelligence improves the abilities of the person creating it and increases their value to the organization. As cited in The Organization for Economic Co-operation and Development (2011), "Leiponen (2000) found that, in contrast to non-innovating firms, innovators' profitability was significantly influenced by the amount of higher education, higher technical skills and research skills possessed by employees."[3] When these skills are embedded within the procurement function, the combination of external understanding and internal visibility has direct bottom-line impact. Beyond the financial rewards, the opportunity exists to differentiate the company's offering in the marketplace, and improve top-line performance, something included in an increasing number of procurement organizations' performance goals.

It is not unusual for professionals to find themselves in procurement after an unexpected twist in their career path, as opposed to a purposefully selected destination. As a result, talent acquisition, management, and retention are always high priority challenges for CPOs. In some cases, these professionals had not previously found the right environment for their skills, and they flourish in procurement. They learn to evolve in order to become successful individual contributors. There are a wide range of skills that are assets in procurement, including analysis, cost modeling, and negotiation. In addition to these "hard" skills, soft skills such as communication, creativity, and project management are critical to procurement's success. When any subset of these capabilities is combined with a general interest in learning how things work and why, empowering a person to answer their own questions through research leads to greatly improved results.

Just as procurement professionals often learn how to source on the job, it is realistic to expect that a person with the desire to develop their skills can learn how to conduct secondary market research in the same way. This is especially true when the motivation for the research is the pursuit of intelligence that can be immediately applied to a task at hand. When supply market intelligence capabilities are layered on top of existing knowledge of the processes and disciplines required to source products and services, the results can be surprisingly good. Research and analysis are best performed with a solid understanding of the end purpose as well as sufficient subject matter expertise.

An even better approach ensures the person doing the research has a vested interest in applying the resulting intelligence to improve their own job performance. Owning the process of creating intelligence provides procurement with an incentive to dig deeper into relevant supply markets, and for the rest of the organization to support them in their efforts and trust their recommendations.

An important distinction should be made between analyzing information in the context of creating intelligence and the process of conducting spend analysis—a discipline most procurement professionals are familiar with. When internal data sets and third-party data enrichment are combined during spend analysis, the resulting conclusions usually take the same quantitative form as the information on which they are based. Technology and automation are requirements for making spend analysis implementations and timely refreshes possible. With supply market intelligence, qualitative and quantitative elements are combined during the analysis process. The resulting intelligence reflects the qualities of both, creating a context specific combination of data and subjective information. While spend analysis has long been supported by a number of well-designed technology solutions, there is no corresponding tool for analysis in the pursuit of supply market intelligence. The closest resources assist professionals in accessing information (fee for use databases) or in managing the physical deliverables created as a result (knowledge management applications).

The quantitative, or measurable, information commonly used by procurement includes supplier financial data, market growth trends, raw material pricing, and currency conversion rates. Qualitative information is not captured as succinctly, but carries equal weight in the intelligence creation process. This information provides insight into emerging markets, competitive technologies, the implications of regulatory requirements, and innovative applications of existing solutions. Qualitative information enables the foresight required to craft a visionary supply management strategy. Neither type of information can be used in isolation to generate supply market intelligence. Qualitative information without data lacks substance and validation. Quantitative information without context does not reflect the full potential or risk level of the situation at hand. It is in their consideration and combination that quantitative and qualitative information are able to inform corporate supply strategy.

As we have said, intelligence is not big, fast, or loud, but it is also not fact. There is inherent risk when a judgment call has to be made that no amount of research or analysis will ever overcome. Within that risk exists the opportunity for differentiation. No other company in a market will see information or perform analysis in the same way because it is tied directly to the long-term strategy, internal view, and market position of the company in question. Certainty is an unreasonable expectation in today's rapidly evolving business climate, and decisions must be made in accordance with the best intelligence available at each moment. All information gathering and analysis must be done with an eye to the actionability of the conclusions and recommendations because only in its application does intelligence truly exist. When decisions are influenced as a result of research, the supply market intelligence process is complete. The company that does the best job riding the unpredictable tides of their supply markets is the company with the greatest potential for growth, innovation, and shareholder value creation.

MARKETS

In the most general sense, markets are groups of sources where companies locate the products and services they need in order to operate. They are also where companies sell their solutions or finished products. Just as each company must identify their addressable or available market as a way of assessing demand and determining revenue potential, they must also define the relevant markets when looking for a specific source of supply.

In the past, markets have been bound by traditional industry definitions and dominated by large players. Geography and the relative size and corresponding negotiating leverage of the buying and supplying organizations were defining factors, as well. A company's market share reflects "the percentage that a company has of the total sales for a particular product or service"[4] and demonstrates the strength of the connection between a company's identity and the sphere in which they actively compete.

In *The End of Competitive Advantage*, Columbia Business School professor and strategy expert Rita Gunther McGrath discussed the requirement that businesses today be dynamic in order to compete, simultaneously looking for new markets to enter and watching for unexpected competitive threats. She illustrated this dynamic by highlighting the contrast between Sony and Apple in the music industry. This case shows how an established player (Sony) can quickly lose control of a market to a newcomer (Apple). According to McGrath (2013), "Sony provides a clear cautionary tale. It yielded dominance in portable music to Apple."[5] No one would have expected Apple, a company historically focused on hardware devices and operating systems, to enter the music content business, let alone to undercut the prevailing physical delivery model of CDs with an entirely digital approach.

As electronic commerce improved and logistics costs fell, companies were able to expand their addressable markets. This expansion had a correspondingly positive impact on revenue, as new companies became prospective customers. These changes also required prevailing ideas about market share to become more flexible. Companies started competing in geographies that were previously beyond their reach. They also started marketing their products and solutions based on successful applications rather than remaining bound by traditional industries.

> One of the biggest changes we need to make in our assumptions is that within-industry competition is the most significant competitive threat.… It isn't that industries have stopped being relevant; it's just that using industry as a level of analysis is often not fine-grained enough to determine what is really going on at the level at which decisions need to be made.[6]

The changes seen in the strategies, techniques, and technologies of modern companies are reflected in the markets they are a part of, as well as the markets they source from. When growing levels of competition are viewed from procurement's perspective, they translate into an indication of the potential for price compression. An increase in the number of qualified supply options gives procurement better negotiating leverage, and forces competing suppliers to improve or differentiate their offerings in order to stay competitive. Taking advantage of such an opportunity requires a well-informed procurement function. Procurement must evaluate traditional industry players as well as new entrants and alternative solutions for each bid. New market entrants now include not only startups or emerging economies, but cross industry sources of supply. The resulting competitive pressure can be applied in a number of ways, but only when procurement knows of their existence, and is able to structure bids so that nontraditional solutions are not disadvantaged because they don't fit in the expected box.

The process for turning information into intelligence through analysis hinges on the perspective of the person conducting the research. In the same way, the definition created for the relevant market reflects the understanding of the individual responsible for managing a category of spend or a group of suppliers. It is no longer sufficient to define a source market by looking at incumbent or well-known suppliers and inviting their primary competitors to bid against them. Rather than basing forward-looking requirements on a historical contract, procurement should allow the business' needs to serve as the center point, with any viable solution, regardless of industry, and in some cases location, receiving due consideration in the bid process. The market for any spend category should be objectively identified, taking particular care that the definition does not impose artificial limitations on supplier participation resulting from traditional thinking.

Approaching supply markets with an open mind is not easy. It requires a clear understanding of the identified need, as well as of all of the solutions that may be qualified options. It also presents a strong opportunity for the application of supply market intelligence in procurement, and since markets continue to change, category expertise is harder to maintain today than it was in the past. Even experienced category managers should strive for a fresh perspective on the suppliers and solutions that are viable candidates for their business, whether they were traditionally considered part of the industry in question or not.

Another impact of changing supply markets takes place in the second tier of the supply chain, which is made up of a company's suppliers' suppliers. As shifts occur in how second tier supply partners source and pay for their raw materials and supporting services, there are corresponding changes in the cost drivers of first tier supply partners. An effective bid process increases visibility into all elements of price and cost. Whenever possible, it is ideal to have all prequalified suppliers provide insight into their cost structures and profit margins so that negotiations can take a "cost plus" approach like the model often used with services. Efficient suppliers will make use of the best available supply options just as procurement professionals strive to do on behalf of their own company. Suppliers that hold the same attitudes about resource efficiency as their customers do will make the best business partners.

As procurement looks to identify the suppliers that offer them a competitive edge, they need to build their understanding of the markets in play. Depending on the context, and their level of experience in managing a given spend category, procurement may examine a market from the top down or bottom up. There are other authoritative perspectives of markets that come into play as procurement seeks to become better informed. Analysts provide an outside in view of a market by building a broad understanding of all the players in a space, and tracking changes in the influence and innovation associated with long-time market dominators, as well as new market disruptors. Suppliers, including incumbent and prospective business partners, have an inside out view of a market, and have their own incentives for understanding the competitive pressures from traditional sources and new market entrants. The extent to which procurement can combine these four approaches to define a market—up, down, in, out—as shown in Figure 1.1, will determine their ability to maximize the potential of the associated spend and to consider all possible alternatives.

When procurement looks at a market from the top down, they start with a general understanding of an industry or broad group of well-known suppliers. This approach is common in spend categories new to the company, where there are no incumbent suppliers under contract, or when procurement has not previously had access to manage the spend. If the spend has not been contracted in the past, the intelligence opportunity for procurement is significantly larger, as there may not be experience with the market elsewhere in the company. This means that their internal stakeholders are free from the "baggage" associated with traditional thinking and incumbent supplier relationships. As the market comes into focus, procurement will segment the suppliers into groups or types of companies and compile knowledge about relevant associations, cost drivers, and new developments or substantiated risks. This learning is weighed against corporate requirements to better define minimum qualifications for supplier participation. Finally, procurement selects the subset of the market that best fits their business requirements, and continues to develop an increasingly granular understanding, until they have identified the suppliers that will be invited to compete for a contract and gathered the necessary information to collect pricing.

The opposite approach is taken when procurement defines a market from the bottom up. This is a supply- or supplier-driven exercise, and starts with the companies that are known to be relevant. Procurement then backs up to increasingly higher-level perspectives that not only include other qualified companies and products, but also reveals the forces at play in the market as a whole. It is those

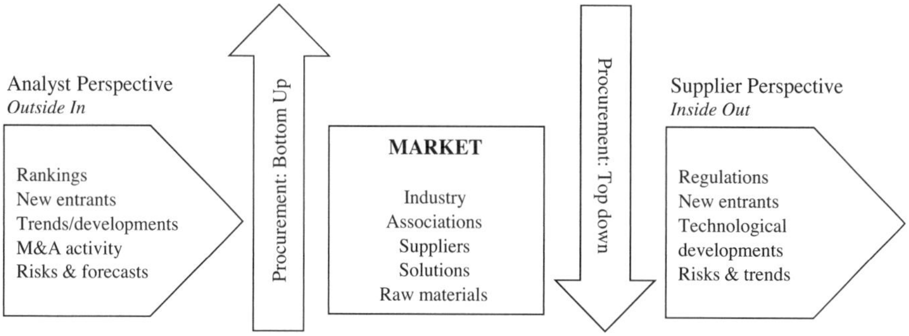

Figure 1.1 Supply market perspectives

forces that procurement will need to understand in their effort to document the risk profile, cost structure, negotiating leverage, and relative opportunity represented by the category of spend. When procurement is compiling intelligence about a market where contracts already exist, the day-to-day managers of the contract are likely to have relevant expertise that should be taken into account. This is not, however, a substitute for procurement developing their own understanding. As in the example of J. P. Morgan, Edison, and DC electricity, the perspective of the person providing market intelligence is crucial. Procurement's objectivity may open the door to savings and value that internal stakeholders would rather not have to consider. As Payne and Dorn (2012), the authors of *Managing Indirect Spend,* wrote, "What end users probably cannot give you, but may think they can, is an objective perspective of the marketplace as a whole."[7] Balancing the need to build relevant intelligence with the politically savvy ability to make internal stakeholders feel respected is a constant challenge for procurement.

Procurement teams are often organized around categories of spend. These are high-level portions of the company's expenditures, and they loosely match the organizational structure of the operations portion of the company. Examples of these categories are maintenance, repair, and operations (MRO), logistics, hired services, marketing, capital equipment, information technology, and indirect (or not for resale) goods. Each company has their own category structure and places more emphasis on the categories of particular importance to them in the form of increased granularity and procurement headcount. For example, a freight company will have far more purchasing activity around equipment parts, repair, and fuel than a banking or pharmaceutical company.

Procurement professionals associate themselves with a category of spend much like the company as a whole does with their target customers. While building up this expertise is critical, as soon as it prevents a person from objectively evaluating potential sources of supply, it has become more of a liability than an advantage. Individuals should beware of the same pitfalls that prevent companies from being flexible enough to survive shifts in consumer demand. If procurement is to be objective, while also maintaining good working relationships with their operational category counterparts, they need to strike the right balance of industry knowledge and reliance on process discipline.

The very idea of a *market* is in flux, and all indications are that we should expect nothing but continued change in the years to come. Companies must learn to adapt to more dynamic environments just as they have learned to take advantage of additional sources of supply in the form of new materials and emerging economies. The extension of modern supply chains has created a globally competitive landscape. This raises new challenges and opportunities that are felt on both the sales and procurement sides of every organization.

As competition for business increases, profit margins are driven down. In response, innovative companies look to increase efficiencies or experiment with alternate materials and delivery models. When this is not enough to fuel healthy revenue growth, companies must look further and with an open mind to increase their addressable market, finding new applications for the products and services they sell. This not only puts pressure on the sales force, it creates a competitive dynamic that well-informed procurement professionals can leverage to the benefit of the whole organization in the quest to manage their sources of supply better than the competition.

SUPPLY

From procurement's perspective, a company's spend is evidenced by the transactions for all of the products and services purchased in the course of operation. Since each organization has a finite amount of working capital that they are able to spend or invest in the most strategic way possible, procurement—as the steward of that capital—is best positioned to create a competitive advantage through its use.

At a high level, procurement is tasked with bringing as much spend under management as possible. The conditions required to consider spend 'under management' vary by organization. At a minimum, spend that is under management has been analyzed, competitively bid, and put under contract. Lower company margins demand elevated requirements for spend management techniques. "Broadly speaking, professional cost management practices have been adopted by industrial sectors in the sequence one might have expected. That is, the higher the proportion of a company's revenues that are spent with third parties, the greater the need to manage the spend professionally."[8] Bringing spend under management is so critical to the success of organizations that it is one of the top metrics used to track procurement's performance, in many cases second only to realized savings. That being said, not all spend is addressable, or eligible to be affected through the competitive bid process. Examples of non-addressable spend are taxes, tolls, postage, and some salaries. These categories of spend should be designated and isolated immediately when spend management strategies and baselines are established.

All of the remaining addressable spend is divided up using a category hierarchy and then associated with the appropriate function in the organization. The goal of this process is to ensure that, at least in theory, all spend is being actively managed by someone: procurement or otherwise. Ideally, procurement should have some role in managing all addressable spend, even if they are not responsible for making award decisions. Procurement is an objective internal third party, that can identify and enable spend management improvement opportunities through consistent processes, centralized technology, and of course, supply market intelligence. In some cases, the goal may be to include the same payment terms, service level agreements, and liability limitations in all contracts. In others, the benefits of having procurement manage all spend are associated with the solutions they administer, such as eSourcing, eProcurement, or ERP systems.

The benefit of having procurement serve as an internal consultancy, has led to the prevalence of the Center of Excellence (COE) model. This organizational model enables a relatively small yet strategic and empowered group of professionals to serve as a central anchor for the procurement processes, solutions, and results that allow purchases to be made in a distributed fashion throughout the organization. In a COE, procurement professionals may be dedicated to an industry or category of spend. Alternately, they may be industry generalists but process experts that are able to work across any number of categories. Often, procurement professionals combine strong general business skills with high-level category understanding. They then acquire relevant, highly-detailed category knowledge at the outset of each project. During the ramp-up for each sourcing effort, procurement benefits from the experience of their operational colleagues. They must also be prepared to investigate cost drivers, new solutions, and alternative sources of supply on their own for the purposes of validation and improvement.

There are common types of supply, although the categories of spend associated with each type vary by company and industry. There are also a variety of organizational models to be considered for procurement, and the size of the team relative to the amount of spend to be managed often determines how much ownership they will have. *Indirect spend,* or not for resale, is almost always owned by a centralized procurement function. Indirect spend is necessary for running the company, but does not go into the product or solution delivered to the company's customer base. *Direct spend,* on the other hand, is associated specifically with producing, manufacturing, and delivering the company's offerings to clients. Many companies also separate the handling of products and services, citing complexity concerns with services, although both types of spend benefit equally from strategic sourcing. Each type of spend or supply has unique internal requirements and is bid out, negotiated, and purchased in the context of relevant external markets.

Indirect spend includes office supplies, facility maintenance services, and temporary labor. These categories of spend are usually owned by procurement, and are often considered low-hanging fruit because they require relatively little effort to source and negotiate, but may deliver significant results through increased visibility and simple efficiencies. There is also less risk associated with switching suppliers and less internal attachment to incumbents. Despite this relative simplicity and ease of access, strategy and intelligence must play a role in indirect spend management. In many companies, categories of indirect spend have been overlooked as opportunities for value creation. As a result, completely new approaches to contract structure or materials use are available, resulting in significant savings for the organization from an unexpected source.

As an example of strategic results generated from an indirect spend category, the relationship between Procter & Gamble (P&G) and Jones Lang LaSalle, a commercial real estate services provider, was so transformational that it was featured in the book *Vested* by Kate Vitasek and Karl Manrodt (2012). Within that relationship, a "reinvention of the approach to facilities management potentially could save P&G a great deal of money, generate efficiencies and process standardization, and enable resources to focus on key priorities."[9] No one would say that P&G, a global consumer packaged-goods company, is in the facilities management business. Most of their customers interface with them through third-party retailers. However, this did not stop P&G from seeing the potential impact of a more strategic approach to managing this indirect spend category or from taking a risk to approach it in a truly innovative way.

Unlike indirect spend, direct spend is used in the creation or delivery of a company's core product or service. In P&G's case, this would include the chemicals, paper, and pulp used to make their products, as well as their consumer packaging. Due to the fact that direct spend categories and suppliers are critical to the operation, there are likely to be non-procurement professionals in the company that have deep experience in the relevant markets. In direct material sourcing projects, procurement needs to fully exercise their supply market intelligence capabilities in order to hold their own with internal stakeholders and to stand on equal footing with suppliers that understand their value to the business. While intelligence about a market may already exist internally, applying that understanding using a process as detailed as strategic sourcing or supplier relationship management may require additional research specific to the purpose, and procurement is best positioned to meet this need.

Beyond the ownership of a spend category by an internal function for operational reasons, products and services are often addressed differently. Products, whether they are part of direct or indirect spend, can be described quantitatively with specific measurements and specifications. Demand quantities are tied directly to sales projections or production estimates. Inventory management can be improved through internal efficiencies and properly structured restocking agreements with suppliers to provide further opportunities to save money and optimize working capital. Quality measures are a critical aspect of any material contract, as squeezing suppliers on price without specifying quality and design will result in unacceptably high levels of unusable product. The relevant supply market intelligence will be material, supplier, and source location focused.

Research must cover price volatility and product availability, as well as new materials and their impact on in-place processes and equipment.

Services, on the other hand, give many experienced procurement professionals pause. Yet with the right understanding and effort, services can be sourced like materials. Skills or capability requirements parallel the specifications seen with items. Demand is based on headcount or hourly effort estimates in place of unit count quantities. Quality measures are equally important, as are cost structures, and demand management is handled not through inventory but through internal approval processes and human resource policies. Just as pressing too hard on supplier margins results in poor quality products, forcing services contract pricing too low results in suppliers that hire minimally qualified people at lower rates in order to preserve their margins. For this reason, many services are bid using a "cost plus" model where the hourly wage paid to the worker is established up front but not negotiated between the buyer and supplier. Research and supply market intelligence for services includes skills shortages, new program management models, alternate source geographies, and going rates for the services and skills required.

One services model that requires a considerable amount of time from procurement is outsourcing. When an organization decides to outsource a function, they hand the associated tasks—and sometimes the employees—to a third-party provider. Usually, this is done because the third party can manage the function better and more cost effectively, leaving the company's direct employees to focus on the core business. When possible, the contract and cost structure governing such agreements should be tied to fixed deliverables. This properly motivates the supply partner to ensure a successful outcome with minimal administrative overhead. Supply market intelligence may include if and how other companies have outsourced a specific function, and what the benefits and complications are. Although outsourcing does not always mean offshoring, procurement must research the locations, both domestically and abroad, that can provide the skills required at a competitive cost, and balance the outsourcing against the risks and complications associated with time differences, language barriers, and intellectual property concerns.

Every type of supply that is purchased and used by an organization, whether a product or service, is better managed with an understanding of relevant markets. Many companies have grown through acquisition, as well as through organic means. As a result, procurement's first task is often to centralize corporate spend in order to get better visibility into current supply practices. The processes, agreements, and suppliers in place represent one half of the opportunity associated with the spend category in question. Alternative approaches, structures, and providers represent the other half of the opportunity. When procurement can assess the as-is situation and compare it to qualified alternatives in place outside of the company, the resulting gap between the two represents the value creation opportunity for the organization. Part of the effort required to get the company to consider changing its current practices is informing internal stakeholders about them, something procurement can not do without a good understanding of the practices themselves.

CONCLUSION

In this initial consideration of supply market intelligence, there are a number of moving pieces, processes, and resources that must align for intelligence to be created. This effort takes place at the strategic level of a project, and as such, the desired results may be hard to visualize until the moment that alignment takes place. For procurement departments or professionals looking to elevate themselves and their performance, making an investment in developing the necessary research and analytical skills may present the value creation opportunity they seek.

Fortunately for the professionals who have these skills, there are a variety of applications in any business along with a scarcity of automated substitutes. Even when supporting talent is available for hire from external firms, having an internal perspective not only improves results, it brings with it a long-term, vested interest in the organization's success.

As markets continue to evolve, information and intelligence need to be refreshed and kept current. Emerging sources of supply and competition provide simultaneous pressure to manage the company's working capital as efficiently and strategically as possible. The process of gathering and maintaining supply market intelligence is never complete. This means that there are perpetual opportunities to improve the ways that resources are spent and requirements are fulfilled.

When procurement continually refines its interpretation and application of intelligence, intellectual property and a competitive advantage are created. These increase procurement's contributions to the organization and increase how much we are valued in return.

REFERENCES

1. "The Men Who Built America: J. P. Morgan," in *ValuesandCapitalism.com*, Accessed June 25, 2014, http://www.valuesandcapitalism.com/dialogue/society/men-who-built-america-jp-morgan/.
2. "Always Listen to Your Peers and Know When to Obtain a 3rd Party Opinion," *The Wright Interface*, October 31, 2012, http://thewrightinterface

.com/blog/always-listen-to-your-peers-and-know-when-to-obtain-a-3rd-party-opinion.
3. The Organization for Economic Co-operation and Development, *Skills for Innovation and Research*. OECD Publishing, 2011, 18.
4. "Market share," in *Merriam-Webster.com*, Accessed June 25, 2014, http://www.merriam-webster.com/dictionary/market%20share.
5. Rita Gunther McGrath, *The End of Competitive Advantage: How to Keep Your Strategy Moving as Fast as Your Business*. Boston: Harvard Business Review Press, 2013, 78.
6. *Ibid.*, 9.
7. Joe Payne and William R. Dorn, Jr., *Managing Indirect Spend: Enhancing Profitability Through Strategic Sourcing*. Hoboken, NJ: John Wiley & Sons, Inc., 2012, 30.
8. Mike Buchanan, *Profitable Buying Strategies: How to Cut Procurement Costs and Buy Your Way to Higher Profits* Philadelphia, PA: Kogan Page Limited, 2008, 4.
9. Kate Vitasek and Karl Manrodt, *Vested: How P&G, McDonald's, and Microsoft Are Redefining Winning in Business Relationships*. New York: Palgrave MacMillan, 2012, 18.

2

SUPPLY MARKET INTELLIGENCE AS PART OF THE PROCUREMENT SYSTEM

Procurement is more than the linear process of finding, contracting, buying, and paying for products and services. Most procurement organizations have built up systems of initiatives that incorporate all of these things, and more, in an effort to create a sustained competitive advantage for the company. Each initiative offers some improvement to performance and results. A system of loosely interconnected disciplines and solutions guides procurement's efforts through the source-to-pay process, and beyond.

Rather than being a new initiative pursued in parallel to those already underway, creation of supply market intelligence intersects with the rest of the procurement system and improves the results associated with each effort. Common procurement initiatives include strategic sourcing, spend analysis, supplier management, risk management, category management, and procurement transformation. Although members of the same team often pursue these initiatives simultaneously, they are not always as synchronized as they could be. When the force of supply markets is considered as an ever-present dynamic, affecting all of procurement's initiatives, it improves the consistency of approach and balancing of corporate priorities.

In this chapter, we will discuss each initiative in the overall procurement system and consider how the context of supply markets allows procurement to perform to their full potential. We will also outline the role that supply market intelligence should play in improving execution and identifying value creation opportunities.

STRATEGIC SOURCING

One of the most common initiatives leveraged by procurement organizations is strategic sourcing. As an improved approach to purchasing, strategic sourcing is applicable regardless of industry, company size, and level of supply management maturity. The benefits associated with an expanded and consistent process for selecting suppliers are significant. According to Charles Dominick and Soheila Lunney in *The Procurement Game Plan* (2012):

> Strategic sourcing is generally defined as a rigorous process of identifying the right supplier. Not necessarily the cheapest or highest quality supplier, but the supplier that offers the greatest overall net benefit to the organization, all things considered.[1]

Often, organizations begin following a strategic sourcing process in conjunction with the implementation of an eSourcing solution, making a deliberate and coordinated investment in people, process, and technology. This three-pronged approach maximizes the benefits of an eSourcing solution by reconsidering existing processes and providing current team members with the skills necessary to fully leverage its capabilities.

It is in the reconsideration of processes that supply market intelligence can contribute the greatest value to strategic sourcing. Supply market intelligence allows for better visibility into the opportunity associated with each spend category through increased understanding of cost drivers, levels of competition between suppliers, and alternate solutions or sources available. Most procurement organizations use a strategic sourcing process with six to eight steps, starting with internal data collection and concluding with the signing of a contract and the beginning of ongoing supplier management. Although any effort undertaken by procurement is improved through a greater understanding of the larger market context, there are some specific points in the strategic sourcing process where it is particularly critical: identifying prospective suppliers, designing data collection tools, and developing a negotiation strategy.

Identifying Prospective Suppliers

In the overview of supply market intelligence in Chapter 1, we stated that there are two ways for procurement to approach a market: from the top down or the bottom up. In the top-down approach, procurement starts with a broad understanding of a source market and digs deeper to determine which subset of suppliers should be evaluated further. In the bottom-up approach, procurement starts with one or more known suppliers and looks to maximize competition and value by increasing the pool of candidates. In either case, procurement must be able to articulate their requirements using the terminology appropriate for the market in question. This makes it possible to locate suppliers that offer what is currently purchased, as well as to locate qualified alternatives from emerging markets and new market entrants.

There are benefits to having procurement lead strategic sourcing projects as an objective, internal team. However, in order for that objectivity to pay off, procurement must also be educated enough to mount a category specific effort every time. Without a solid understanding of the markets in question, procurement is confined by the boundaries of their company's historical purchasing habits. Researching the materials and services required by the organization in a more general sense identifies types and sources of supply that otherwise would not have been considered for inclusion. This expanded view of how to meet requirements creates value beyond negotiating lower prices for the same goods and services. When suppliers using traditional approaches are evaluated alongside innovative alternatives, procurement gets the opportunity to shed new light on the methods and cost structures, and the capabilities of both.

Sources of information on prospective suppliers include industry associations, directories, analysts' reports, and bloggers knowledgeable about the market. The level of difficulty associated with locating alternative prospects is often tied directly to their size relative to dominant players and the existing market. A large company moving into a new market will generate significant discussion, whereas a startup may develop and refine their offering for years with minimal press or analyst coverage. In many cases, awareness of their existence is spread through word of mouth, making it necessary for procurement professionals to reach out to their network of colleagues in order to locate little-known alternatives to large, dominant players in a specific market.

Designing Data Collection Tools

As the range of solutions and providers under consideration is broadened, the tools that procurement uses to evaluate them must expand in kind. Procurement organizations use a series of data collection tools to collect qualitative and quantitative information from their prospective suppliers. Collectively referred to as RFxs, these tools solicit different types and combinations of data.

- Requests for Information (RFIs) collect qualitative information through a series of questions,
- Requests for Quote (RFQs) collect pricing and other quantitative information about specific line items, and
- Requests for Proposal (RFPs) collect both quantitative data about line items and qualitative information about the bidding company as a whole.

In more extensive strategic sourcing projects, these tools may be used repeatedly or in conjunction with each other to evaluate and qualify suppliers through a multi-round process.

Most organizations ask standard questions in the course of each strategic sourcing project, resulting in the use of RFx templates. The common questions asked of each prospective supplier usually request contact details, financial information, and IT security details. Although there is value in consistency, these questions should not represent the largest portion of any RFx. Procurement must be well informed enough to ask questions that extend beyond basic screening information. The most valuable responses will motivate strategic actions specific to each category. There is some leeway when procurement has time to run an RFI in advance of an RFP or RFQ because they can collect information from suppliers in time to put it to use in their price collection strategy. Organizations that press forward without the proper foundational understanding sacrifice the opportunity to improve the way they collect information from suppliers in the bid process, as well as how they manage the category internally.

Procurement teams can insulate themselves from this missed opportunity by running an RFI in advance of finalizing the pricing model used to compare solutions. If there is not sufficient time available, the best alternative is a focused investment in supply market intelligence. Procurement must understand the relevant cost drivers and how they are reflected in supplier pricing strategies in advance of RFx data collection. This contextual knowledge puts procurement in control of the process rather than in a reactionary or dependent position. They must be able to reconcile each supplier's prices with internal historical spend and projected costs, as well as to compare details across all qualified proposals. In addition to the benchmarking of quantitative information, procurement should include questions that reveal the use of recognized best practices specific to each market. There is no worse realization in the late stages of a strategic sourcing project than that a certain piece of information known sooner would have changed the strategy employed and the results generated.

Negotiation Strategy

Solid negotiation skills have long been the stock-in-trade of the seasoned procurement professional. Some parts of the strategic sourcing process can, and have been, automated through online supplier feedback functionality or dynamic online negotiation through a reverse auction. Automation notwithstanding, many projects still arrive at the point where procurement must sit across the table from representatives of each qualified supplier to hash out the details of what might become a successful agreement. Each negotiation cycle addresses pricing and a range of other components, such as service level agreements, contract length, and payment terms. For the suppliers awarded a portion of the available business, the output of these sessions forms the foundation of the resulting contractual agreement. Adding to the significance of the agreed upon outcomes, the evaluation and compensation of both sides is at stake. Procurement is evaluated (if not directly compensated) based on savings, as well as the other beneficial terms they are able to negotiate. Supplier sales representatives have even more to gain or lose in a negotiation through quotas, bonuses, and favorable territory assignments.

Good negotiators have sometimes been stereotyped as tough or even aggressive people. These hypothetical negotiators are willing to take any approach necessary to ensure an optimal outcome for themselves and their organizations, regardless of the impact on future business partners. This supposed need to intimidate others has the unintended consequence of scaring many procurement professionals away from building negotiating expertise. Fortunately for the organizations and individuals on both sides of the table, that stereotype has given way to a more collaborative approach. While no less driven to optimize their own results, effective procurement negotiators are enabled and even encouraged to consider the needs of their suppliers in pursuit of mutually beneficial or "win-win" partnerships.

When this is the case, professionals with access to supply market intelligence, will excel based on their knowledge of potential bargaining chips and collective value-creation opportunities. There is no need to bang on a negotiating table when it is possible to be more effective by demonstrating an understanding of cost drivers and market conditions. That information, in the right hands, can motivate informed questions about specific components of a supplier's pricing or proposal that seem less than competitive. "Information or knowledge is definitely power, but in information-based negotiations, the supply chain professional gains a deep knowledge of the supplier's industry, their margins, and their culture. In essence, this is a deep immersion or empathy with the supplier and their competitive landscape."[2] Negotiations are a direct opportunity for the value of supply market intelligence to be demonstrated as well as measured using traditional procurement performance metrics. When procurement is successful in establishing long-term relationships with their suppliers, they also open a channel for supply market intelligence to come directly from these trusted partners.

SPEND ANALYSIS

One of the critical inputs to the strategic sourcing process is an understanding of historical expenditures. Like strategic sourcing, spend analysis is often associated with the implementation of technology. These solutions allow organizations to view their spend dynamically segmented by a combination of dimensions such as supplier, invoice date, category, and corporate hierarchy or business unit. In many cases, this is the first efficient way for a company to see how much is spent with whom, by whom, and on what. Spend analysis is much like the information that must be processed in order to become intelligence. In order for spend to motivate strategic actions and decisions, additional analysis in the form of an opportunity assessment must be conducted.

Opportunity assessments may be completed by procurement or by a third-party service provider brought in expressly for the purpose. They combine historical spend data with the strategic plans of the organization and current market conditions to identify and prioritize potential strategic sourcing projects. That prioritization reflects the relative savings opportunity, contract expiration dates, resources available to assign to the effort, and an organization's specific goals such as supplier rationalization and minimization of complexity or risk. Opportunity assessments, and the recommendations that result from them, are as fluid as the company's operational plans and the markets in which they function. Since these plans are constantly revisited and updated, all internal and external inputs must be kept current.

Supply market intelligence is critical to the execution of an opportunity assessment because it provides visibility into the current internal handling of each category of spend relative to available external alternatives. A number of external data points are required to reflect the market potential of each category. At a high level, these data points reflect relative buying power by establishing total market size and maturity so that the company's demand can be weighed against them. Inputs "range from the annual spend and contract end date, to understanding the supply market and how much of the suppliers costs are outside their control."[3] At a more detailed level, external data may be used to benchmark current prices or assign a specific risk level to an incumbent supplier. From procurement's perspective, two key factors that should be captured by an opportunity assessment are how much competition exists for the available business and how much control each supplier has over its costs.

Relative Leverage

The ultimate goal of an opportunity assessment and the resulting sourcing recommendations is to secure optimal pricing and contract terms for spend as it is brought under management. As a result, determining the organization's total leverage is an important early step. The opportunity that exists within each category of spend is directly tied to the buying power of the organization. This power is based on a number of external factors such as the valuation of the total supply market, the number of qualified suppliers, the level of differentiation, and the range of supplier sizes. The combination of these data points with the planned spending of the organization determines how much leverage procurement can expect to have in a negotiation and, therefore, how high of a priority the project should be.

When approached purposefully, relative leverage can be improved by more than just consolidating spend into a larger contract award. If a category of spend is of strategic importance to the company, the decision may be made to find the right size supply partner rather than to maximize savings. For instance, if the buying company wants to have input on a supplier's product road map or design priorities, they must select a supply partner that is not so small that they introduce risk and instability, but is also not so large that the available spend or volume does not carry the desired level of influence. In these cases, the decision may be made to pay incrementally more for a product or service in exchange for sway with the selected supplier. If forging a partnership with the right supplier creates a competitive advantage, the foregone cost savings can be considered a worthy investment.

An opportunity assessment collects both the current conditions as well as the forward-looking priorities for each spend category. The organization can make the decision to work with a certain size or scope of supplier in order to achieve the desired results. Staying with the idea of relative leverage, a starting point for procurement may be to determine whether more or less influence is required. They can then consider the profiles of incumbent suppliers and collect market intelligence about companies that may be a better fit, or who offer opportunities for innovation. This context helps procurement realize what characteristics they must look for in prospective suppliers. These characteristics may be captured by a combination of qualitative and quantitative market intelligence elements, such as a supplier's annual sales, the size of its customer base, how active its user community is, and how responsive its design team is to customer feedback and requests.

Supplier Cost Control

Although the quantitative focus in a competitive bid process is usually prices, the actual opportunity represented by each category of spend is better assessed through an understanding of supplier costs. More specifically, procurement must determine how much of the supplier's price is tied up in their costs and how much profit they earn. Larger or more efficient suppliers keep costs low through strong negotiating leverage and economies of scale. This gives them an advantage by protecting profit margins, while also allowing them to offer competitive prices. In general, however, the percentage of supply costs that suppliers have control over will apply to an industry as a whole. In an opportunity assessment, it is critical to determine what level of control the suppliers in each category have over their costs because that information is directly tied to the savings potential.

As discussed in the section on negotiation strategy previously, negotiation relationships with suppliers have become more collaborative. When it is deemed beneficial to do so, procurement should help their supply partners identify costs that are out of line with the rest of their market. When procurement is well informed about what supplier overhead and material costs should be and how they can be optimized, they are in a position to provide valuable feedback to suppliers. This cycle of communication improves their prices in return. Costs may be reduced by using alternate materials or by improving the efficiency of processes to minimize waste and increase inventory turnover. In these cases, procurement has a vested interest in helping their suppliers improve, as those cost savings are passed back to them. Suppliers that operate cost effectively are positioned to offer competitive pricing without sacrificing their ability to compete and innovate in a market over the long term.

Gaining an understanding of a supplier's costs and cost structures is an exercise in second-tier supply chain management. Part of procurement's information on this topic will come from data collected in the RFx process. The rest of it must be uncovered through their own research, as suppliers are not always willing to expose granular cost details. Sources of information that may be used for validating supplier costs include raw material indexes, industry associations, and analyst reports. For public companies, quarterly or annual reports can be a source of profit and loss numbers and gross margin percentages for a specific division or product line. Even when suppliers are willing to share information, procurement is responsible for validating its accuracy. By increasing their visibility into the primary cost drivers for a product or service, procurement can not only benchmark or baseline the prices they are paying now, but also identify the trends and cost drivers that need to be monitored on an ongoing basis to mitigate future price increases.

SUPPLIER MANAGEMENT

Despite the central role that strategic sourcing plays in procurement's responsibilities and performance goals, interactions with suppliers extend through the length of each contract or buying relationship. Once suppliers have been selected through strategic sourcing and brought under contract, their performance must be managed. Given the size of any organization's supply base, it stands to reason that not all suppliers will be managed by procurement in the same way with an equal level of time and attention. The factor that determines what sort of relationship will be put in place is the potential return for the organization. Depending on the circumstances, the return may be measured in terms of savings, risk minimization, efficiency, or creation of a competitive advantage.

Procurement has no choice but to prioritize their efforts when faced with the master list or database of the company's suppliers. This includes companies that are under contract and those that are not. Prioritization is often achieved through supply base segmentation, where procurement looks at suppliers through the lens of corporate objectives. It is common practice to rely upon the Pareto Principle, also known as the 80/20 rule, when managing the supply base. The application of this principle in supplier management is the idea that 80 percent of the company's spend will be associated with 20 percent of the suppliers. In the words of Mike Buchanan (2008), "All else being equal, you'd make an effort to reduce to costs of spend areas at the upper end of the list, rather than at the lower end of the list—because the potential cost savings should be higher."[4] This rule of thumb can be applied to the whole supply base at once, or within each category of spend, to segment line items or transactions.

Upon first consideration, supplier management seems to be an internal initiative and not a candidate for improvement through supply market intelligence. On the contrary, best practices for managing suppliers must employ a category specific context driven by an understanding of the relevant market forces. The knowledge required to implement such a tailored supplier management program must undergo constant validation through qualified external sources and experts. Key performance indicators (KPIs) are a specific example of this need, both in their articulation and in procurement's response to the supplier performance they measure. It is also critical for procurement to recognize when a supplier or category is a "Pareto-buster" or a case where additional attention is required, even though the total spend value or transaction count would otherwise cause the opportunity to be overlooked. Procurement is faced with the challenge of balancing projects where they can achieve a maximum return for their effort in the form of savings and projects that are based on the recognition that a supplier offers a unique or critical solution. Striking this balance is aided by an understanding of all supplier relationships in the context of the market as a whole.

Key Performance Indicators

The core task associated with supplier management is the regular review of supplier performance against the KPIs or service level agreements (SLAs) outlined in a contract. This may take the form of quarterly meetings where procurement reviews current status, open challenges, and potential opportunities with their supply partners. As we mentioned in the opening to this section on supplier management, it is impossible (and inefficient) for procurement to make the same investment in every supplier. The suppliers that are designated as having sufficient strategic importance to warrant focused attention, will also be in a position to impact the buying organization's performance. How suppliers are measured, and how they perform against those metrics, must drive the desired results in each circumstance.

In *Vested Outsourcing*, Kate Vitasek (2010) talks about the risk of what she calls "perverse incentives." Although her use of the phrase refers to situations where an entire function has been put in the hands of a third-party provider, the concept applies to all supply relationships. Since "you get what you measure," it is important to make sure you want more of the behaviors encouraged by KPIs. According to Vitasek, "We define a perverse incentive as 'An incentive that is intended to promote a desirable effect, but instead creates and nurtures a negative and unintended outcome.'"[5] Although there are many internal groups that have a hand in the execution of each contract, procurement's role should be to ensure that contracts deliver the desired results in the long term. The satisfaction with the commercial relationship between any two organizations must be founded on clear and applicable KPIs. The buying organization should feel that they are getting the anticipated value, and each supplier should be clear about what is expected of them.

Some KPIs are category or supplier agnostic. Examples of these include on time delivery and adherence with commitments about reporting and communication. Other KPIs are tailored to a supplier or spend category. Procurement must know what metrics are appropriate, how often they need to be remeasured, and what reaction each score or trend requires. The most meaningful KPIs are tied directly to a supplier's operation and address internal effectiveness, as well as how the supplier responds to external challenges. Reducing the cost of waste, decreasing turnaround time, and increasing productivity per full-time equivalent (FTE) are category specific metrics that procurement may track with their suppliers. The baseline for each should be established with a recognition of the performance levels of the supplier's competitors. In order for procurement to be an effective advocate on behalf of their organization, they must gain insight into leading and average performance levels from analysts and experts recognized in a supplier's market.

Unique or Critical Suppliers

When procurement is tasked with sourcing direct spend, the materials or components used to produce the products sold to consumers, it is not unusual to find that a critical input is only available from a limited number of sources. In some cases, the product may be unique as the result of a custom specification, designed and produced specifically for the buying organization. It is always appropriate for procurement to validate that there is not a more standard product that could be used in order to minimize risk and to manage costs. This inquiry must go beyond a simple exchange between procurement and internal stakeholders, and should involve documentation or process observations to validate the requirement.

In other cases, it is possible that an innovative supplier is offering a product that is not available through any other source, even though it is not a custom specification. That company is in a position to influence the performance and buying decisions of their customers as long as their advantage exists, a situation that is fortunate for them but less desirable for the companies that buy from them.

From procurement's perspective, being reliant on a critical but limited source product is a high-risk situation. The fact that there are no alternatives makes it much harder to negotiate. If anything goes wrong at the supplier, including disruptions in the supply chain, there is little that can be done. If the determination is made that there really is no substitute, procurement will need to work closely with internal design, engineering, and research and development teams to understand the role this product and the supplier will have in future designs. They must make sure those groups understand the associated risks, and constantly monitor availability and inventory levels. It is possible that a supplier or product has become critical unintentionally, meaning that it was selected before strategic sourcing was an accepted discipline in the company, and its importance has grown over time as more internal designs require the product. The organization must carefully track and plan for usage and anticipated demand. If at all possible, the product should be flagged on development road maps as a design element to change.

The role of supply market intelligence in managing these critical suppliers is twofold. First, procurement must capture a comprehensive and detailed assessment of any and all risks associated with the supplier. This includes their throughput, financial standing, and supply chain reliability. If the product or material is patented, procurement should investigate to find out when the patent expires and if it is likely that other companies would make their own version available. Second, if the product is truly worth the risk, procurement should also propose the option of *reverse integration*: buying the company or the product line to ensure that it continues to be available as required. This step has an added benefit in that it gives the organization an advantage over their competition, who will not have access to the product unless it is financially beneficial to the organization to make it available. In the case of reverse integration, supply market intelligence may include the identification and assessment of other prospective buyers.

RISK MANAGEMENT

Apart from doing an assessment of each supplier during the strategic sourcing process, ongoing risk management and assessment are critical procurement activities. Extended global supply chains have presented companies with an enormous opportunity to secure the products and materials they need at competitive costs. But with these longer, more complex supply chains comes increased risk due to natural disasters, geopolitical instability, capacity constraints, and reputational damage. According to Gary Lynch (2008): "The key to avoiding or reducing risk in the new interrelated world is to develop the intelligence and the flow of information—anticipating, avoiding through agility and flexibility, or reacting to warning signs, containing, and responding."[6] Just as the need to understand a supplier's costs requires increased visibility into the second tier of the supply base, many risks lurk beyond the direct sight and reach of a buying organization.

Each potential source of risk requires a different approach to gathering supply market intelligence. Geographically based risk is caused by natural disasters, supply chain disruptions, and geopolitical instability, and requires research into countries, transportation methods, political movements, and severe weather zones. Financial risk must be determined one company at a time, and can be evaluated based on annual reports and filings for public companies. Private companies are more difficult to evaluate, as information is not readily available because they are not required to release it. Risks associated with capacity constraints may be tied to the availability of raw materials or production capacity. Reputational risk is more difficult to identify as it is heavily dependent on perceptions of a company's decisions. There are some common sources of reputational risk, such as sourcing from countries with questionable labor standards or from places where there may be negative environmental impact from a production process. When this is a concern, broad intelligence gathering activities are required, including monitoring general news sources, as well as the websites of watchdog organizations.

While risk management sounds like one activity, in order to be conducted effectively, it must actually be broken down into three subcomponents: risk assessment, risk monitoring, and response planning. During a risk assessment, concerns are identified, articulated, and prioritized. Once a list of risk factors has been compiled, the effort transitions to risk monitoring: watching for signs that a response is necessary. If action is required in response to changing conditions, plans should already be in place. These plans may include alternate sources of supply, whether they are already under contract through a split award or from prequalified suppliers. Although an increasing number of companies have teams or individuals responsible for general business continuity, supply chains may be overlooked. Procurement is often responsible for making sure supply risk is minimized through fully informed supplier selection and predictive monitoring of risk indicators.

Since one or more risk factors may come into play with each product or service purchased, risk factors need to be studied in isolation and in combination to insure that response planning does not rely on sources of supply equally likely to be affected by the disruption. Fortunately for procurement, the information required to assess, monitor, and respond is often easily available through general news sources. The challenge lies in the time required to search for actionable information by supplier, industry, or country, and then filter that information and assess its severity before making a decision about what actions need to be taken. Any resulting delay may cost the organization the opportunity to take preventative measures or to mitigate the impact of a full-fledged disruption or public relations crisis. Procurement must provide market intelligence to the organization through the development of a risk profile, focusing on relevant factors during supplier qualification and the development of the award strategy for each category.

Risk Assessment

A risk assessment is used to determine the type and severity of risk associated with a supplier, an industry, or a location. The information gathered represents a snapshot in time and is ultimately used as a baseline for ongoing monitoring. Procurement may conduct risk assessments for a number of reasons, including at the outset of bringing a new category of spend under management, in the process of evaluating current and prospective suppliers for new contracts, or as a broad general exercise aimed at improved overall risk management. In order to be thorough, procurement should start by making a list of all possible types of risk to use as an assessment checklist and eliminate nonrelevant concerns one by one in each category. Any confirmed risks must be monitored on an ongoing basis. Just as supplier management requires unexpected information from outside the organization, effective risk management requires internal inputs to be actionable.

The practice of conducting a risk assessment makes it possible to determine what level of risk will be tolerated. Procurement cannot usually make risk-based decisions on behalf of their organization, but they are in a position to lead cross-functional or executive conversations on risk. These conversations enable the company to make governing decisions and provide procurement with visibility into the management team's perspective.

Lower risk often means higher costs. As a result, risk tolerance levels in a sourcing project or an opportunity assessment have a direct impact on the opportunity for savings. This puts procurement in the unique position of balancing the desire to reduce costs, while also minimizing risk. Being able to identify present risks, and to explain the cost impact of any one of them, positions procurement as a strategic resource with the security and stability of the organization at the center of their efforts.

The supply market intelligence required to support risk assessment is closely tied to why the assessment is being done. Supplier-based risk is likely to start with an evaluation of their finances and capacity, then broaden to include connected markets that introduce second-tier risk. Current news stories on pending labor strikes, material or component shortfalls, or elevated risk in the countries that supply originates from or passes through are good starting points. For each identified risk factor, procurement must also define the frequency with which they will update the status and best sources of information. Although the priority of a risk assessment is to identify sources of concern, any information that can be gathered about anticipated trends or risk indicators is valuable as the effort transitions to risk monitoring.

Risk Monitoring

When risk monitoring is an active effort because of the materials, locations, organizations, or countries involved, procurement has the opportunity to partner with their internal stakeholders. Having more eyes and ears looking for changes in risk status improves the results and forges a trusted working relationship between procurement and other functions. The timeliness and accuracy of the information is key. Since even the best-prepared organizations require time to respond, procurement must monitor elevations in risk indicators rather than waiting for a risk to completely materialize. There is some level of risk in every supply relationship, but those risks are not equal. Each internal stakeholder will see the risk that affects their spend as critical, and so it will be up to procurement to determine relative risk based on the anticipated impact on revenue, operations, regulations, and reputation.

Since procurement is likely to be brought in to help manage situations of elevated risk later than they would like, they must monitor these pre-identified categories of spend even when the day-to-day management has transitioned back to internal stakeholders. Sustaining a long-term effort like risk management is as challenging as identifying areas of concern in the first place. It is easy to become complacent over the term of a contract. News stories come and go, and with very few exceptions the changes in each supply market become background noise. In some cases, risk monitoring may be incorporated into annual or quarterly supplier review meetings. Anything that procurement can do to maintain the effort through consistent updates, executive engagement, and supplier participation will improve the position of the organization, as well as relevance of the procurement function within it.

Risk management is undoubtedly an important activity for procurement organizations, but it is another area of responsibility on top of other supply management tasks. Whenever possible, risk monitoring should be automated by signing up for appropriate industry alerts or using search engines to create custom alerts. In organizations where procurement is aligned with a category of spend (IT, marketing, MRO, textiles, etc.) it may be possible to monitor risk by reading the news sources dedicated to the industry in question. When procurement is process focused, and team members move from one unrelated project to another, the effort to monitor risk may need to be centralized so that there is appropriate coverage for relevant risk indicators without a duplication of effort. The effort will be split between monitoring the indicators identified in the risk assessment and making sure new, previously unidentified risks, are recognized.

Response Planning

When an identified risk is significant enough to change the management of a category, plans must be put in place to mitigate as much risk as possible. Responses may include the pre-identification of alternate sources of supply, managed inventory levels, and other internal steps that can be taken to keep the operation moving. These plans should be frequently updated, and must be managed separately from the people who put them in place. Records should be clear and detailed enough so that anyone in the organization could execute them without more than basic or high-level knowledge.

Risk mitigation plans can be anticipatory as much as they are reactionary. For instance, in a strategic sourcing project for a product with high-risk components, or a supply chain susceptible to disruption, the decision may be made to split an award between two suppliers in order to have more than one contracted source available at all times. The presence of risk factors also increases the importance of the supplier qualification process. The suppliers who participated in recent bids but were not selected for contracts become the first alternate sources when contracted suppliers are unable to meet demand for any reason. All plans should be prescreened to make sure that alternate sources of supply are not rendered ineffectual by the same disruptions that eliminated the primary sources.

One of the most effective uses of supply market intelligence in risk response planning is getting a better understanding of how other companies responded under similar conditions when risks materialized. For instance, consumer electronics companies may wish to study the tsunami that affected consumer electronics and automotive manufacturers in Japan in 2011. Multiple impacts of each risk should be considered as a disruption that could affect availability, cost, or both. Successful reaction planning is helpful for companies looking to make their own plans, but failed or missed reaction opportunities should be studied as well.

ADVANCED PROCUREMENT INITIATIVES

While all procurement organizations will see a benefit from incorporating a supply market perspective in their initiatives, mature procurement organizations will allow the market to drive their efforts, priorities, and even the organization of the procurement team itself. The more advanced a procurement function is, the more closely intertwined its people and priorities are with the rest of the organization. Advanced procurement initiatives are applied when a greater business need requires them, or when procurement matures to the point that they are no longer able to generate the same results using conventional methods. These initiatives may require that procurement be reorganized in order to carry them out.

Category Management

In the early stages of a procurement or strategic sourcing program, the focus is likely to be on one project at a time. Even when the team is aligned along category lines, there may still be opportunities to improve results by managing each category as an interconnected set of suppliers, purchases, and cost drivers. As Jonathan O'Brien wrote in *Category Management in Purchasing*:

> "Category management is about changing sourcing in a radical way or a way that gives radical improvements. Whether it is in using competition to drive down prices, changing the internal processes, using suppliers to change the value of your products or simply eliminating needs, category management is about delivering far better value to the organization than traditional incremental improvement activities such as ad hoc negotiations can deliver."[7]

Another way of looking at category management is as the improvement of all initiatives in the procurement system at once.

The value of a well-executed category management program to the organization includes improvements beyond savings. Category management takes into consideration the entire source to pay process. It includes opportunities to improve internal demand and supplier contributions to product development. These factors certainly improve the cost or margins of an operation, yet do not usually fall within the scope of procurement responsibility. With this expanded approach comes the opportunity to apply existing procurement capabilities to new areas and to develop new skills. In order to succeed, the organization as a whole needs to be open to change and willing to work more cross functionally than they have in the past.

Just as category management requires a new perspective of the spend and suppliers that have been managed in the past, it also requires a different understanding of the relevant markets along the entire supply chain. Rather than starting with historical spend, category management may be most successful when it is used to understand where the organization is positioned relative to its competition from a sales perspective. How do prices compare to the available alternatives? If they are high or low, procurement can start looking at why. The answer may be outside of procurement's usual approaches, and may include a recommendation to spend money (such as on a new machine or altered process) rather than to shave costs by trying to accomplish the same old things in an incrementally improved way.

The role of supply market intelligence is to make all decisions, even new types of decisions, within the context of total cost. Comparing direct and indirect costs, as well as the relative success rates associated with an investment, requires research into the available options and how they have been employed in similar operations. In some cases, procurement may need to mock up a business proposal of sorts so that the executive team can preapprove a new approach before procurement goes to market to collect bids.

Procurement Transformation

There is no initiative in the procurement system more discussed recently than that of *procurement transformation*. The idea that procurement could achieve a higher level of performance and strategic value is sought by leaders and practitioners alike. The meaning of transformation is different for each organization because it is directly related to their beginning-state maturity and execution. Examples range from the implementation of a strategic sourcing program in a more tactical purchasing organization to the total reorganization of procurement as a distributed function in a more mature organization. It is important to note that unlike many of the other initiatives in the procurement system, procurement transformation is not a way to make an average- or under-performing function better. Procurement transformation is the way to help a well-performing organization achieve excellence.

Ironically, a procurement transformation may break down the function as it is traditionally structured. In order to take performance and results to the next level, it may be necessary to remove the people and responsibilities from the procurement organization and distribute them in the organization with solid and dotted line reporting to operational and shared service leaders. Carrying out such a complex restructuring requires complete support, ownership, respect, and agreement from all executive leaders in the organization. It is also necessary for all functional leaders to have bought into the value proposition of strong procurement processes, hence the need for transformation to be based on demonstrated performance rather than in response to missed expectations. Although such broad restructuring efforts are difficult, they may present the best opportunity for procurement to maintain and improve their stature within the organization.

Supply market intelligence must be at the heart of a procurement transformation because by completely overhauling the way procurement is structured and executed, the organization makes the connection between procurement and their operational health. Pre-transformation procurement organizations often focus on the competitive landscapes in the markets they buy from because they dictate the level of savings opportunity and the strategies required for their realization. Transformed procurement organizations focus on the competitive landscape of the company itself, prioritizing their efforts and selecting spend management strategies because of the improvement they will drive in revenue, profit margin, market share, and operational decisions.

CONCLUSION

After reviewing some of the initiatives that may be underway in any procurement system, it is easy to see how they can become disconnected. By keeping supply market intelligence at the center of all efforts, strategies and decisions are soundly based on factors such as savings opportunities or risk mitigation. Procurement's job is to optimally manage all spend, given the conditions that affect it. This may include levels of competition, scarcity of supply, relative leverage, and indicators or performance. Although some of these may be influenced by internal decisions and conditions, most of them are the result of market context. These conditions provide the opportunity for procurement to position intelligence at the forefront of organizational strategy.

REFERENCES

1. Charles Dominick and Soheila R. Lunney, *The Procurement Game Plan: Winning Strategies and Techniques for Supply Management Professionals*. Fort Lauderdale, FL: J. Ross Publishing, Inc., 2012, 69.
2. Tom De Paoli, *Common Sense Supply Management: Tales from the Supply Chain Trenches*. North Charleston, SC: Createspace, 2012, 89.
3. "2014—The Year of Category Dojo!" *The Secret Diary of Market Dojo*, Accessed June 26, 2014, http://blog.marketdojo.com/2014/01/2014-year-of-category-dojo.html.
4. Mike Buchanan, *Profitable Buying Strategies: How to Cut Procurement Costs and Buy Your Way to Higher Profits*. Philadelphia, PA: Kogan Page, 2008, 26.
5. Kate Vitasek, *Vested Outsourcing: Five Rules That Will Transform Outsourcing*. New York: Palgrave Macmillan, 2010, 24.
6. Gary S. Lynch, *Single Point of Failure: The Ten Essential Laws of Supply Chain Risk Management*. Hoboken, NJ: John Wiley & Sons, Inc., 2009, 239.
7. Jonathan O'Brien, *Category Management in Purchasing: A Strategic Approach to Maximize Business Profitability*. Philadelphia, PA: Kogan Page, 2012, 33.

3

SUPPLY MARKET INTELLIGENCE CREATION PROCESS

To this point in the book, we have defined *supply market intelligence* and looked at how it fits into the rest of the procurement system. Now, we will review the process for creating supply market intelligence within a specific procurement effort, such as a sourcing project or a supplier performance review. Although leveraging intelligence is the end goal, it is the end-to-end process for creating it that we address in this chapter.

At a high level, the supply market intelligence creation process consists of four steps, plus an independent approval hurdle that must be met before the intelligence documentation is shared with stakeholders outside of procurement. The steps, shown in Figure 3.1 are:

1. Identify and Define,
2. Research, Read, and Refine,
3. Analyze, and
4. Document.

The second step, Research, Read, and Refine, is an iterative process that should be repeated multiple times before procurement moves on to steps 3 and 4. Although we will overview that step from a process perspective in this chapter, we will focus on tactics for executing this step in Chapter 4. There are a few keys to success embedded within the details of this process, including how to get started and how to process the information that is collected.

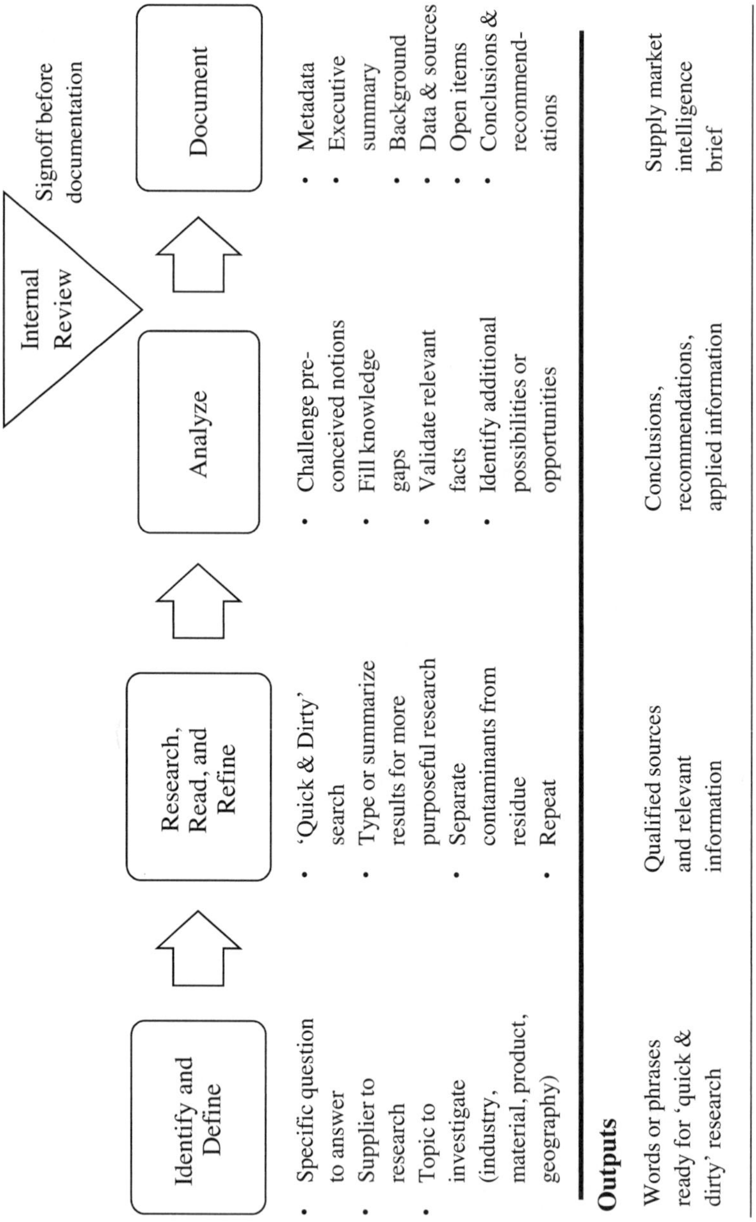

Figure 3.1 Supply market intelligence process

When applied to research and supply market intelligence, the Pareto principle suggests that 80% of the intelligence will come from 20% of the information reviewed. Procurement must balance the need to gather sufficient information to support informed recommendations with the other tasks waiting for their attention. This presents the constant challenge of knowing when further research represents an opportunity for intelligence and when it will only result in diminishing returns.

STEP 1: IDENTIFY AND DEFINE

It is critical to clearly articulate the requirements for supply market intelligence before the work to create it begins. Being able to define the pieces and types of information required can be a deceptively complex step, and should not be rushed.

The Identify and Define step of the supply market intelligence creation process is akin to research strategy development. Information needs must be mapped out and associated with clear applications for the business. The value of intelligence is represented by its eventual relevance and actionability. It must accurately reflect the current state as understood by the daily owners of the category or suppliers in question. Leveraging the existing knowledge held by these stakeholders advances the discovery process and improves results. At this step in the intelligence creation process, information needs are one of two kinds:

1. A defined need such as a question on a specific topic, or
2. An unexplored, abstract sense that there is an opportunity to improve the management of an ongoing effort.

The research approach may differ, but the output of the Identify and Define step is always the same: a basic framework for the initial search. Once procurement has articulated the words and phrases for use in the first round of research, the work can begin.

The Role of Collaboration

While step 2, the process of Researching, Reading, and Refining information, is usually carried out independently by one individual in procurement, the work to Identify and Define specific information needs is improved through collaboration with internal stakeholders. Not only does this inclusion breed additional ideas, it may also clarify the subject being researched as it relates to the business opportunity, supplier, or industry in question.

It is true that there are some projects so new to a company that there is no existing in-house knowledge base, but this is the exception. Procurement is usually acting on behalf of or in cooperation with another group in the organization, and that group of colleagues should be considered the first source of potential information. Even if they do not possess a clear market perspective, they can provide immediate insight into how the information, as well as the improvements it is expected to lead to, will be applied as intelligence.

Procurement should not waste opportunities to collect information from internal stakeholders because of concerns about appearing ill informed. Asking intelligent, open-ended questions is just as good a way to demonstrate strong capabilities as possessing significant knowledge on a topic. In some procurement organizations, the staffing philosophy is based on process discipline rather than being category centric. Process-oriented organizations manage a broad range of spend categories and suppliers with good results by applying a solid, well-documented process and the right input from category experts. Getting input from internal leaders and stakeholders early and often allows them the opportunity to contribute materially to the success of the project. Perhaps more importantly, it reassures them that they are being heard and provides procurement with the opportunity to incorporate their knowledge and experience.

The other valuable input that comes from internal collaboration is the history of the relationship between the category and operational decisions. There are often good reasons for decisions that otherwise seem difficult to explain. Donald Jean, co-founder of FocusedBuyer® and career procurement professional, refers to the importance of organizational history, or tribal knowledge, to successful procurement: "We all know companies spend untold amounts of money to capture their history and then leverage it—after the fact. But specific history, continuous history, and historical patterns represent one of the most essential keys and gateways to a better procurement future."[1] This history may even predate the establishment of a formal procurement organization. When procurement is organized along category lines, the knowledge held by colleagues managing the spend on a day-to-day basis will always be more detailed and nuanced. Collecting it in advance leads to better results.

Some of the information collected through internal collaboration serves as background or context for procurement to start their research. The most useful information in early rounds of research includes relevant terminology, acronyms, authoritative organizations and associations, and reputable sources of news.

Overt Information Needs

While we have been discussing supply market intelligence and research as opportunities for procurement to create value, both are already baked into many familiar processes. Research is a prescribed step early in the strategic sourcing process and in opportunity assessments. This application of the research process assumes an overt information need that impedes progress. Examples of overt information needs include the names of qualified suppliers and the annual value of a market. At the very least, most standard procurement processes require the validation of current information. Sample information needs for each of the initiatives in the procurement system, as defined in Chapter 2, are identified in Figure 3.2.

In some cases, overt information needs are answers to specific questions. For example, ethylene is a derivative of natural gas and petroleum used in many plastic shopping bags. Procurement professionals in retail may ask, "What is the projected pricing trend for ethylene?" Most of the time, however, an overt information need is associated with a subject that procurement must learn more about. Since not all pricing is based on the cost to manufacture, information

Initiatives in the Procurement 'System'	**Sample Information Needs**
Strategic Sourcing	• Identify prospective suppliers • What to ask in RFx • Pricing structure • Negotiation strategy
Spend Analysis	• Determine relative leverage • Determine supplier's control over costs • Identify key performance indicators • Profile unique suppliers
Risk Management	• Anticipated material shortages • Geopolitical instability • Changing regulations
Category Management	• Common points of leverage across projects • Suppliers offering cross category products or solutions • New contract models
Procurement Transformation	• Market forces affecting the company • New sources of competitions • Emerging technologies

Figure 3.2 Information needs by procurement initiative

about supply versus demand and perceived real value must be investigated. The topic may be a supplier, an industry, a material, a product, or a source market. The approach for conducting supply market research varies for different types of information needs and their eventual application. When preparing a research strategy, there are three details that should be defined up front:

- What is known,
- What is unknown, and
- What will be done with the information.

Articulating what is known and what is not known are simple steps that breaks the inertia for researchers with more of a need for information than they have knowledge of the subject. Whether the information is coming from internal stakeholders, incumbent suppliers, or historical spend, known terms and phrases form the foundation of a search and define the parameters for useful information. As items in the "need" category are crossed off as a result of research and reading, the information in the "known" category grows.

The reason it is helpful to note the eventual use of the intelligence being created is that it helps procurement determine when enough research has been done. The point of diminishing returns is not precise. It occupies an area on procurement's learning curve where each additional piece of information uncovered requires a disproportionate amount of procurement's time to locate, while adding negligible value. Making the determination that this point has been reached is a difficult decision, but is made easier with an immediate reminder of the reason for the research. Overt information needs are often associated with specific tactics, such as finalizing a list of prospective bidders. Being able to gather information quickly enables the project to keep moving forward. Maintaining momentum should be balanced with the desire to know as much as possible before progressing.

When procurement first identifies and defines their information needs, the details may not be in the best format to conduct research. They may have a list of specific companies or geographies, but need to generalize the details before additional information can be collected. For instance, if additional suppliers are sought for a bid, the initial "known" information will include all current and former suppliers of the product or service. Procurement can then articulate the characteristics and capabilities that qualify those suppliers and search for other companies with similar profiles.

Opportunistic Intelligence

Beyond the predetermined project milestones that call for research, procurement professionals must recognize unique opportunities to improve an ongoing effort through supply market intelligence. In many ways, a spontaneous pursuit of additional information generates better results than prescribed research. When an information need is tied directly to a value-based opportunity for results improvement, the person conducting the research has a clear motivation to increase their understanding.

An opportunistic need for information is often abstract even when the reasons for collecting it are clear. This initial need may feel like an unidentified piece of the picture is missing. Find the time for the need to materialize into a specific, concrete inquiry, no matter how amorphous it seems. Writing down the most basic thoughts is helpful when converting an abstract idea into a defined need for further research. It may not be much, but those words and phrases are the start of the research phase.

Often, a researcher does not know what they do not know. When this is the case, the research starts by learning enough about the topic to identify what additional details are required.

For experienced procurement professionals, the desire for opportunistic intelligence starts with the instinct that there is a "better way to do this." It may be a product that (according to internal stakeholders) can only be purchased from one supplier. Alternatively, there may be a nagging sensation that identified risks are higher than previously thought, or that the current risk profile is incomplete. The greatest mistake a professional can make in this moment is to dismiss their concerns and instincts, and push ahead with the project just to meet deadlines. Completing a project that is on schedule and below its potential is a wasted effort and a lost opportunity.

For this and other reasons, time is a critical success factor when it comes to the creation and application of supply market intelligence. Even in the face of brisk project timelines and the need for results "yesterday," a skilled professional knows when it is time to stop and think. Opportunistic supply market intelligence is most likely to have value potential in more complex, strategic efforts than in transactional ones. At every turn, the project lead should be evaluating the available information and strategy for weak points and growth opportunities.

The fact that opportunistic intelligence starts with more of a "sense" than a question or topic makes the process to Identify and Define that much harder. On the other hand, it is exactly the reason that Research, Read, and Refine is an iterative process. Any search term or phrase that helps the information need materialize is an acceptable place to start.

Output

At the end of the Identify and Define step, the person(s) who will do the research should have words and/or phrases ready to use in their initial search. More specifically, these notes should include what is known, what is unknown, and what the information will be used for. If there is anyone internally with relevant information, procurement should collect it. There is nothing theoretical about the next part of the process. It is time to sit at a computer to Research, Read, and Refine.

STEP 2: RESEARCH, READ, AND REFINE

As mentioned at the outset of this chapter, the second step in the supply market intelligence creation process is iterative, meaning that the same steps are repeated over and over in pursuit of an improved knowledge position. We could also have called this step "Research, Read, Refine, and Repeat, Repeat, Repeat, etc." In Chapter 4, we will look at research tactics, or how to combine the right search strings and sources to get the required information output. In this chapter, the focus is on the process itself.

Unlike step 1: Identifying and Defining information needs, Researching, Reading, and Refining are solitary activities. This responsibility can be intimidating and isolating, especially when time is of the essence, which it always is. For that reason, we advocate getting started as quickly as possible. Take what is known and enter it into an Internet search engine just to get moving. The researcher serves as a filter for all the information they read. Reading it, or more importantly, Refining it, allows known information to be processed so that more targeted rounds of research can be done. This is where the iterative nature of this step pays its greatest dividends. However, just because a researcher is more informed after conducting the first cycle of Researching, Reading, and Refining does not mean that s/he is sufficiently informed to complete the business task, depending upon the supply market intelligence.

The level of knowledge that procurement holds at the outset of this step should be recognized as an influencing factor. For the sake of applicability, we will assume a knowledge base of zero when describing how to Research, Read, and Refine. Although the process is iterative, additional knowledge held by procurement at the outset does not change the steps taken, although it may speed it up or improve the end result. The other implication of this second step is that it is never done, although the natural limitations of time and resources require a decision to be made about when further effort promises only diminishing returns. Since procurement is responsible for more than research, comparing the potential associated with more research to the potential benefit from pursuing other tasks usually makes the decision clear.

Research

Given that most procurement professionals do not have formal training or professional experience in conducting research, getting started can be the most difficult step. It is more comfortable to take on tasks that are straightforward and familiar. The Latin phrase *tabula rasa* or "blank slate" was used by the Romans to describe the wax tablets used by scribes for taking notes. An unused tablet, or simply a "blank page" in modern lingo, suggests a readiness for productivity, but it also represents the unknown. It can be paralyzing. Getting started fast on research is more important than getting started well, especially when additional iterations are expected. For that reason, the first part of the research process is what we call a "quick and dirty" search for information. In other words, mark up the *tabula rasa* quickly so that it becomes a work in progress and breaks the inertia of the unknown.

While most of the research itself is done online and the final deliverables are likely to be in an electronic format, one of the best tools for a "quick and dirty" search is a tried-and-true pen and paper. Especially in cases where procurement is starting with little to no prior knowledge of the subject being researched, anything that is known forms the basis of the first query. These written notes, words, and phrases should be simple facts, such as one or more supplier names, a service or product to be sourced, or the name of an industry or commodity. If there are specific questions to be answered (overt information needs) or objectives to be achieved through the resulting intelligence, write those down as a reminder of the role they should play in the research effort. This seems like a simple step, but it is empowering. Each additional detail learned is noted on paper, which will quickly fill to become a first pass overview of the subject.

The goal of research is to collect information that advances procurement's current understanding of a subject. The process is the same in the first, second, and third iterations, and so on. Once the cycle of Research, Read, and Refine is begun, it is the starting point, or the level of understanding held by the researcher, that changes—not the process itself. The only other change is the volume of relevant information. When starting from a knowledge base of zero, procurement needs to consume a large volume of information on a subject. As their knowledge position improves, the information taken in may be more detailed and refined, or may represent incremental additions to the information already collected.

In order to make the research phase as productive as possible, creativity and interest in the subject are critical. Coming up with queries or search strings can be a challenge early on, when you don't know what you don't know. It may be helpful to create specific questions for yourself, like someone else would do if they were auditing your work. Identify both on point and surrounding or descriptive terminology, as well as authoritative (and hopefully objective) sources. With the exception of the reading that needs to be done to determine the value of the information or source at hand, focus on becoming immersed in the search and collecting information that can be read without the distracting lure of gathering additional information. Continue researching until enough information has been collected to enable a new level of understanding, and then move on to the reading phase.

Read

At its core, successful research is about careful reading. Casting a wide net for information at the outset generates a more refined end result. This fact brings us back to the importance of the person conducting the research. In his or her capacity as a filter, this person distills a broad pool of loosely interconnected information into to a concentrated nugget of tailored intelligence. A larger pool of initial information allows for the included subset to be that much more on point and actionable. The details that are excluded from the final documentation still become part of the researcher's knowledge base, and give him or her an elevated comfort level when presenting and discussing the intelligence.

If the researcher is serving as a filter, the information that he or she allows to pass through unused is just as important as what is held back for later use. Being able to effectively sort the information into relevant and irrelevant categories requires a clear understanding of the intelligence needed, and an accurate perspective of the business conditions the intelligence will impact. As stated by Christian Madsbjerg and Mikkel Rasmussen (2014):

> A perspective implies that you have prioritized certain things—relevant things—and by consequence let some things go. This risk—letting profitable opportunities go for the sake of others—is the essence of all value propositions.[2]

Letting profitable opportunities go does not mean that value is not created from them. The researcher is still being exposed to new ideas.

There are two categories of information that do not find their way into the final intelligence documentation: irrelevant and contextual. Irrelevant or unusable information may be out of date or of suspect quality, or require different circumstances than those at hand in order to be applicable. The second kind of ultimately undocumented information is *contextual*, and should be thought of as more of a hold back than as irrelevant. This information provides the larger context for the facts that are directly on point. In many cases, contextual information explains why the documented information is important. It may also simply be interesting to procurement, and although interest does not seem critical to a business mission, we should never underestimate the value of being generally conversant on a topic. The additional insight resulting from contextual information allows procurement to have productive conversations with suppliers and stakeholders, and may even prove invaluable for recognizing the difference between average and market-leading solutions.

As the information collected in the research phase is read, procurement will be making notes about additional topics to research, knowledge gaps to fill, and questions to answer. Attention should also be paid to sources and authors so that they can be prioritized or avoided in later rounds of research. Once all of the information has been read and reread, it is time to refine the search strategy in preparation for another round of research.

Refine

As noted earlier in this chapter, the process of Researching, Reading, and Refining does not change regardless of how many times it is repeated. What does change is the starting point, or the level of knowledge and understanding held by procurement on the topic in question.

Since the end goal of the supply market intelligence process is to have a document that contains information able to support informed business decisions, any documentation done along the way increases the end-to-end efficiency of the process. A practical way to fold this into the Research, Read, and Refine process is through typing or editing a master notes document at the end of each iteration. As new information is added to the document, a logical structure should emerge, allowing similar or related pieces of information to be recorded side by side. New details may increase the accuracy or applicability of existing information, or they may shed new light on previously held assumptions.

As procurement bolsters their own understanding of a subject through research, they should always remember that while the final information has to be actionable, it also has to be more than just accumulated facts. The majority of this work is done in the Analyze step of the supply market intelligence process, but procurement should be asking increasingly complex questions about the information during the research process. Refining the information in hand by applying a critical eye allows procurement to change or modify their approach and collect the information required to support a new direction. Ideally, once procurement has reached the Analyze step, they are beyond the point where significant additional information is required.

With revised notes and search strategies in hand, procurement can then return to the research phase and collect additional information. It is hard to know when it is time to proceed to Analysis, rather than perpetually collecting more information. If the research is being done to answer a specific question or collect a particular detail, the work is done when the answer is found or when it is determined that the answer is not available. When the goal is to expand procurement's knowledge on a topic so that they can be more strategic, the completion point is less clear. In some cases, time will simply run out and force procurement to move on. In other cases, they will reach a point of diminishing returns and need to acknowledge that any further investment of time and effort is better spent elsewhere.

Output

At the end of the Research, Read, and Refine step of the supply market intelligence creation process, procurement will have collected and reviewed a body of information relevant to the business need at hand. Qualified sources will be identified and properly cited for reference in the final document. The next step, Analyze, begins the process of transforming the collected information into intelligence.

STEP 3: ANALYZE

In Chapter 1, we discussed the fact that there is no automated substitute for a professional armed with basic research skills and a good understanding of a business challenge or information need. The Analyze step of the supply market intelligence creation process is where the majority of this "magic" happens. According to Madsbjerg and Rasmussen (2014):

> After all, humans will, at some point, have to analyze the data, no matter how it is sliced and diced. Someone needs to have a perspective on what the algorithms deliver. It is this perspective—the moment of clarity—that requires time, deep thinking, and experience.[3]

If successful research is ultimately about careful reading, effective analysis is dependent upon thinking and reflection. Taking an analytical approach to information requires time to consider what it really means and how it can be applied to the situation in question. This time may also allow procurement the opportunity to "sanity test" what they have collected, so that the resulting conclusions and recommendations are not only based on facts, but also grounded in reality. This is especially true when the information collected results in unexpected insights or presents a direct challenge to preconceived notions.

For the most part, supply market intelligence should be reviewed within procurement and formally documented before being shared with others in the organization. One exception to this is when the information uncovered might be considered a surprise. Surprises are bad! If truly unexpected information is discovered in the research process and validated, it should be brought to the attention of relevant stakeholders immediately—no formal documentation required.

Examples of surprises include approaching deadlines for changing regulations, an unexpected merger or acquisition that will alter the supplier landscape, or suddenly elevated risks for raw material shortages or supply chain disruptions.

When organizing information for the purpose of supporting analysis, having a structure to work within helps procurement be as thorough as possible. There are a number of popular frameworks for analyzing information, markets, and suppliers. Porter's Five Forces, SWOT, and PESTEL are all familiar tools to professionals in many disciplines. Later in this chapter, we will review the advantages of using these models for analyzing information collected in the supply market intelligence creation process as examples, rather than required approaches. If there is another framework that is more applicable or comfortable, especially if it is used elsewhere in the organization, that approach should take precedence.

Regardless of the framework chosen, procurement should use the Analyze step of the supply market intelligence process to look at the information they have collected and determine how it applies to the organization. In order for information to be actionable, procurement must articulate how it affects negotiating leverage or recommends a change to corporate or category strategy. The conclusions and recommendations that emerge as a result of procurement's analysis of the information are the concrete results of the entire effort.

Analysis versus Synthesis

Although we generally refer to step 3 of the supply market intelligence process as Analysis, it includes both analysis and synthesis. The primary difference between the two approaches is in how the different pieces of information relate to each other.

Analysis is the deconstruction of a topic in pursuit of increased clarity and improved understanding. In other words, analysis is "the process of breaking a complex topic or substance into smaller parts to gain a better understanding of it."[4] The value proposition associated with analysis is in the granular understanding of a topic, whether it is a supplier, a material, or an industry. The resulting improved visibility allows procurement to isolate and affect precise factors of cost, risk, or innovation that may be obscured from a higher vantage point. An analytical approach to information may be used to build a cost model or dissect a competitive landscape.

Synthesis, on the other hand, takes two or more pieces of related information and combines them to create a new idea. As *BusinessDictionary.com* more eloquently puts it, the synthesis is the "systematic combination of otherwise different elements to form a coherent whole."[5] Unlike analytical situations, where the value lies in the details, synthesis is best suited for idea or strategy creation activities. For instance, when procurement is asked to determine a category level spend management approach or compare supplier proposals to determine the right negotiation strategy.

Regardless of whether analysis or synthesis is applied, what procurement is really looking for is a new way of looking at and applying information. Truly unique thoughts are hard to have on demand. The more ways that information can be regarded, the more likely it is that procurement's consideration will result in strategic conclusions. To this point, it may also be a valuable exercise to run the information and preliminary thoughts past an informal panel of colleagues. If procurement is organized along category lines, objectivity may be best found in colleagues accustomed to managing different industries.

Analytical Frameworks

For a more formal approach to analysis, it is advisable to use one of the common strategy frameworks to dissect and consider supply market information. Porter's Five Forces, SWOT, and PESTEL are well-known frameworks for analysis, and each has its niche. As much work as it requires to complete the chosen framework, it is important to remember that this effort is not analysis in and of itself. Only once the collected information is placed in a framework can conclusions and recommendations be drawn from it.

Porter's Five Forces: Competition

Porter's Five Forces, principally created by Harvard University Professor Michael Porter, combines competition from external sources with internal threats to represent the attractiveness of a market. This framework is highly effective for understanding strategies or conditions that will affect all or most of the suppliers in an industry. From a procurement perspective, Porter's framework is suitable for identifying sources of risk, as well as the potential opportunity associated with new market entrants or emerging substitute solutions.

The intended perspective of Porter's model is that of a company looking at the competitive landscape in which they operate. If procurement can accurately understand the competitive landscape their suppliers operate in, they can improve their own bargaining position. A detailed understanding of competitive pressure points allows procurement to see where they have the greatest leverage. On a collaborative note, Porter's model may also give procurement a better idea of what they can offer their suppliers in lieu of cash and what value it is likely to hold in the negotiation process.

SWOT: Simplicity

The Strengths, Weaknesses, Opportunities, and Threats (SWOT) model is usually completed using a two-by-two matrix. Like Porter's framework, SWOT recognizes the differences between internal forces (strengths and weaknesses) and external forces (opportunities and threats). Procurement may use this model to analyze their organization's potential in a market or to better understand suppliers' leverages relative to their own buying power.

The simple matrix format of a SWOT analysis places the focus on the most critical details when the complexity of a situation threatens to obscure the true story:

> SWOT is a useful tool to help marshal insights into a cohesive form. It should only be used to record the most important findings, not every piece of detail; otherwise there is a risk of the story being missed.[6]

When procurement has been effective in their efforts to collect sufficient information through research, yet does not have much experience with a market or category, the volume of details can be paralyzing. When all of the information is new, it is difficult to prioritize it by accurately assigning importance to each detail. Forcing procurement to distill a situation down to the most critical factors may foster the clarity required to accurately represent the current situation.

Since SWOT is commonly used by an organization's sales and marketing teams to assess external competition and customer positioning, using this model may present an interesting opportunity to incorporate their feedback, simultaneously improving the usability of the model and building positive internal working relationships.

PESTEL: Change

The Political, Economic, Social, Technological, Environmental, and Legal (PESTEL) model framework looks at specific macroeconomic factors that influence the appropriate strategy for a given situation. In addition, the initials may be used in different combinations or order, including PEST and PESTLE. Regardless of which components a company chooses to focus on or the order used, this model provides both a broad and detailed overview of a subject, with particular attention given to the anticipated changes each factor may have on strategy.

The amount of change anticipated in a category is usually tied directly to the volatility of the related markets. Procurement organizations tend to select category strategies that can be executed within the term of the contract they intend to sign. As a result, having a sense of the relative stability or instability expected during that time frame will have an impact on the details of the agreement with their suppliers. This may be looked at as a representation of risk, but it can also be a straightforward decision to tie pricing to an index rather than to lock in itemized rates. Since suppliers are likely to be highly aware of these possible changes, and will naturally pursue an opportunity that tips the scales in their favor, procurement should be equally well-informed and consider all possible options for negotiating before making an agreement.

Drawing Conclusions and Forming Recommendations

Once information has been qualified, analyzed, and collected into some kind of logical structure, there are two requirements remaining in the supply market intelligence creation process: drawing conclusions and forming recommendations. These form the core of what will be presented to the business. A simple visualization of how the pieces fit together is shown in Figure 3.3. This is where the critical tie is made between the information collected and the interests of the business. Anyone who has had the unfortunate experience of getting blank stares after the presentation of information has missed this part of the process. The best way to avoid such a situation is to answer the question, "And so what?" for one's self before sharing information.

Conclusions capture procurement's interpretation of what will happen in a market based on the research and reading they have done. Conclusions are predictive in nature, and therefore, are best accompanied by a representation of certainty or the subsequent events that the predictions are tied to (if A and B, then C). Conclusions cannot be statements of fact because judgment is required to form them. Although conclusions are not facts in and of themselves, they should be stated clearly so as to avoid misinterpretation and tied to the facts that motivated them. Any qualifications or dependent conditions should be stated outright.

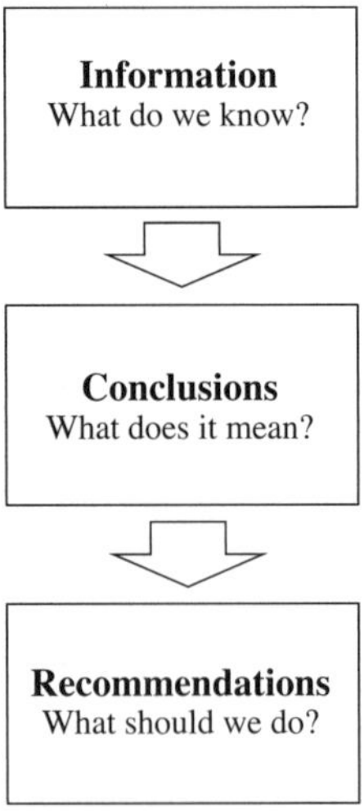

Figure 3.3 Supply market analysis

Recommendations represent procurement's opinions about how the company should act, given the conclusions they have drawn. If the conclusions are brought into question, it follows that the recommendations will need to be revised, as well. Just like conclusions, recommendations should be straightforward and contain any necessary qualifications. Since it is possible that procurement has identified more than one qualified direction for the organization to take, it should be clear what will determine the right path and what conditions are associated with competing recommendations. Just as information must be made actionable in order to be considered intelligence, recommendations should be action steps that can be executed by the company or an individual within it. Whenever possible, procurement should also articulate the expected outcome that will result from each recommendation.

Output

At the end of the Analysis step, procurement will have assembled all of the pieces of information that will ultimately make up the intelligence brief, which is the output of the final step of the supply market intelligence creation process: step 4, Document. As stated above, procurement's conclusions and recommendations form the heart of the output, not just of this step, but of the entire supply market intelligence creation process. In addition to conclusions and recommendations, it is wise to articulate additional questions, and information that was desired or sought but not found. Since we recommend pausing after analysis to pass an Internal Approval Gate, these questions and remaining open items help procurement leaders and managers assess the level of certainty behind the intelligence before it is shared.

INTERNAL REVIEW: APPROVAL GATE

After all of the work procurement needs to do leading up to the documentation of supply market intelligence, it might seem natural or even easy to proceed with all due haste to present their findings to the rest of the project team or organization. For that exact reason, we advocate that a procurement-only review session be held to evaluate the information collected, and the resulting conclusions and recommendations. Once this Approval Gate is passed, the final document should carry the name of the procurement manager or leader who signed off on the intelligence.

There are two primary reasons this is considered a prudent approach:

1. To make sure the work is done as best possible, and
2. To guard against errors.

Both reasons for approval are closely tied to the fact that supply market intelligence ultimately lives as a document. This document, once it is distributed beyond procurement, may travel quickly to unexpected individuals and groups within the organization. The document will contain information that indicates the company's intended strategy or perceived risks, so it should be made clear through distribution and in the document itself that it is for internal use only, and is not to be shared with supply partners.

Conducting a constructively critical review of the intelligence provides an opportunity to expand or improve the work before it is distributed. Any additional work should be weighed against the downside of investing more time and effort. The person doing the review should be in a leadership position within procurement, such as the CPO or other head of the function. If possible, the same person should review all intelligence. This allows for greater consistency and serves the double purpose of keeping the approver informed.

Rather than being an administrative rubber stamp, supply market intelligence approval warrants a meeting where the researcher shares what they have learned and presents their conclusions and recommendations. All relevant procurement team members should be present, including the researcher, category managers, and analysts. During the discussion, everyone present should make sure there are no glaring omissions and that the work generally passes a "smell test" as relevant work that is based in fact. Once this meeting has been conducted, and any additional work is done, procurement can move to documentation in step 4 and create the supply market intelligence brief.

STEP 4: DOCUMENT

We have referred to the documentation of supply market intelligence as a "brief." Strategic research and analysis should not result in a long document. To the contrary, the brief should be a dense document that includes references to the source material for anyone interested in reviewing the primary sources for themselves. Just as the research process is about critical reading skills, procurement's ability to summarize is critical to the creation of this document. The brief should be constructed with efficiency of expression, conveying maximum information in as few carefully chosen words as possible.

The components of the document are:

- Metadata,
- Executive Summary,
- Background,

- Data and Sources,
- Open Items, and
- Conclusions and Recommendations.

We advise putting together a template containing each of these sections, with relevant notes, so that all supply market intelligence briefs created by procurement have a consistent look and feel. Part of this consistency includes the documentation of sources, which is covered through examples in Chapter 6. All supply market intelligence briefs should be stored centrally in an electronic format.

Since the document must be as condensed as possible, every opportunity to convey information should be taken. Even the order of a bulleted list may contain meaning. Each section within the document should have a relevant order such as date (newest first), importance (most critical first), or applicability (most on point first). When the order has an express meaning, it should be noted in the section heading. Nothing should ever be alphabetized just for the sake of injecting an artificial order.

Metadata

Metadata is defined as "data that serves to provide context or additional information about other data."[7] Metadata is a critical part of the documentation of supply market intelligence. There are some details that must be recorded as part of every brief to provide context. They include the relevant spend category, annual spend, key incumbent supplier names, the researcher's name, the approver or approvers' name(s), the completion date, and a recommended schedule for refresh. The person within procurement responsible for leading the intelligence effort should track the metadata from all briefs in one place. We will further discuss the considerations related to knowledge management in Chapter 6.

Executive Summary

An Executive Summary represents the hope that executives within the organization will find the time in their schedules to read at least this part of the brief. It should not contain background information or a lead-in paragraph, but is the information that will be of greatest interest to decision makers. This summary is the brief within the brief, and should be—brief. Measured in sentences rather than paragraphs, the Executive Summary should be straightforward and provide an incentive to read the rest of the document. When possible, procurement should take advantage of the opportunity to represent data in a graphical format rather than in straight text.

Background

Once the reader has been grabbed by the information in the Executive Summary, the Background section provides procurement with an opportunity to take a step back and share the greater context of the topic. It may include information on the organization's history with the category, recent changes in relevant markets, or the challenge that led to the research being done in the first place. Likely to be several paragraphs in length, this section of the brief should increase the reader's understanding, just as procurement increased their own knowledge during the research process. It should not assume a history of experience with the category, and so procurement must balance the inclusion of basic information with the need for efficiency of expression.

Data and Sources

Since hard facts are often critical to the credibility and actionability of the brief, a bulleted list of relevant numbers or data points should be included. While references in the rest of the document are cited through footnotes or endnotes, they should be cited in text next to specific data points because the source of each fact contributes to overall reliability. For example:

- 2012 U.S. Sales of Commercial Ultra Low Sulfur Diesel: 1,662,447 thousand gallons (U.S. Energy Information Administration)[8]
- U.S. Average Ultra Low Sulfur Diesel Price Per Gallon Week ending 3/31: $3.975 including taxes (U.S. Energy Information Administration)[9]

Open Items

While the ideal supply market intelligence brief will address all open issues, it is not unusual to have follow-up questions, additional points for consideration, or remaining unknowns. In many cases, information may be uncovered that prompts additional decisions to be made that are beyond procurement's responsibility. The desired actionability of the intelligence brief includes informed consideration by decision makers. If actions are identified, they should be included in the brief and followed up on each time the document is refreshed. Open items should be prioritized in order of importance.

Conclusions and Recommendations

The conclusions and recommendations formed during Analysis and confirmed during the Internal Approval Gate are presented at the end of the intelligence brief. Although not all of the information collected and reviewed is included in the final document, conclusions and recommendations should seem like logical outcomes, based upon the data and background given. If asked, procurement should be able to point to the facts that justify their recommendations.

CONCLUSION

The supply market intelligence creation process takes procurement from a knowledge base of zero through the creation of a documented deliverable. With experience, researchers will transition from following the process in four distinct steps to growing their knowledge through a smooth learning curve. The process represents value to the organization through actionable information discovered in response to both overt and opportunistic information needs, as well as the improved understanding held by procurement. This understanding results from the details that are captured in the final brief and in the contextual background that are absorbed.

We covered a significant amount of critical information in this chapter, but there are six suggestions that can make all the difference in the supply market intelligence process:

- Err on the side of inclusion when gathering information internally. It improves procurement's understanding of the information and how it will be used. Inclusion also builds positive working relationships and trust with internal stakeholders.
- Why procurement is researching is every bit as important as the information being sought. Clearly articulate business drivers in any notes that will motivate a search.
- Research inertia can be paralyzing, especially when the topic is new. Do not wait until the search strategy is flawless. Gather enough terms or ideas to start researching, and then begin. Later rounds of research can be used to fill in any gaps.
- Knowing when to stop is equally as challenging as getting started. Be on the lookout for the point of diminishing returns, balancing additional time invested against other tasks competing for procurement's attention, and the incremental value associated with potential new information.
- Surprises are bad. When unexpected information is uncovered, share it as soon as possible. Do not delay communication for the sake of formal documentation.
- When documentation is completed, it must be as brief as possible. Procurement must write with the executive team in mind, particularly the need to make the most of their time and to clarify what has been learned.

REFERENCES

1. Kelly Barner, "Who's Got Your Back in a 'Beware' Business Environment?" *Buyers Meeting Point*, March 10, 2014, http://buyersmeetingpoint.com/news/latest-news3/745-3-10-2014-who-s-got-your-back-in-a-beware-business-environment.
2. Christian Madsbjerg and Mikkel B. Rasmussen, *The Moment of Clarity: Using the Human Sciences to Solve Your Toughest Business Problems.* Boston: Harvard Business Review Press, 2014, 155.
3. Madsbjerg and Rasmussen, *Moment of Clarity*, 71.
4. "Analysis," *Wikipedia.org*, Last modified 25 April 2014, http://en.wikipedia.org/wiki/Analysis.
5. "Synthesis," *BusinessDictionary.com*. Accessed June 25, 2014, http://www.businessdictionary.com/definition/synthesis.html.
6. Jonathan O'Brien, *Category Management in Purchasing: A Strategic Approach to Maximize Business Profitability*. Philadelphia, PA: Kogan Page, 2012, 165.
7. "Metadata," *BusinessDictionary.com*. Accessed June 25, 2014, http://www.businessdictionary.com/definition/metadata.html.
8. "Distillate Fuel Oil and Kerosene Sales by End Use," *U.S. Energy Information Administration*. Release date November 15, 2013, http://www.eia.gov/dnav/pet/pet_cons_821use_a_epd2dxl0_vcs_mgal_a.htm.
9. "Weekly Retail Gasoline and Diesel Prices," *U.S. Energy Information Administration*. Release date April 28, 2014, http://www.eia.gov/dnav/pet/pet_pri_gnd_a_epd2dxl0_pte_dpgal_w.htm.

4

SUPPLY MARKET INTELLIGENCE RESEARCH TACTICS

In Chapter 3, we outlined the entire process for supply market intelligence creation from the identification of a need through the finished document. The second step of that process, Research, Read, and Refine, is iterative, and should be repeated multiple times to gather sufficient applicable information to address the inquiry at hand. The techniques and tactics required to successfully execute this step are not often a formal part of the training that procurement professionals receive in school or on the job.

In this chapter, we will focus exclusively on the step of Research, Read, and Refine. We will dig into the details of:

1. Conducting research;
2. Collecting information; and,
3. Documenting sources in preparation for analysis.

The research process must be iterative because each piece of information, and corresponding increase in understanding, changes the perspective of the professional conducting the research. Part of the impetus for this book is our belief that any intelligent, motivated professional can learn to research for the purpose of creating supply market intelligence. In this chapter, we demystify the techniques used by professionals who have earned the applicable graduate degrees and dedicated their careers to this discipline. By learning to take on this responsibility for themselves, procurement teams can experience the benefits without seeking help outside of the organization, or worse, proceeding while ill-informed.

The components of this step, Research, Read, and Refine, provide the primary structure for this chapter with the addition of two more R's: Repeat and Record. In addition, we will delve into special cases where information may be particularly hard to find. It is important to note that while we refer to *tactics* throughout this chapter, the research process is anything but tactical. With the pressure for procurement to take on increasingly strategic efforts, the word *tactical* often designates tasks that do not provide an opportunity for value creation. Nothing could be further from the truth. Creating supply market intelligence requires advanced, critical thought, as well as the drive to learn more about whatever topic is being researched—precisely for the purpose of creating value.

RESEARCH TECHNIQUES AND TACTICS

There are a set of basic skills that can be applied to any research activity, whether it is via the Internet, open web, or carried out using commercial services that offer enhanced quality and relevance of research results in exchange for a fee. Like the skills required for running a marathon, performing surgery, singing an opera aria, or smoking award-winning ribs, practice is critical in research. Researching regularly not only hones skills such as building effective search strings and knowing which sources are best, it provides each individual with the opportunity to develop his or her own particular way of finding, collecting, and organizing information.

The following recommendations for research are based on years of experience in conducting business research. They combine the formal instruction that we received in pursuit of our Masters degrees in Library and Information Science, as well as the routine, often messy reality of conducting Internet research under the pressures of limited time and high expectations. Always remember that *research* means to search, and then re-search, and re-search again until you find the required information.

Get the Terminology Right

Using the wrong terminology or keywords when searching is one of the primary factors leading to poor or irrelevant results. The best prevention is to brainstorm and identify various keywords and terms that can be used before starting to search. This is one of the best applications of the pen and paper method, and may even be the natural outcome of collaborative sessions with internal stakeholders. For more on this, read the section on "The Role of Collaboration" in Chapter 3. As informal as these hastily scribbled notes may be, it is important to regard them carefully because they simultaneously speed up and improve early research results.

Terminology can also be improved by reading basic background and introductory material to better understand the subject or industry being researched. Most professional associations and trade publication websites have an overview or background section that can be useful in increasing understanding for the purpose of better defining results. Thorough websites also offer glossaries. Online dictionaries, thesauri, and Wikipedia provide good definitions for terms key to the understanding of a subject. Graphical versions of dictionaries, such as Visuwords.com provide an interesting alternative to traditional reference materials, and emphasize the connections between related terms.

Look for opportunities to leverage related searches or related terms features in databases. These tools help to identify alternative terms that can be used to reach a refined result quickly. Even Google offers this feature. For example, searches related to "strategic sourcing best practices" could be: strategic sourcing process, best-in-class strategic sourcing, and procurement best practices benchmarks.

Always absorb the information contained in the structure of a website, page, or article in addition to its explicit content. In almost all commercial databases, subject headings and subheadings are assigned as part of the formatting. If you find a good site, see what subject headings have been assigned and incorporate them in subsequent rounds of research.

Use Boolean Operators

Even as search tools move towards natural language commands, which allows queries to be entered in the same way a question would be asked if using written or spoken language, Boolean operators (such as AND and OR) are broadly used and very effective. The need to use Boolean operators is based on the idea that more refined search results require less of procurement's time to read and review before adjusting search terms and moving on.

The Boolean search term AND can be used to narrow results by requiring that a combination of words or phrases be present in a document for it to be returned as a search result. A search for "supplier" AND "manufacturer" will retrieve articles that contain both of those terms. Some sites, such as Google, automatically apply the AND operator when there is more than one keyword in a search. This Boolean term is particularly effective when a supplier name or product is so general that it returns a wide range of results, most of which are not applicable. Adding an industry or headquarters location makes it possible to get directly to the right company.

The Boolean search term OR works by allowing substitute terms to expand the results returned. A search that includes "supplier" OR "vendor" will retrieve articles that have at least one of those terms. Also, use this Boolean term if there are different ways to enter a term: "IBM" OR "International Business Machines." The

Boolean OR is best used for a problem quite opposite the one that a search using AND will address. While AND will return fewer, more applicable results, using OR expands the number of website results, making sure desirable results are not excluded because a word that might be considered a synonym was not included in the search string.

Make Use of Other Key Operators and Symbols

While not all websites and databases employ the same search mechanisms, there are some common operators that can be used to support advanced research needs.

Use an asterisk (*) to find *all* forms of a search term. For example, a search for "hack*" will find hacks, hacker, hacked, hacking, etc. In some cases, the asterisk can be used at the beginning of a word, as well as at the end. With Google, the asterisk functions as a placeholder for any word in a longer search string. Searching for "Institute for * Management" returns the Institute for Supply Management, as well as the Institution for Nonprofit Management and Leadership, and the Institute for Ranch Management.

Quotation marks (" ") in a search string indicate that you want results that contain the entire, exact phrase. For example, searching for "market share" with quotation marks will find results that discuss the market share of a company rather than results that contain both words individually.

Similarly, proximity searching requires that words be close to each other, but not necessarily together. With Google searches, use the AROUND( ) feature. Searching for "Franklin AROUND(2) Roosevelt" will pick up any variation of middle name or initials for the thirty-second President of the United States. In other databases, use the NEAR and WITHIN operators. Operators are different for each database, so make sure to check available Help features. A LexisNexis database example is "Cadbury w/10 Godiva," which will return results where the word *Cadbury* is found within ten words of the word *Godiva*. This technique incorporates context into a search without looking for a short, exact phrase.

Put It All Together

Keep in mind that while each of the above recommendations is useful in its own right, combining them can be incredibly powerful. For instance, using the right terminology in conjunction with a phrase designated by quotation marks, and two alternative terms designed with the Boolean operator OR, may allow the right results to be found very quickly, achieving precision and speed at the same time.

Special Cases in Google

Google is the world's most popular search engine, with more than 80% of unique searchers choosing their search site over its competitors.[1] A solution does not dominate a market without being the best, and the honor is well earned. Not all searches will start at an Internet search engine, but the odds are that when they do, Google will be the website of choice. This fact requires that we provide some search recommendations specific to Google.

Google's Advanced Search is a fantastic resource. In addition to making it easy to combine search techniques such as phrases, Boolean operators, and exclusions, the Advanced Search helps instill advanced research *thinking*. Remembering to take advantage of all of the query options in any search is a discipline built up over time, and seeing individual fields for many of the available search approaches serves as an active reminder for new researchers.

Here are a few of the other search tools and options available through Google:

- Comparison searching: Using "vs" after a product or company name will find comparison articles. For example, "NetSuite vs" will return alternatives to NetSuite.
- Dictionary definitions: To find the definition for a word or phrase, type the word "define" then a space, then the word(s) you want defined, such as "define compliance."
- Number ranges: Separate numbers by two periods without spaces (..) to see results that contain numbers in a given range of things like dates, prices, and lists; for example, enter "top 50..100 companies" or "camera $50..$100."
- Site: Use this if you only want to search one specific website, for example, "site:linkedin.com contract manager." This approach is part of the Advanced Search feature and is particularly helpful when a site is known to be a good resource but has poor embedded search functionality.
- Word exclusion: Use the minus (–) sign to exclude terms. Place the minus sign right before the term you want to exclude, for example, "cardinals–Arizona" that will emphasize birds rather than football in the search results.

USING RESEARCH RESOURCES GIVEN IN PART II

Part I of this book covers the importance of supply market intelligence for all of procurement's initiatives, and details a process and methodology that can be put into place to implement a successful intelligence program. The number of supply market intelligence sources that are available for research purposes can be overwhelming, especially once all of the industry and market specific resources are considered. The Internet makes information readily available, but it is easy to become frustrated with search results that are not specific enough. It is an inevitable truth that the valuable information used for critical decision making is often not free, and can actually be quite expensive. As a result, identifying, evaluating, and choosing the correct resources are a key component to successful supply market research. It is important for procurement to understand how to identify and evaluate the sources they find in the research process.

The resources in Part II of this book address the need for supply market intelligence by listing and describing the best resources available to procurement professionals for both general and specialized information requirements. The sources included in Part II, which are listed by content type, were evaluated and are considered to be authoritative. Further evaluation done by each procurement professional will help determine if the resource covers his or her own specific information need, and if it is within the available budget. The chapters included first in Part II provide listings of general category sources and those specific to the practice of procurement. The remaining chapters list resources that are dedicated to a particular industry, market, or spend category, whether it is associated with direct or indirect spend. Each chapter includes a combination of the following: Background Information; Supplier Identification; Pricing and Market Analysis; Market Research Reports; Publications and Websites; and Associations and Organizations.

Background Information

As pointed out in the above section, Research Techniques and Tactics, identifying the correct terminology as soon as possible improves the efficiency and accuracy of a research effort. The sources that we designated for the purpose of collecting background information will help identify the correct terminology and increase general understanding of the topic in question.

The sources may be particularly helpful in advance of meeting with internal stakeholders when procurement has not previously sourced spend in the category or industry. Additional details will unquestionably have to be collected after such meetings or discussions. Entering each meeting with enough background knowledge to ask intelligent questions improves the productivity of internal sessions, allows procurement to ask more informed questions, and earns the respect of the stakeholders who manage the spend and suppliers on a regular basis.

Supplier Identification

This section includes various buyers' guides and resources designed specifically for the purpose of collecting and providing information about sources of supply. When, as some guides do, they break lists of suppliers down into similar groups, they also provide insight into the structure of the industry and capability types held by suppliers.

These guides may provide two types of useful information for procurement. The most evident type of information is to identify new suppliers who may be interested in participating in a bid. Contact information and capability details are also commonly included in buyer guides, making them an ideal source for this needed information. One risk of relying on the contact information from guides is that they may provide a general "info" e-mail address or phone number. If a supplier seems qualified, it is always appropriate to visit their website directly, assuming they have one, and request a sales or account representative.

Another application for buyer guides is getting a better understanding of how incumbent suppliers fit into the larger market in which they compete. Most of the information available to procurement about incumbents is insular. Spend data only tells procurement about the history of their purchasing activity with the supplier, and information from internal stakeholders only represents their opinion about the company. While both pieces of information are important, neither provides the contextual information that may be gained when a supplier is compared alongside its primary competitors.

Pricing and Market Analysis

This section arguably lists the most valuable information to procurement, as these resources are crucial for getting direct insight into market trends and cost drivers. These sources usually provide current, historical, and forward-looking market data, and may also include trend identification.

Gaining access to this data is hugely helpful to procurement when benchmarking contracted pricing, either for an opportunity assessment or in a strategic sourcing project. When it is possible to estimate market share, procurement may be able to use this information to determine whether the prices that the organization is currently paying are competitive. When the pricing information is associated with input costs, or materials that suppliers are purchasing for inclusion in a finished or assembled product, procurement can assess the buying power and usage efficiency of their suppliers.

Market Research Reports

This section identifies the providers of packaged market research reports. While resources in the Pricing and Market Analysis sections tend to be data focused, market research reports are more about analysis and interpretation of that data. Depending on how current and analysis-intensive the information is, these reports can be prohibitively expensive. In other cases, they are made available for free. When reports are made available at no cost, it is important to read them carefully for information on which companies may have sponsored (and potentially influenced) the content.

Market research reports provide information that procurement may find useful for the development of a category strategy. Well-written analyst reports will include major industry trends and developments, as well as emerging technologies or disruptive innovators. When the reports are targeted enough, and when the buying power of the company matches the size of the suppliers included in the report, they may be another source of prospective suppliers for bid invitations.

Publications and Websites

Listed in this section are the key trade, journal, and industry-specific publications along with their accompanying websites, if available. Where Pricing, Market Analysis, and Market Research sources are likely to provide updates monthly, quarterly, or annually, publications and websites often provide updates on a daily basis, especially if they have blogs.

These resources may be useful to procurement professionals who are dedicated to an industry or category of spend and need to stay on top of regular developments for the sake of responding appropriately to or taking advantage of unanticipated opportunities that arise. Since publications and websites are likely to have revenue models based on advertising or marketing arrangements, it is always advisable to look closely for the motivation and objectivity of their writers. Author credibility, impartiality, and motivation are covered in detail in Chapter 6.

Associations and Organizations

This section includes prominent and influential professional associations and organizations. These are often the associations that internal stakeholders belong to, and therefore, influence their opinions. Associations are key providers of market and industry information, along with opportunities to network with like-minded professionals. They are the entities that develop and enforce industry standards. Almost all of these groups report on key legislative and policy issues and intelligence that are crucial to understanding a specific market.

Many times, procurement makes the assumption that the best source of information is a website or publication, when in reality it is a person. Many thought leaders are more than willing to make themselves available over the phone to answer questions within their area of expertise. When a company is advanced in their management of a category, it may be highly effective to go straight to the source to ask context-specific questions, rather than trying to make do with general information.

READ AND REFINE

It is a rare search, even for a professional researcher, that returns the exact, correct result the first time. Common problems are too many results, not enough results, or results that somehow miss the mark. In addition to building search skills, procurement professionals must remember that it is important to understand how each search engine or database works, and how those implied constraints will affect their results.

One of the best tactics employed by professional researchers may be the simplest. Know when to take a break or stop, and try a new approach. If you have been researching for a while and are starting to see the same (ineffectual) results returned, take this as a clue that it is time to change the strategy and/or search terminology. If searches have not been successful, it also helps to take a break for as long as a day before re-approaching the effort with fresh eyes. In the best-case scenario, zero results mean a search term has been misspelled. In the worst case, it indicates a deeper misunderstanding of the subject. Search fatigue makes it hard to diagnose which of these problems is the likely cause, let alone solve the problem.

Use the Find Command

When first reading a long document, article, or report, use a browser's or document's Find command to highlight and jump to where your keyword or search term appears. This technique lets you see how many times the term is used and in what section of the document it appears. Having the term appear in a reference list or in footnotes is not likely to be associated with sufficient content. Terms that appear in the introduction, a section heading, or the text will produce more relevant results. The Find command can also be used to locate all forms of the root search term.

Know How Search Results Are Sorted

The first thing to do when viewing your results after entering a term in a search engine is to determine how the results are being sorted. Most of the time, the default is set to relevance, meaning the results with the most occurrences of your search term appear first. In most cases, this is sufficient, but it is not as appropriate when researching something that needs to be current, like supplier financials. In this case, it is necessary to sort or filter the results by date. If the default is by date, and the first round of results misses the mark, it is possible to think the problem is with search terms rather than display settings.

Take the Opportunity to Search within Results

Effective databases and websites offer various ways to narrow and refine search results. An advanced search will almost always allow searching for words in the title only. Narrowing the effective date range can either target a specific point in the history of a company or news story, or be used to eliminate anything other than the newest results. Overly general results may benefit from adding limits or narrowing terms to the search string.

Actively Seek Out and Use the Help Feature

Many search engines and databases offer online or live customer support. Take the time to refer to the Help feature in the database you are searching. Search functions vary from database to database, but the Help feature shows what search options are available and how to use them.

When available, support teams can help set up searches to get the right results because they want their customers to be successful using their product or service. Take any Help training that is available before using the resource. When specialized help is not provided by the resource, try to locate forums or discussions online from other users.

Be a Good Steward of Fee-for-Use Information Spend

Procurement spends the majority of their time looking at the efficiency of resource use. We often run into cases where one part of the organization has made a purchase without first validating that no one else in the organization had already done so. We need to practice what we preach, and should always investigate what fee-for-use resources are already available within the organization before signing a contract of our own.

Investigate any firm-wide subscriptions your company uses. Many companies subscribe to at least one resource like LexisNexis, Factiva, or Hoover's. Departments that use these types of resources are Marketing, Research and Development, and Legal. Even if the precise, desired solution is not already available in-house, it may be possible to meet information needs cost effectively by adding onto an existing contract and splitting the cost between all involved departmental budgets.

If your budget is lean, yet your information needs are robust, consider accessing information services through local libraries. For example, the New York Public Library provides access to respected resources like Bloomberg, Business & Company Resource Center, Business Monitor Online, Business Source Premier, Emerging Markets, First Research, IBISWorld, Mergent, and many others. It may also be worthwhile to determine whether anyone in procurement earned a business degree through a local school with a library, where they can leverage their alumni status to make use of otherwise costly resources.

RECORD

The essential idea of research is that information that was already collected or documented by others is being sought for a new use. While it is not wrong to leverage the work of others, it is mandatory that the proper attribution be given. Properly documenting sources should not be considered an administrative task. Accurate citations allow valuable sources to be consulted as necessary, and provide the appropriate credibility to the quotes and statistics cited.

This requirement may present a challenge in organizing sources during the research process: "Since the beginning of the written word, individuals have been struggling with the dual problems of organizing and retrieving information."[2] Today, we are dealing with "information overload," a term that was popularized in the 1970s by Alvin Toffler's bestselling book, *Future Shock*.[3] When mind-numbing advances in technology are combined with the ever-increasing creation and sharing of content, information overload is not going away. According to a McKinsey (2013) report, "Employees spend 1.8 hours every day—9.3 hours per week, on average—searching and gathering information. In other words, businesses hire five employees, but only four show up to work; the fifth employee is off searching for answers, but not contributing any value."[4] According to Interact, "19.8 percent of business time—the equivalent of one day per working week—is wasted by employees searching for information to do their job effectively."[5] IDC data shows that "the knowledge worker spends about 2.5 hours per day, or roughly 30 percent of the workday, searching for information."[6] Procurement professionals perform daily general research tasks in addition to market intelligence research. Becoming efficient at finding, organizing, and retrieving research materials ensures a professional's ability to be more effective and successful at his or her work.[7]

Document As You Go

Documenting as you go might seem like a minor point, but it is much more efficient to document a possible source before moving on to the next one than it is to relocate that source later. This is especially true in the opening rounds of research, when the primary drive is to gather information quickly. For instance, an early article may be dismissed for being off topic, even if it is close. A researcher mentally notes it and moves to the next article. After viewing many articles, s/he realizes that the early article was more relevant than initially thought and would be good to use. Now, s/he is performing another search to find that particular article.

Documenting during research, or at least copying the citation information or a URL, allows for quick reference of articles that have potential. Research is a valuable activity, but rediscovery is an inefficient use of time.

Tools for Organizing Links

The following tools and services, many of which are available at no cost, provide convenient capabilities to easily capture, annotate, organize, and retrieve content in all of its forms. Many of these tools and services also support the ability to share information with others, an important capability when one person is conducting research for information that will be leveraged by an entire team. As for the rest of the knowledge management topics that we address in Chapter 6, it is wise to establish standards for which services to use and how to manage access, so that work and information are not lost through employee turnover.

Some research tools and services that offer information sharing are:

- **Box**
  https://www.box.com
  Box, named as a leader by Gartner and Forrester, offers scalable content sharing. Its mission, as stated on its website, is "to make sharing, accessing and managing content ridiculously easy." Its note-taking app, called Box Notes, lets teams collaborate on ideas and information, using a simple format.
- **Delicious**
  https://delicious.com
  Delicious is a free bookmarking service for collecting, organizing, and searching web links. This site was founded in 2003 and relaunched in 2011 by YouTube founders Chad Hurley and Steve Chen.
- **Diigo**
  https://www.diigo.com
  Diigo describes itself as a multi-tool for knowledge management. Diigo is an acronym for "Digest of Internet Information, Groups and Other stuff." Here, researchers can annotate and highlight sections in web pages; tag, organize, and build personal libraries in the cloud with links and other favorite items (with search functionality); and build a group knowledge repository.
- **Dropbox**
  https://www.dropbox.com
  Dropbox is not a note-taking or bookmarking service, but a cloud file-storage service. It can be used to securely store photos, documents, and videos, with access from anywhere. There are three plans: Basic,

which is free; Pro, which is for personal projects; and Business, which provides unlimited space with centralized administration features.

- **Evernote**
  http://evernote.com
  "When power users talk about Evernote, they call it their brain."[8] This highly rated service is great for collecting information anywhere and making it readily available. It is possible to save web pages including text, images, and links via the web clipper function. Evernote Business offers features for enhanced collaboration in organizations.
- **Google Keep**
  https://drive.google.com/keep
  Google Keep is Google's note-taking service, where researchers can create, access, and organize notes that are automatically stored on Google Drive.
- **OneNote**
  http://office.microsoft.com/en-us/onenote
  OneNote is Microsoft's note collection offering, which competes with Evernote. Notes in any form—typed, handwritten, or drawn—can be captured, saved, organized, and searched. According to Microsoft, it is also possible to "clip links and web pages, insert photos and videos, embed tables, and attach files."
- **Pocket**
  https://getpocket.com
  Pocket is a save-for-later service that supports the need to save items from the web, such as articles and videos, so they can be read or viewed later, when more time is available.
- **Scrible**
  http://www.scrible.com
  Supported by the National Science Foundation, this tool (in beta at the time of publication) makes it possible to organize, search, and retrieve research from a personal library. It also provides the ability to annotate web pages and share them with others.
- **Springpad**
  https://springpad.com/about
  Springpad is a free digital note-taking application that saves favorite items into an easy to organize visual platform and adds useful information. Researchers can save and access information from multiple devices and the web.

SPECIAL RESEARCH CASES

Most of the research done by procurement follows a similar pattern, starting with the identification of a need and making the most of the time available to fill the gap in their understanding. There are, however, some special research cases that require a different approach.

One example of a special case is in researching privately held versus publicly held companies. The difficulty in this case is the lack of information availability rather than the experience of the researcher. We have become accustomed to information being widely available in straight data form, and even analyzed or interpreted for us by industry analysts and bloggers. When it is not, it is easy to feel "against a wall" without an available next step.

Another special case is when information does not need to be collected because it is already in procurement's hands. If it came from a supplier or another third party, it must be validated as current, accurate, and applicable before being passed along internally as fact.

Public versus Private Suppliers

Finding supplier information depends on many variables, including whether the supplier in question is a publicly or privately held company. Detailed financial information is generally more available for publicly held companies because they are required to disclose financial information, and most make this information easily accessible on their website.

In the United States, a public company has issued securities that are traded on the open market. Public companies are required to file reports and data on their finances and operations. This information is filed with the Securities and Exchange Commission (SEC) in the form of annual reports, 10Ks, and other filings. A company may also be a parent or subsidiary of another corporation. This is important to note because the financial information for a subsidiary is filed under the name of the parent company.

Private companies, as a general rule, are not required to reveal anything, thus making it more of a challenge to find information. The best sources to use include local, regional, international and business newspapers, trade journals, press releases, executive interviews, directory information, research companies, credit reports, analysts, and social media (e.g., LinkedIn, Twitter, Facebook).

Overall, more information is available on suppliers that are larger, publicly held, more established, and/or operate in a regulated industry. Conversely, you will find less information on smaller, privately held, new, or emerging suppliers, and/or those that operate in nonregulated industries.[9] This research can be a particular challenge for procurement when a category evaluation or bid process includes both public and private companies, as the same information is not available for all prospective suppliers. Some information may be provided by the private supplier at the appropriate time in the bid process, but procurement should still make an effort to discover as much as they can from third-party sources.

Validation versus Discovery

Although most of this chapter, and in fact this book, assumes that procurement is looking to gather information on a topic, sometimes we find ourselves in the position of having a fact or detail that we need to validate. When suppliers provide information, there will be a natural level of skepticism, especially when the information is in their favor. Other times, procurement may need to validate (or contradict) a belief held by an internal stakeholder. In either case, procurement must find an authoritative source that definitively supports (or contradicts) the information. If the information turns out to have both reputable supporters and deniers, this is also important information and should be used to temper how motivating the fact is.

Searching to validate is something like the television game show *Jeopardy*, where all correct responses have to be presented in the form of a question. Preparation for validation research may start by generating a list of questions that would lead to the fact in hand. Alternately, this is a perfect opportunity to reach out to an industry expert directly, as suggested in the section above on Associations and Organizations. If procurement takes this approach, they should make the most of the opportunity by preparing additional questions or topics to inquire about.

CONCLUSION

The fact that professionals get graduate degrees in conducting research indicates that it is a formal discipline, deserving respect and requiring training, specialized knowledge, and practice. That being said, the tactics and techniques provided in this chapter, along with quality sources and critical thought, make it possible for any motivated professional to locate the information they need to complete an open assignment.

REFERENCES

1. Danny Sullivan, "Google Still Most Popular Engine by Far But Share of Unique Searchers Dips Slightly." *Search Engine Land*, February 11, 2013, http://searchengineland.com/google-worlds-most-popular-search-engine-148089.

2. Mary Axford and Crystal Renfro, "Noteworthy Productivity Tools for Personal Knowledge Management," Academic Search Main Edition. *Online* 36 (2012): 33.
3. *Ibid.*, 33.
4. Beth Burgee, "Top Three Reasons Why We Spend So Much Time Searching for Information." *UTR*, May 14, 2013, http://utrconf.com/top-3-reasons-why-we-spend-so-much-time-searching-for-information.
5. "A Fifth of Business Time Is Wasted Searching for Information, Says Interact," *ITAnalysis*, May 2, 2013, http://www.it-analysis.com/services/outsourcing/news_release.php?rel=38149.
6. Doug Loo, "Information: The Lifeblood of the Enterprise," *Armedia*, October 30, 2013, http://www.armedia.com/blog/2013/10/federated-search-the-importance-of-being-able-to-find-information.
7. Kasey Fleisher Hickey, "Eight Ways Evernote Can Help You Get More from Your Research in 2013, and a New Ambassador!" *Evernote Corporation*, December 18, 2012, https://blog.evernote.com/blog/2012/12/18/8-power-ways-evernote-can-help-you-get-more-from-your-research-in-2013-and-a-new-ambassador.
8. "The World's Top Ten Most Innovative Companies in Productivity," *Fast Company*, February 11, 2014, http://www.fastcompany.com/most-innovative-companies/2014/industry/productivity.
9. MIT Libraries, "Business Research Workshop," *Docstoc*, February, 2008, http://www.docstoc.com/docs/14974480/Business-Research-Workshop.

5

THE BUSINESS CASE FOR SUPPLY MARKET INTELLIGENCE

When procurement allows their work to be driven by external information and advised by internal data, rather than the reverse, they position themselves closer to the operational pulse of the organization. As we have demonstrated through our review of processes and tactics in Chapters 1 through 4, leveraging supply market intelligence in procurement is not another initiative running in parallel to other efforts. Instead, it forms the basis for an execution philosophy that should be internalized by procurement and consistently carried out across all initiatives.

Each organization must make the conscious decision to place supply market intelligence central to their procurement priorities. In most cases, this decision signals a significant change in how procurement aligns with the rest of the organization. When markets are at the center of procurement's strategies and decisions, they take on the same view and performance drivers as sales, account management, and marketing.

Careful planning is required to deliver results that demonstrate procurement's strategic relevance to executive leadership through supply market intelligence. Any effort or expense associated with introducing a supply market intelligence program must be offset by sustainable returns. Procurement must design a program that makes the right information available to the right people at the right time. Vision, objectives, and goals need to be articulated in a formal business case that can be presented internally. The business case must also include any additional talent and staffing requirements, and outline the methods and metrics that will be used to track results.

One of the secondary benefits of supply market intelligence is that it offers advantages beyond helping procurement improve their own performance. The intelligence created holds value for multiple internal and external stakeholders. Once the effort has been invested to create and document intelligence, procurement should not miss a single opportunity to use it to build additional bridges and relationships. Like the supply market intelligence program and the supporting business case, this outreach should not be haphazard. Procurement must deliberately identify what information holds value for each group of internal stakeholders or suppliers, and when it is appropriate to distribute documented intelligence. This extension of the core supply market intelligence business plan allows procurement to create value by making the most of their effort and the organization's investment in them.

BUILDING THE BUSINESS CASE

We recommend taking the time and effort to build a business case despite the fact that procurement could arguably begin executing a supply market intelligence program on their own, with little fanfare or resistance from the rest of the organization. When supply market intelligence occupies its rightful position at the center of procurement activity, the improvement in results merits the proper recognition. While we make the argument that it is possible for professionals with the right training and motivation to create their own supply market intelligence, we do not mean to imply it is easy. The fact that procurement has made the decision to attempt such an effort deserves the respect of executive leaders. Making a formal business case presentation is the right way to simultaneously inform them of procurement's intent, earn their respect, answer their questions, and solicit their input. It also presents the opportunity to sell other functions on the potential of getting market intelligence through procurement.

The components of such a business plan are not fixed. At a minimum, the plan should demonstrate that the supply market intelligence program is appropriate, given the associated opportunities. Much of the advice we provide in the section about intelligence briefs in Chapter 3 applies to a written business case.

The business case should be brief. It should contain clearly documented facts and figures. Most important of all, procurement should be ready to present the business case comfortably. By this, we mean that the person making the case should be well versed enough in the supporting details that the session is more of a strategy discussion than a one-sided presentation followed by a yea or nay vote. Procurement should expect constructive (and not so constructive) criticism, and be ready with responses as well as the confidence to ask for more input in the face of uncertainty.

Before presenting the business case, procurement should know specifically what they are asking the executive team for. Although it will feel like a tenuous moment in the discussion, procurement should demonstrate the same level of respectful tenacity that the organization would expect them to exercise in negotiations with suppliers. In order to be fully prepared, it may be wise to run a pilot of the supply market intelligence program. Select one project and incorporate the supply market intelligence creation process as though the business case had already been granted executive support, or select a number of staggered projects so that each point in the sourcing process can be improved in a compressed timeline. When presenting the findings from the pilot, be sure to include what was learned, as well as any successes achieved. Be prepared for mitigated approvals, such as requests for further consideration or additional pilots. Procurement should take whatever measure of approval or support is offered and press forward, returning to executives as appropriate to demonstrate their initial wisdom in "approving" the program.

Vision, Objectives, and Goals

Part of what makes a business case effective is that it forces presenters to articulate things that seem obvious, and the case can improve through discussion and debate. The vision, objectives, and goals of a supply market intelligence program are perfect examples. Any procurement team that has made the decision to invest in a supply market intelligence program has intrinsic knowledge of why they are doing it, what they hope to accomplish, and what the high level motivating factors are. Being able to clearly and succinctly communicate these thoughts to executives in a high stakes presentation is another thing entirely.

Vision

In forming procurement's vision for a supply management program, it is important to consider how a supply market intelligence program will positively alter the organization as a whole. The fact that procurement is taking a proactive rather than reactive position on supply market intelligence creates an opportunity to determine and live up to their own vision for the future. The vision should demonstrate procurement's current and aspirational maturity. It should focus on the potential for evolution rather than struggle to meet current expectations. The vision is what will likely win over executives. If the vision aligns with executives' own perspectives on the organization's needs, it increases the odds that they will support the need to commit corporate resources such as people, time, and money to the effort.

The vision statement should be no longer than two sentences, and should lead the business case. Opportunities for improving procurement's performance should be included, as should the risk of not adopting a supply market-driven philosophy. Although it is brief, the vision is the sort of statement that will be written and edited repeatedly. The reality of working with executives is that they are accustomed to making decisions quickly, and with minimal information. Get the vision statement right, and the deal may be sealed quickly. Miss the mark in either content or delivery, and the meeting may be over with equal haste and less satisfactory results. If approval is given, and the supply market intelligence program is launched, an annual review of the vision should be done by procurement and then shared with executives and stakeholders. This will ensure that the vision continues to match overall organizational strategy and reflect what procurement has learned as the program matures. It also makes sure that the use of supply market intelligence remains in the consciousness of busy executives.

Objectives

When forming objectives, procurement must be prepared to articulate why the organization needs a supply market intelligence program. In order to resonate with executives, objectives must be directly on point for the organization. The vision should capture the potential associated with making an investment in supply market intelligence. Objectives provide concrete examples of how that potential will change or improve execution. There are likely to be a few examples in any business case, such as:

- To increase corporate leverage through stronger negotiating positions.
- To minimize risk in the supply chain by understanding the factors that introduce potential disruptions and raise confidence in decision making.
- To support the ability to build better cost models in order to benchmark the resource efficiency of suppliers and increase internal profit margins.
- To ensure that market conditions are incorporated in decisions to prioritize and set the schedule for strategic sourcing projects.
- To support product differentiation and create greater perceived customer value, resulting in a higher selling price.

Goals

For each objective, procurement should outline what specifically will be accomplished. Each goal in the business case for a supply market intelligence program should align with an objective. If an objective provides the reason why, each goal should show how procurement will demonstrate their achievement of the objective. For example:

- To conduct a SWOT analysis in advance of every negotiation.
- To document at least three potential risks associated with every new sourcing project.
- To have the Chief Procurement Officer (CPO) review a cost model before every RFP or RFQ is opened for bidding.
- To flag sourcing projects when the timing of a contract expiration would result in suboptimal negotiating conditions for procurement, and to avoid the situation in the future.
- To include at least one nontraditional, qualified, and competitive solution in each sourcing project to force participants and decision makers to be imaginative.

Talent and Staffing

While talent and staffing are human resources or management issues for procurement, executives will look at them as investment requirements. More bluntly, they will need to understand what the supply market intelligence program will cost the organization. This brings procurement to the classic make vs. buy decision. Is it better to upskill internal resources, following the process and tactic recommendations outlined in this book, or do the needs of the organization merit hiring someone with market research skills and experience?

The decision will be based, at least in part, on the available budget. Any recommendation that procurement makes should reflect the workload capacity of current team members and the likelihood that they will successfully absorb the process and skills required to create supply market intelligence in the time available to them.

Make: Train Current Procurement Resources to Create Supply Market Intelligence

Managing talent is a primary challenge for any CPO. Fortunately for managers and practitioners alike, the identification, research, analysis, and documentation associated with supply market intelligence are relatively concrete, making them easier to learn.

The advantages associated with training current resources include little to no budgetary impact and the positive work environment created when professionals feel that their organization has confidence in them and is willing to make an investment to see their potential materialize. The benefits of acquiring these skills will be of use to professionals through a long successful career in procurement or any other part of the organization they join. Empowering procurement team members to own the creation of supply market intelligence reduces lost efficiency due to response delays, misinterpretation of requirements, and lack of ownership over the information collected.

The disadvantages of a "make" approach include frustration from overworked sourcing or category managers, and delays in the positive impact of supply market intelligence due to the natural learning curve. The learning curve has two effects. The first is associated with a longer lead time before improved results are realized as training is carried out and absorbed. The second is the lesser quality associated with work done by researchers in training. Experience is the best teacher, and cannot be rushed. Realistic expectations must be set regarding the time frame for positive impact when selecting the "make" approach.

Recommendation: If the organization, procurement or otherwise, has no budget for hiring market research talent, this is the best option. The "make" approach will be the most successful when carried out with a motivated, energetic procurement team who can see the potential upside for themselves and the function associated with taking on this additional work. The communication of a "make" supply market intelligence program should include clear examples of how it will pay dividends in terms of better project results and higher executive team respect and visibility. Fortunately, as discussed in Chapter 6, it is possible to contract professional researchers on a project-by-project basis. When high-stakes efforts come along, their assistance will not only ensure a quick, quality result, it will elevate the perspective of the in-house team.

Buy: Hire Dedicated Professionals to Conduct Research on Procurement's Behalf

If the budget and the right candidate or candidates are available, it is a valid option to consider hiring experienced research professionals to conduct research on behalf of the entire procurement team. The model for this approach would be similar to having a dedicated analytic resource that steps in to assist all project or category teams as needed, and then disengages once their role is complete. An alternative to hiring a permanent, full-time staff member is bringing in a professional resource on a contract basis to train existing procurement resources and then gradually transition the responsibility to them in full.

The advantages of hiring a professional already trained in corporate market research extend beyond bringing the intelligence program online quickly. Research professionals are accustomed to conducting research for colleagues that do not fully know what they are looking for. They know how to lead exploratory discussions or conduct an intake interview to collect the context and questions on which their research activity will be based. They will also see potential applications for market intelligence that procurement has not yet envisioned. If the opportunity and the desire exist, they may even transfer some level of their knowledge to the entire team over time, allowing them to focus on more complex, strategic research.

Having a centralized ownership and point of contact for the market intelligence function offers many strategic advantages. By having designated professionals field requests and conduct research, there is a decreased chance of "recreating the wheel" each time a new research project is initiated. Most importantly, that professional will become increasingly adept at understanding the unique intelligence required by the department. This allows them to anticipate and predict coming information needs, which creates value by demonstrating procurement's deep understanding of the organization. It also allows procurement to command a deeper respect and contributes to their success in getting budgets approved for increased resources. To internal stakeholders, it demonstrates skills and knowledge that other groups in the organization do not possess.

The most obvious disadvantage of hiring is the cost of an additional salary, or the reallocation of a salary that would otherwise be dedicated to core procurement work. Even if this is not a constraint, it is likely to take procurement professionals some time to become accustomed to making use of this resource. Procurement often faces the reality that their non-procurement colleagues find it easier to keep buying the way they always have, without strategic sourcing, even if they pay incrementally more. In the same way, procurement may find it easier to keep market intelligence at arms length, accepting similarly less optimal results.

Recommendation: If procurement makes the decision to increase the focus on supply market intelligence by hiring one or more experienced professionals, they should be fully aware of what else will be required to make the choice a success. In addition to needing to learn more about procurement as a discipline, the person or persons selected should be prepared to operate in an entrepreneurial environment. They will need to sell the benefits of research and intelligence and actively seek opportunities to contribute to the team's performance. A Master's Degree in Library and Information Science is ideal, as is relevant work experience or an academic specialization in corporate libraries. Demonstrated proficiency in knowledge management and market intelligence program design are highly desirable as well.

Running a Supply Market Intelligence Pilot

Conducting a supply market intelligence pilot takes the effort and its associated benefits out of the realm of the hypothetical and into an appropriately confirmed position of certainty. The experiences associated with a pilot allow procurement to engage executives in a narrative that is based on specifics of time, talent, and tools. It also allows them to make a more compelling argument as they can base their statements and responses on firsthand knowledge.

An additional decision that procurement will need to make is whether the pilot can be run openly, or whether it should be a "stealth" pilot. In some cases, procurement will need to determine the likelihood of executive approval by doing actual hands-on work before publicizing the effort in. If the pilot can be run openly, whether executive approval has been given for a full program or not, procurement may want to consider establishing a "war room" where all discussions regarding the pilot take place. Having open and visible evidence of the effort and its results welcomes any interested parties to take an active role, track progress, and stay informed.

The timing of a pilot should be based on a calculated understanding of what procurement expects the business case presentation to be like. If it is probable that there will be vocal skeptics involved, running a pilot in advance of the presentation is wise. If executive support is likely based on a well-presented case alone, procurement has the option of recommending a pilot before a full scale roll out of a supply marketing intelligence program is begun. The primary differentiator between these cases is the anticipated attitude of corporate leadership toward the idea, and how much unknown there is on the part of procurement leaders. If uncovering additional unknowns in advance will allow for a stronger presentation, the pilot presents the opportunity for procurement to get their proverbial "ducks in a row." This would be the most likely scenario for a stealthy pilot.

There are two approaches to a pilot. Generally speaking, we recommend running the pilot on a process that is repeated often, such as strategic sourcing, rather than one time or intermittent efforts such as opportunity analysis. Procurement can either select one project and make sure that supply market intelligence processes and tactics are fully incorporated from start to finish, or they can take a number of projects simultaneously underway and designate the step in the sourcing process where supply market intelligence will be emphasized for each one. Although there is a loss of continuity, this approach allows a pilot to be run in a compressed timeline while still seeing how the overall process would be improved.

The hardest part of running a pilot may be selecting the right project. It is an understandable instinct to choose the simplest available project for a pilot, but this may not be the most effective choice in the long term. The chosen project must at least be representative of the other efforts likely to be undertaken by procurement. Favorable results from an overly simplistic project may not be as influential for decision makers who need to endorse the idea of applying supply market intelligence across a broad range of projects. In addition to the category of spend, thought should be given to the procurement resource leading the pilot project. They should be experienced enough to handle the pilot in addition to their usual strategic sourcing and project management responsibilities. They should also be in a position to make in-the-moment and after-the-fact observations about what should be improved before supply market intelligence is rolled out to all other projects.

Last, different supplier profiles and relationships should be considered. This presents another opportunity to appeal to executive leadership, as troublesome incumbent suppliers often create more difficulty for the business than they provide value in return. If procurement can demonstrate that supply market intelligence is a path to a more supportive, collaborative supply base, their approval will likely be forthcoming.

As effective as a pilot can be, procurement should not expect to have a perfect business case as a result. It would be easy to get caught in an indefinitely phased pilot rollout of supply market intelligence. At some point, someone in procurement with the right support from executive leadership must make a clear decision to move ahead with the proposed changes, or not.

METHODS AND METRICS FOR MEASURING RESULTS

Procurement professionals are all too familiar with the challenges of tracking and getting credit for qualitative results. Savings continues to be the primary metric by which procurement's performance is measured. This is especially true as an increasing number of organizations have procurement reporting into finance. Given that this is the case, how can procurement track the results of supply market intelligence?

It is easier to outline how *not* to track results than it is to make one recommendation that will be received well in a majority of organizations. It would be difficult to assign a portion of negotiated savings or cost avoidance from each sourcing project to supply market intelligence, even though it likely makes procurement's performance incrementally better across the board. We advocate against making broad assumptions, such as a 2 to 3 percent improvement in each project where supply market intelligence is leveraged. Not only is this impossible to support with facts, it does not capture the impact supply market intelligence has on non-sourcing related efforts, such as opportunity assessments, supplier management, and category management. The ability to create and leverage supply market intelligence is a skill that should be considered central to procurement's ability to get the job done, just like negotiation and analysis.

All that being said, it is possible to report on the impact supply market intelligence has had on procurement's results by tracking events that would not have been possible without it. Examples of these events, which can be tracked on a per project basis and then rolled up, are:

- New suppliers or solutions evaluated
- Risk categories identified
- Risk responses documented

- Strategic alterations to project timing
- Additional supplier performance key performance indicators (KPIs)
- Modified cost models
- Improved contract terms

The idea behind identifying and then tracking these events is that they become the metrics for desirable or prioritized procurement behavior that are made possible as a result of additional understanding and emphasis on external information.

When presenting a business case for supply market intelligence, procurement should also be able to articulate the potential costs of poor or lacking supply market intelligence. While it is harder to measure, these examples should be every bit as motivating for executive decision makers as the potential improvements. These "costs," which include the cost of doing nothing are likely to be the sort of missed opportunities that keep executives awake at night. Seeing them listed as avoidable with the right investment in supply market intelligence should help procurement's case. For example:

- Poor negotiating position relative to suppliers
- Missed risk categories or elevated but unmonitored risk levels
- New regulatory requirements
- Unconsidered alternate specifications that increase efficiency or reduce costs
- Substantial anticipated changes to supplier capacity

While these opportunity costs are likely to be documented negatively, when procurement discusses them there should be a positive spin, focusing on what supply market intelligence will enable them to accomplish on behalf of the organization by avoiding or mitigating these risks.

The presentation of the benefits of supply market intelligence should include a narrative of learnings and successes as well as counts of positive events. In order to provide depth and credibility to event-based details, procurement must be able to explain which projects were associated with each category of results, as well as which categories of results came from any given project. For instance, if a location-based services sourcing project was positively impacted by supply market intelligence by having two new suppliers invited to participate, one risk category uncovered and addressed (authorized worker documentation), and three additional KPIs used to manage the supplier relationships for the term of the contract, procurement should be able to look at the record of that project and state what the impact of supply market intelligence was. If four events in the third quarter had new risks identified based on supply market intelligence, procurement should be able to access the details that they were floor cleaning services, corrugated packaging, polyethylene, and HVAC maintenance services.

Whether procurement makes the decision to hire a dedicated resource to conduct research for supply market intelligence or to have everyone on the team build some level of proficiency, at least one person must be designated as the lead for metrics tracking and reporting. Building this into the internal approval hurdle makes sure that the impact is acknowledged and recorded while the project is still open, rather than as an afterthought when looming projects take precedence and the specific role of supply market intelligence has begun to fade in the memory of the project lead.

SUPPLY MARKET INTELLIGENCE AS OUTREACH

In addition to improving how well procurement performs the tasks they are already responsible for, supply market intelligence can help build bridges to other functions in the organization. In many organizations, procurement has been given complete access to, if not total ownership over, indirect or not-for-resale spend. Other spend categories remain off-limits to procurement because the organization does not see the benefit of getting them involved or because the executive owner of the spend does not want to relinquish control. Supply market intelligence may create an opportunity for procurement to open the door to these categories of spend by fostering the relationships required to build trust.

The external view made possible by supply market intelligence can be combined with the internal data procurement has access to through spend analysis and ERP systems. The resulting insight and intelligence reflects positively on procurement and recommends them as a strategic internal partner for spend management, as well as any special projects that arise. The functions and departments that may be good candidates for this approach include marketing, human resources, legal, IT, logistics and supply chain, and sales. In addition to internal outreach, suppliers may be interested in what procurement has learned. New information may improve current contracts and provide suppliers an opportunity to have value-oriented discussions with procurement.

There are a few approaches that can be used to increase the likelihood of success across all of these groups, especially when procurement is met with resistance or has been met with resistance in the past. Request that an executive supporter make a formal introduction. Make sure the terminology used, either in discussions or documentation, reflects a value-oriented approach rather than overemphasizing cost savings.[1] Listen carefully to the challenges and priorities of the function before making recommendations. The broad applications of supply market intelligence are the news stories, geographies, suppliers, and regulations of interest to each function.

Marketing, Human Resources, and Legal

Marketing, human resources, and legal are traditionally the most procurement-resistant functions in the organization. Their spend is services-dominant, sensitive in nature, and highly strategic to the success of the organization as a whole. While some of the tactical or material categories they own are increasingly managed through standard procurement processes, the majority of their spend is not. In addition, whether or not they realize it, each of these groups has an interest in how the rest of the organization warms to centralized procurement, and procurement should not miss an opportunity to leverage that.

As we explained in the beginning of this section, the immediate goal for conducting outreach through supply market intelligence is not to get access to spend for the immediate purpose of strategic sourcing, but to build relationships. Finding ways to assist aloof functions by collecting and analyzing information on their behalf demonstrates procurement's full range of capabilities while also opening a dialogue. Marketing may be interested in the campaigns of direct competitors or of creative approaches used by on-contract agencies on behalf of noncompetitive companies. Human resources may appreciate help tracking changing regulations in locations where the organization has direct hires. Legal may also be interested in changing regulations, or the progress and outcomes of relevant cases or suits. Conversations with legal also provide an opportunity for procurement to ask what fee for use services (such as LexisNexis) they have access to so that procurement can add onto or legally leverage existing accounts.

From an overall perspective, each of these groups can be offered increased guidance and visibility into other procurement efforts. Marketing could gain valuable insight if the company's supply partners share their knowledge about end markets of interest. Smart suppliers should understand their customer's customers and should be willing to demonstrate that knowledge. Legal may see value in finding ways to ease their involvement on the contracting process by reviewing contract terms and conditions such as liability, indemnification, intellectual property ownership, and warranties. As more contracts involve a labor component, human resources is likely to want to set ground rules or make sure existing contingent labor contracts are leveraged to their full extent.

Logistics and Supply Chain

Although logistics and supply chain are often grouped together with procurement in the larger corporate context, they usually operate independently from each other in an organization. Whether the organization manages its own fleet or works with third-party logistics providers (3PLs), there are opportunities for procurement to support them through supply market intelligence.

When the organization operates their own fleet, trends in packaging, materials handling, warehousing, driver safety regulations, and fuel may be of interest. There is a large volume of websites and periodicals covering this space, and if procurement can help their supply chain colleagues monitor relevant topics, both groups stand to benefit. One topic that may be of particular interest is sustainability. Any opportunity to improve the sustainability of a supply chain by lessening its negative impact on the environment is beneficial to shareholder and public relations efforts.

When the organization's logistics are managed by third parties, procurement may be able to find cost effective ways to locate and benchmark freight capacity and cost. When seasonality is a factor, procurement can help supply chain anticipate and plan to minimize the impact to operations. When multiple modes of transportation are used to move goods from a supplier to an organization's own production facilities or from that same facility to customers, procurement may be able to help arrange for and negotiate optimal Incoterms to minimize risk and cost through well-timed transfer of ownership.

Engineering, Operations, and Research and Development

Depending on the industry an organization is in, the majority of direct spend may be associated with engineering, operations, or research and development. The more procurement can learn from these teams, the better informed they will be about the core business of the organization. Even when procurement does not have responsibility for or access to direct spend categories for strategic sourcing and spend management, every opportunity should be taken to increase their visibility.

From a supply market intelligence perspective, procurement is best positioned to create value for these groups by assessing and mitigating risk. This might include the identification of pending capacity constraints or geopolitical instability in an important source region. For risks that are identified and agreed upon, procurement can pull information on alternatives that, once reviewed by operations, should be documented in business continuity plans. Qualified alternatives include new suppliers of the same items or new materials that can be tested as replacements. Incidentally, the work that procurement does to identify and qualify these alternatives will be very handy if procurement does get the green light to undertake a strategic sourcing project in the future.

Information Technology

In many organizations, the information technology (IT) function operates as independently as marketing, human resources, and legal. Especially when there is a CIO that is equal in rank and influence to the CFO, they are likely to have the clout to manage and retain negotiating and contracting responsibility for their own spend. Depending on the IT requirements of the organization, their spend may involve hardware, software licenses, and outsourcing or contract labor. Procurement can create intelligence to help manage all three types of spend.

IT hardware is often produced in geographies that are subject to supply chain disruptions, like the tsunami in Japan in 2011. According to a *Forbes* article, written one year later, "Damage and workforce displacement left critical suppliers and subcontractors for auto-makers, technology firms and countless other industries short on parts or completely out of supply."[2] Software licenses that provide access to offsite solutions may introduce risk through security breaches, such as the 2013 Target Corporation point-of-sale credit card reader breach that enabled hackers to access customer credit card information. Outsourcing agreements can always be improved through better incentives and performance drivers that make sure providers focus on the activities that create the greatest value for the contracting organization. Contract or contingent labor arrangements may require additional attention to intellectual property terms or a fact-based understanding of when it is preferable that work be done by employees.

Sales

Of all of the functions that procurement should reach out to, sales may be the most unexpected. After all, what spend (and therefore opportunities for strategic sourcing and savings) are they associated with? It is true that sales usually represents a significant portion of travel spend, and they use an inordinate number of business cards, but why should procurement use supply market intelligence to improve their relationship with sales?

Sales is an example of where procurement needs to start thinking about the combination of internal and external information in a more visionary way. There are few functions that have the opportunity to carry information as cross functionally as procurement. If they can see beyond the most direct performance metrics, procurement can work with sales to improve their perception and relevance in the organization. Other functions are likely to attribute low sales to poor selling skills than they are to recognize the role of inferior product design issues. Procurement can assist sales by providing evidence in the case that issues are with the product itself.

Sales can offer information on consumer demand, feedback on current products, and requests for future capabilities or functionality. In addition to improving the conversations procurement has with other customer-facing functions, listening to sales can also broaden the perspective and understanding of procurement professionals who are responsible for performing supply market research and analysis. In return for this visibility into market and client demand, procurement can track key customers and prospects, and report significant findings to sales. They may also be able to help prepare sales representatives on the decision drivers and motivating factors at play in the industries where major prospects conduct business.

Suppliers

Procurement may make the reasonable assumption that their suppliers have more supply market intelligence in certain areas than they do. Like any other assumption, it will sometimes turn out to be accurate, and other times not. While there should never be an expectation that procurement would improve their suppliers' intelligence just to be neighborly, opportunities for improvement or innovation that come to light may be shared if there is sufficient mutual benefit.

Supply market intelligence will be best received in collaborative supplier relationships. When procurement and the company's suppliers are empowered to take on a new opportunity together, the business and relationship will both benefit. In the course of reading, procurement may come across an alteration to the product or service currently being purchased. This could include a process or material that has been successfully incorporated with higher quality or lower cost. Alternately, procurement may approach a supplier who is positioned to help address a challenge in the organization based on a new application of their solution, rather than waiting for a suppliers' sales team to approach them.

Regardless of the exact intelligence, procurement should pause and consider before approaching a supplier with anything that might be considered confidential. Even indirect information, such as materials or approaches that are of interest to the company, may reveal more than is prudent. This is another good use for the internal Approval Gate discussed in Chapter 3. If the case is strong enough, and the circumstances warrant it, procurement may go ahead and approach a supplier with intelligence that can improve results and create value in the short term and beyond.

CONCLUSION

If procurement is determined to demonstrate how relevant they are to the long-term health and success of the organization, they should go about it in a proactive way. Striving to be more strategic, but waiting for executive leadership to notice, is a doomed approach in an agile, highly competitive landscape.

When procurement makes the presentation of a business case to decision makers, they should have the right balance of prepared documentation and internalized understanding of what is being requested and why. Once the required approvals have been received, procurement should look for every opportunity to maximize the return to the organization, as well as how they are regarded by other internal functions. In this way, procurement can simultaneously improve their immediate results and the position they occupy in the organization in the long term.

REFERENCES

1. "Fueling Effective Collaboration: How Strategic Sourcing Delivers Results for Marketing Groups," *Source One Management Services*, Accessed May 28, 2014, http://www.sourceoneinc.com/downloads/Marketing-Sourcing-Insight-Report.pdf.
2. Eric Savitz, "Japan One Year Later: The Long View on Tech Supply Chains," *Forbes*, March 13, 2012, http://www.forbes.com/sites/ciocentral/2012/03/13/japan-one-year-later-the-long-view-on-tech-supply-chains/.

6

QUALITY ASSURANCE

In a manner of speaking, supply market intelligence provides quality assurance for all of procurement's market-driven efforts. Without validation from third-party sources, procurement may be overly reliant on current and potential suppliers to build an understanding of a market. While suppliers are a legitimate and realistic source of information, it is wise to test their objectivity. Procurement should exert their information independence by making their own inquiries into topics of importance. Procurement should also take the time to build deliberate quality assurance measures into their supply market intelligence efforts to ensure that, to the best of their ability, their quality assurance is quality assured.

Since the information collected during supply market research forms the basis for procurement's subsequent analysis, recommendations, and conclusions, it is essential that it be thoroughly screened. While information found in a fee-for-use context is usually objective, it should still be evaluated for timeliness and accuracy.

Internet research is another matter entirely. Information found on the Internet, even from reputable sources, must be checked for timeliness and accuracy before being further scrutinized to ensure the source and author's credibility, motivation, and impartiality. In case something surprising is uncovered, procurement should take care to validate it through references or multi-source triangulation.

Once an investment has been made to document supply market intelligence and procurement's resulting recommendations, a structure must be in place to make it accessible. From a knowledge or content management standpoint, this includes the administration and maintenance of the documents themselves, as well as the efforts required to make their content sustainably useful. Category playbooks are a popular approach for centralizing and maintaining information. Since companies are rarely willing to share their playbooks, organizations new to the idea often have trouble visualizing what they are and how they can address the information and knowledge needs of procurement professionals.

Although we have made the case that procurement should be able to create their own supply market intelligence, there are always exceptions. Even when most of the research and analysis is done in-house by procurement, there may be circumstances when it is expedient or strategic to bring in a third party to lead the research effort or to take full responsibility for the work. Time or resource constraints, and market or category expertise, are the most obvious reasons for having a third party conduct market research, but the internal climate toward the likely recommendations should be considered, as well. In some cases, decision makers are better able to hear and accept information that comes from outside the organization than they are to accept the same recommendations from procurement.

Even when every effort is made to ensure quality, things can still go wrong. When supply market intelligence is involved in a project where a bad decision is made or an opportunity is missed, procurement needs to be prepared to diagnose the cause of the problem while also improving processes to minimize the chances of a recurrence in the future. Supply market research and analysis are like any other approach that requires a subjective interpretation of conditions and a judgment call as to how the organization should proceed. This is especially true since supply market intelligence's greatest value is derived in situations when factual information is unavailable. In these cases, the focus must be on the quality of the process that led to the intelligence, whether it delivers the right answer or not.

EVALUATING INFORMATION

As stated in Chapter 3, successful research is about careful reading. Our point in the context of that chapter was about the need for each researcher to allow him- or herself the time and opportunity to consider new information as their understanding of a topic materializes. This is no less true in the context of quality assurance.

In some cases, the determination of whether a resource or specific content is of sufficient quality is straightforward. In other cases, it requires a judgment call. Quality is directly tied to the usability and appropriateness of information for the business question at hand. When quality is defined in this manner, we can examine any fact, source, or content in terms of its credibility, impartiality, timeliness, and motivation of the author or creator of the content. This examination is what supports the "assurance" part of quality assurance. When any of the above comes into question, the information does not have to be discarded, but it should be validated by referencing other resources or qualified with a note that there are concerns about the reliability of the data.

Credibility

It is crucial to determine the credibility of the author or institution that published the information in question. There should be proof that the information is coming from an authoritative source. For websites, it should be easy to identify the person or organization taking responsibility for the information being presented. It should be possible to contact the author or organization by e-mail, phone, or mailing address. When reading about the responsible organization, look for any clues that indicate negative underlying motivations, such as prejudice or a compensation-based bias, in presenting the information. In the case of an individual author, look for background information such as other published offerings, education, affiliations, and whether their employment history found them working for a supplier.

Even when the individual or organization associated with the content is credible, procurement should take the active step of determining whether the content is fact-based or opinion. While blogs are a plentiful and useful source of information, they often express the opinion of the writer without making that purpose clear. We have included many blogs in Part II of this book, and the ones we list are the best of the best in terms of content and representation. There is nothing wrong with an informed opinion. For procurement, the best data available is often forecasted or predictive in nature. It is still important to recognize the difference between fact and opinion, and weigh their relative roles in final analysis and recommendations. The proportion of fact to opinion is directly tied to the potential variability of the circumstances and, therefore, the likely success of the chosen strategy.

Impartiality

Even the most credible individual or organization needs to make a living. As a result, some content in supply market intelligence may be sponsored by a company trying to reach the reading audience. As with questions of credibility, procurement does not need to disqualify this information, but must qualify it by recognizing the influence of sponsorship on the content.

There are different kinds of content sponsorship, and each will have a different impact on the information presented and the author's impartiality. In some cases, articles or reports are written for the express purpose of raising the awareness of a company's solution or capabilities. In other cases, a report or article (that would have been written anyway) is sponsored by one or more companies in exchange for the right to brand and distribute the content. In both of these cases, reputable sites will make sure there is a logo or an "About" section in the content, making clear that it is sponsored. More difficult are the cases where sponsorships lead to collegial relationships between authors and sponsors over time. In the best case, the impartiality and objectivity of a writer may lapse without them even being aware of it. In the worst, it may be a conscious decision.

Beyond making clear that content has or has not been sponsored, the best way to determine partiality is to become familiar with the resource over time. Preferences may become evident gradually, and being able to recall a pattern of regard for one company over another without obvious cause is often the best way to spot a news resource in which impartiality has been compromised. This is also a good opportunity to exercise one's professional network. Many times the "experts," who are writing or publishing articles and reports, can be vetted by asking colleagues.

Timeliness

The accuracy of analysis and recommendations is greatly improved when they are based on the most current information available. As a result, the timeliness of information found during market research is an important factor in determining its quality. In some cases, as with subscription-based data or public company stock prices, information is available in real time while trading is taking place. This is a best-case scenario. Most information is not updated with such frequency, and it is not uncommon for some reports to be updated on an annual basis. Usually, the update schedule for these reports matches the rate at which major changes are seen in the associated market. It is procurement's responsibility to make sure that information is sufficiently current, and that significant, unforeseen changes that take place after the fact are incorporated into analysis and recommendations, even when they are not covered in the most recent reports and articles.

Motivation

We acknowledge motivation separate from credibility because it addresses a related yet different quality issue. Motivation is a concern when an author or resource has the desired level of credibility, but is not objective. A perfect example is the story of Thomas Edison and J. P. Morgan given in Chapter 1. There can be no question of Edison's credibility regarding electricity, but his motivation in assessing that DC would trump AC was too personally biased to be objective.

The most common motivation procurement will encounter in Internet research is product or solution marketing. When using a supplier website to gather information, it is wise to remember that the main purpose of a company website is to start the sales process. Critical reviews or negative press articles are unlikely to be posted alongside celebratory press releases or favorable endorsements. When taking information from websites that offer free content, procurement should make an effort to determine the revenue model of the business.

In addition to the motivation of informing potential consumers, motivation can be positive or negative and may not be associated with revenue concerns. Authors can advance a grudge through their content as easily as they promote a favorite theory or cause. It is also not unheard of for an author to favor one solution in order to cast a negative light on (or damage) a company they dislike. In situations where competition is high, bloggers, thought leaders, and analysts may have a slant on the markets they cover that favors specific companies, prefers market leaders over newcomers, or recommends large companies over startups.

The motivation of an author should always be questioned, but is particularly important in cases where an opinion is strong, regardless of whether it is positive or negative. When possible, reach out to the author to gain further clarity on their position by speaking with them directly.

Triangulation

If procurement only bases their supply market intelligence on demonstrated fact, there will be very few documents to manage. As discussed in Chapter 3, the role of the researcher is critical because they are the ones faced with the task of interpreting information. Particularly in cases where there is no budget for subscription-based services or purchased reports, procurement has to rely on a combination of Internet research and discretion.

The best approach for assuring quality under these conditions is triangulation, where a single data point is not allowed to form the center of intelligence. Instead, procurement must find several independent sources that say the same or similar things. The actual truth is likely to be where the information found in those sources intersects or overlaps. Even when there are questions of accuracy, objectivity, or credibility, a plausible conclusion is still possible. It may just require more effort on procurement's part to validate the quality and make the assurances they feel comfortable with. As former President Ronald Reagan notably quoted, "Trust, but verify."

KNOWLEDGE AND CONTENT MANAGEMENT

It is common to hear the need for better knowledge management discussed in organizations. In the case of supply market intelligence, both knowledge management and content management require planning and maintenance. Knowledge management seeks to ensure that what people know, and what is predominantly stored in their minds, is captured in some tangible way so that it can be accessed by other internal colleagues or after they are no longer available. As referenced by Michael Koenig, Gartner Group defined knowledge management as "a discipline that promotes an integrated approach to identifying, capturing, evaluating, retrieving, and sharing all of an enterprise's information assets."[1]

Within the context of supply market intelligence, procurement must first master the discipline of documenting what they learn (knowledge management), so that they can successfully address the challenge of making those documents accessible and keeping them current for future use (content management). There is no need to run distinct efforts to manage knowledge and content. It is the common ground they share, the discipline of recording and maintaining information, which is the most important. We recommend using the phrase *knowledge management* rather than *content management* in internal discussions because it emphasizes the ephemeral nature of strategic, value-oriented information, while content management implies that the information is static and of a tactical nature.

Content management also gives the false impression that all of the intelligence resulting from market research has been captured in a document. The process of filtering information in pursuit of market intelligence creates knowledge that may not be represented in an intelligence brief. This is especially true when procurement is new to the market in question:

> Early-stage knowledge tends to have a much higher tacit component, but in a rapidly changing world this is often the most valuable knowledge—it provides us with early insight into emerging opportunities. So there is a dilemma—the most valuable knowledge is often the most difficult to express and share.[2]

This dilemma is best solved by ensuring the proper centralization, maintenance, and accessibility for supply market intelligence related knowledge. Just as the person who conducts market research plays a critical role in the success of the program, someone must be responsible for handling all of the documents created. While no formal or specialized training is required to fulfill this role successfully, the professional(s) assigned with the task must understand the critical nature of the responsibility they have assumed. Considering the role, administrative misses a broad range of opportunities associated with properly reusing and distributing valuable intelligence.

Centralization

The most basic requirement of a knowledge management program is that the content be available via a centralized location. In addition, there must be a catalog where a listing of all documents is kept and where metadata is captured. As discussed in Chapter 3, metadata is nothing more than data about data. In other words, if there is a central repository of documents, there must also be a catalog that lists information, such as category, author(s), keywords, dates updated, contract expiration date, stakeholder names, incumbent supplier names, etc., for all available documents. The right information to be collected in such a catalog should be directly associated with how it is likely to be retrieved. Searching is improved through standards, such as naming conventions, and having someone to check that they are adhered to before critical details are forgotten and team members move on to other projects.

In addition to the finished documents resulting from the supply market intelligence creation process, there must be a way to centralize the sources that have been the most effective. As evident in the structure of this book, some resources do not fit a category, while others fit into a specific category. Since most sources are likely to be accessed virtually, it is ideal for them to be stored in a way that quickly connects the researcher with the source. In the case that there is account or log in information required to access a resource, those details should also be stored centrally, either in a shared virtual environment or through one person overseeing the use of subscription-based services.

Maintenance

Because the sources on which supply market intelligence is based are dynamic, the associated documentation should be appropriately kept up-to-date. There is almost never excess available time, so documents should only be updated as often as there is a clear business reason to do so.

In the case of project-based supply market intelligence, once the project is over —or once procurement no longer has a role to play—the document should be saved and dated, but does not need to be refreshed until before a new round of effort is to begin. The timing of such refreshes should allow procurement to take advantage of any opportunities to sign a beneficial early contract renewal. When procurement does not disengage from the project or spend category in question, the document will need to be updated on a regular schedule that matches the changes in the relevant markets or the shifting opportunity landscape. In either case, the need for refreshes should be deliberately determined in advance and adhered to by procurement, whether there is a person responsible for issuing reminders and ensuring updates are made, or whether each person is responsible for keeping their own intelligence documentation current.

Accessibility

All of the work to create, centralize, and maintain supply market intelligence is only a good investment if the end result is accessible to the people who can make the best use of it. The most efficient model for saving and sharing documents will vary by company in accordance with policies and habits regarding network drives, internal wikis, and document sharing expectations. The catalog described above, as part of the centralization process, is as important as any one of the documents listed. Knowing what already exists is the best way to prevent a duplication of effort, and may present an opportunity to provide a quick turnaround for an internal stakeholder when an existing document can be updated, rather than needing to start from scratch.

The primary exception to the emphasis on accessibility is *confidentiality*. Some projects are not widely discussed because of the sensitive nature of the people involved or the approach to be taken. An example of this is exploring the option of outsourcing a function that is currently performed in-house. No one, procurement or otherwise, would want one of their potentially affected colleagues to be alerted to such a possibility inadvertently, and certainly not by exposing them to an intelligence brief on the advantages and disadvantages of outsourcing facilities maintenance services, for example. While some mention may be made in the catalog that information is available on the sensitive projects, no detail beyond which management-level contact is responsible should be included.

Category Playbooks

When it comes to the centralization of all the elements of intelligence associated with a category of spend, category playbooks are considered the gold standard. As John Evans, Managing Partner of Denali Group, stated in an article about the importance of procurement knowledge management programs, "Category playbooks are used to document relevant information and strategies for specific spend categories. They are typically created electronically, web-based or on the company file server, so that new hires have information concerning the category."[3] Yet, while it is easy to see the benefits associated with category playbooks, very few actual examples have ever been seen. Beyond a snapshot of the template being used to collect information, it is impossible for one organization to share their playbooks with another. Far too much proprietary information would be revealed.

The chief requirement in designing effective but realistic category playbooks is balancing the need for centralization while avoiding undue duplication. The mythical ideal of a category playbook contains everything one would need to know about a given category of spend: the internal history of the category; annual spend with some level of detail about usage by business unit, geography, and supplier; notes on relationships with incumbent suppliers; item level detail and pricing; market trends and risks; management strategy; and more. The challenge lies in the fact that much of this information resides in solutions or applications where it is easily accessible, such as in a spend analysis solution or ERP system.

Rather than trying to duplicate information into a playbook that cannot hope to be kept as up-to-date as it is in an internal system, details should be recorded about how to access the spend in a solution in such a way that it aligns with the details in the rest of the playbook.

Beyond avoiding obsolescence and duplication, the greatest challenge of playbooks is getting the procurement professionals to complete them. A great deal of vivid information and observations is available at the conclusion of a project, but it quickly fades as a new project takes its place. Capturing that information as completely as possible, before it is too late, holds huge value for the organization. Adherence to such a need should be used as an opportunity to recognize the team members that set themselves apart by being particularly diligent. Some organizations even have gone as far as to clearly include documentation in each procurement team member's performance objectives.

CITATIONS

The authors can attest to how frustrating it can be to stop and take time to properly cite sources when what we really want to do is push ahead with the primary work of the day. Citing sources is, nonetheless, an important part of ensuring due diligence and communicates that the intelligence brief is a professional document to be taken seriously. Procurement should never hesitate to consult, quote, and cite a third-party source. The whole point of supply market intelligence is to leverage the knowledge that exists outside of the organization. It does not reflect poorly on anyone in the organization, procurement or otherwise, to reference a third-party source instead of having found the answer internally.

The primary purpose for proper citation is to ensure that for each reference, the reader can revisit the original source. A secondary purpose is to provide context for the intelligence by capturing the associated source, author, and date. The *Chicago Manual of Style* Notes and Bibliography method was used for the citations in this book. Whether this style is considered the standard for use in a supply market intelligence program or not, it is wise to establish some standards that ensure the thorough capture of information and consistency across documents.

Additional information, in a quick reference format, is available online via the "Chicago Style Citation Quick Guide,"[4] but here are a few of the format examples for sources that are most likely to be useful to procurement:

Book with One Author

Author, *Title* (City of Publication, State: Publisher, Year of Publication), Page number.

Jonathan O'Brien, *Category Management in Purchasing: A Strategic Approach to Maximize Business Profitability* (Philadelphia, PA: Kogan Page, 2012), 33.

Book with Two Authors

Author and Author, *Title* (City of Publication, State: Publisher, Year of Publication), Page number.

Charles Dominick and Soheila R. Lunney, *The Procurement Game Plan: Winning Strategies and Techniques for Supply Management Professionals* (Fort Lauderdale, FL: J. Ross Publishing, Inc., 2012), 69.

Article in an Online Journal

Author, "Article Title," *Journal* Volume (Year): Page, Date Accessed, URL.

Donovan Neale May, "It's Time for Marketing to Buy into Strategic Sourcing," *Peersphere: The CMO Council Journal* 3 (2104): 5, Accessed May 22, 2014, https://www.cmocouncil.org/peer-sphere.php.

Article in a Newspaper or Popular Magazine

Print

Author, "Title," *Publication*, Publication Date, Page number.

Doug Carroll, "Wanted: 4.5 Million Workers, the Most in About 7 Years," *USA Today*, June 11, 2014, 1B.

Online

Author, "Title," *Publication*, Publication Date, Date Accessed, URL.

[1]Doug Carroll, "Job Openings Soar to Highest Since 2007," *USA Today*, June 11, 2014, Accessed June 12, 2014, http://www.usatoday.com/story/money/business/2014/06/10/jolts-april-job-openings-report/10276305/.

Website

"Page Title," Last Modified Date (if available) or Date Accessed, URL.

[1]"Definition of Procurement—Procurement vs. Purchasing," *Purchasing Insight,* November 21, 2010, http://procureinsights.wordpress.com/.

WHEN TO PAY FOR EXTERNAL RESEARCH

Despite our best efforts to make the supply market intelligence creation process accessible for properly motivated procurement professionals, there will be times when it is necessary for more than an investment of time. Depending on the circumstances and the expenses, the additional investment for external research may require budgetary approval outside of procurement. When the circumstances warrant it, this need should not be considered a deterrent. Even when a subscription service or third party needs to be contracted, procurement can still take credit for having made a prudent decision by recognizing that external expertise was required.

Reports

Market research reports can be expensive. While many fee-for-access reports can be purchased on an individual basis, the price tag for each report may range from hundreds to thousands of dollars. While procurement is likely to make every effort not to pay for information that can be accessed elsewhere for free, some highly technical or specialized markets are hard to fully capture without professional analysis. It may also be appropriate when suppliers are highly informed or seem to have an undue amount of leverage, based on their understanding of the market.

Pay careful attention to the report description and table of contents before making a purchase. Some sources of market research reports even make it possible to search inside of the report's contents for a term or phrase before making a purchase. Weigh the cost of the report against the total spend of the category, and consider the cost as being subtracted from any potential savings that are negotiated as a result. This perspective usually makes the purchase decision easier.

Services

Beyond individual market research reports, subscription services allow procurement to access information with one or more account log-ins. It is appropriate to pay for such access in the case of sources that will be used regularly on an ongoing basis, or for a solution that is broadly applicable across a range of categories and markets. Similarly, we have recommended reaching out to other functions in the organization to see what they have access to that procurement can leverage, either by legally using their log-in information or by negotiating additional accounts at an incremental cost.

As with market research reports, procurement should associate the cost of access against any anticipated and measurable benefits. This goes beyond making the case for the investment itself. It helps procurement prioritize which subscriptions will generate the greatest intelligence value for the cost.

Hired Research Services

When a purchased report or subscription service do not meet procurement's intelligence needs, the best alternative may be to hire a researcher on a temporary or project basis. The obvious advantages of hiring a researcher are that they provide quick, high-quality results. There may even be the opportunity for procurement to learn from the reports or documentation they provide as deliverables from the engagement.

It is also an unfortunate yet realistic circumstance that executive leadership may be more receptive to a message coming from an experienced third party. Some executives are conditioned to believe that if a service or deliverable costs more, it also has more value. When this is the case, procurement may take the opportunity to engage a researcher to verify and/or guarantee the work. In the long term, procurement will need to build the organization's trust in their own capabilities, but many times project-specific recommendations need to be made in the short term and must be handled separately from issues of internal perception.

WHEN SOMETHING GOES WRONG

Despite all of the research, analysis, triangulation, and internal approval hurdles that procurement will go through, supply market intelligence is not infallible. The same subjectivity that creates the possibility for a unique competitive advantage introduces risk if supply markets are not interpreted correctly. Relying upon supply market intelligence is not about an active pursuit of risk on procurement's part. There is inherent uncertainty associated with nearly all supply management decisions and activities. Procurement must be prepared to justify and explain supply market intelligence-based decisions, just as they would a chosen sourcing or negotiation strategy.

Regardless of the specific negative perception or outcome that must be addressed when desired results are not achieved, it is important that procurement take the time to understand why a failure took place. That is the best way to improve the processes for collecting, analyzing, and consensus building that allow supply market intelligence to be leveraged for the benefit of the organization.

Bad Information vs. Analysis/Recommendations

Supply market intelligence is based on the information collected through research, and all of procurement's analysis and recommendations rely upon its accuracy. There are several points in the creation process where errors may occur. Understanding the root cause of a specific error, which can be determined in a post-mortem meeting, allows procurement to establish responsibility and prevent the same failure in the future.

When the information itself is the root cause of the problem, the source or sources it came from become suspect. Lack of impartiality or a contrary motivation may have obscured the truth, even when the author or source is credible.

Alternately, the content might not be at fault, but it could be out-of-date. Addressing this sort of content quality issue can often be done through more stringent standards. Establishing a shorter time frame for acceptable content, or increasing the number of sources that must be provided as support for a recommendation, will help. If the author and/or source is found to be at fault through inaccuracy or lack of objectivity, that information should be made known to any procurement resources responsible for research and noted in the centralized resource catalog.

When an error is made as a result of procurement's analysis and recommendations rather than the underlying content, it is more difficult to make changes to prevent a repeat in the future. Unless it can be proven that procurement, and the other internal stakeholders on the project, did not perform the proper due diligence or took information at face value without validating it, the error may need to be accepted as a possible misinterpretation of the market. Research skills can always be improved, as can the understanding of the analytical model chosen. In cases where procurement recommends significant change, a greater number of sources and a higher level of internal scrutiny and approval can be required to validate that analysis and recommendations are sound.

When Sound Recommendations Are Not Taken

Recommendations made by one part of an organization do not always lead to overall agreement and action. Procurement may make the most insightful recommendations possible based on supply market intelligence, but if they are not implemented, negative consequences may result.

Procurement should make it a general practice to get formal acknowledgement of the recommended strategy in a category. In the case that the strategy is successful, everyone shares in the credit. When the desired outcome is not achieved, at least procurement will not hang alone. The reality of supply market intelligence is that it is most critical in cases where changes in the market, or in the company's planned buying habits, require a corresponding adjustment in strategy. While there is also risk associated with not making a change, procurement is less likely to be blamed for holding a steady course.

The need for internal sign-off is even more acute when procurement's recommendations are not taken. Unless there is a significant force that procurement did not anticipate, the reason for procurement's advice being disregarded is likely to have as much to do with political positioning as with the strategy itself. When procurement has invested the time to act in the best interests of the organization, and colleagues do not follow suit, they may have no choice but to protect themselves against future recourse in the case that the pursued strategy fails.

This is also the ideal opportunity to leverage senior management support for supply market intelligence. If procurement's guidance is based on sound research and analysis, and is still ignored by a decision maker, senior management should hold a meeting to discuss what happened, and why. If one or more decision makers disregards legitimate recommendations from procurement, it may be an indication that there are other problems in that part of the organization. Far from "turning in" errant colleagues, this is an opportunity for procurement to demonstrate their concern for the operational effectiveness of the organization as a whole.

WHEN SOMETHING GOES RIGHT

When supply market intelligence is associated with wins or results that go beyond the basic expectations of procurement, they should not hesitate to call attention to this success. Results could include major savings, innovative new supply partners, measurably higher quality, or product improvements that will be recognized by customers. When the circumstances justify it, procurement should not hesitate to highlight examples of excellence, either through established, company-wide employee recognition programs or presentations to senior management.

CONCLUSION

Within the context of supply market intelligence, quality assurance must encompass all of the sources, processes, talent, and documentation required to make the intelligence actionable. The need for quality extends beyond the immediate requirement and should anticipate future use of documented information. Every effort should be made to ensure quality at a detailed level, from the source selection to the citation of sources. There is a great deal of low or no cost information available, but when circumstances warrant it, subscription services and experienced market research professionals should be considered. Whether the final outcome is a resounding success or a strategic misstep, every project should be handled as a team effort. Procurement must ensure that they have the proper buy-in, both for the general value of supply market intelligence and for its application in a specific project.

REFERENCES

1. Michael Koenig, "What Is KM? Knowledge Management Explained," *KMWorld*, May 4, 2012, Accessed June 11, 2014, http://www.kmworld.com/Articles/Editorial/What-Is-.../What-is-KM-Knowledge-Management-Explained-82405.aspx.

2. John Hagel, John Seely Brown, and Lang Davidson, *The Power of Pull: How Small Moves, Smartly Made, Can Set Big Things in Motion.* New York: Basic Books, 2010, 55.
3. John R. Evans, "The Importance of Building Effective Procurement Knowledge Management Programs," *Inside Sourcing Newsletter*, June 2011, Accessed June 13, 2014, http://www.sig.org/newsletter.php?id=5809.
4. "Chicago Style Citation Quick Guide," *Chicago Manual of Style*, Accessed 10 June 2014, http://www.chicagomanualofstyle.org/tools_citationguide.html.

PART II

SUPPLY MARKET INTELLIGENCE RESOURCES

7

RESEARCH RESOURCES

OVERVIEW

All of the resources included in Part II of this book have been vetted by the authors and are considered authoritative and relevant to procurement. Each resource may require further evaluation for use based on the *specific* information need of the professional who is conducting the research. For more details on how to use Part II of this book, please refer to Chapter 4 where there is a section dedicated to the topic. When using the resource lists in the following chapters, please keep the following considerations in mind:

- Some procurement organizations are sophisticated about knowing and effectively utilizing the key resources for a particular market, especially for their direct spend. The intended audience for the resource lists in this book are professionals moving into spend categories and markets with which they are unfamiliar, and those who are new to gathering and evaluating market intelligence resources.
- Resources are listed in the chapter section that best represents the strength or value of the content. This is done to eliminate redundancy. Many resources could be (but are not) listed under practically all sections. Some provider websites, publications, and associations provide comprehensive coverage of content and include, all in one source, information on pricing/market analysis, background documentation, buyers' guides, and several published journals and magazines.
- Pricing has not been included due to the complicated nature of some pricing models and the fact that prices change frequently. The quick view

charts indicate if a source is free, or if it has mixed free and fee-based access. If neither category is checked, it means that the resource is available by paid subscription only.

METHODOLOGY, INCLUDING THE WEB ADDED VALUE™ FEATURE

The methodology used for vetting the resources included in this book utilized the knowledge built over the authors' many years of hands-on experience in supply market intelligence and conducting business research. In addition, the evaluation of resources was done by viewing demos, setting up trials, and having direct conversations with providers. Product reviews and resource lists written by professional and academic searchers, practicing professionals, industry analysts, and others were extensively utilized.

We have followed the many changes in content and format, brought about by the dizzying speed of technology and evolving expectations of accessibility. Many of the resources started out in print format, such as Thomasnet.com and its "green books." Content from Gartner, the IT analyst powerhouse, was originally accessed via binders sitting in offices and on corporate library shelves. In making the adjustment from print to online formats, many of these sources were pioneers in remote access before there ever was an Internet. LexisNexis and Dow Jones News/Retrieval are examples of former print source providers.

Each entry in the following chapters was written with the dual purpose of describing the resource and providing details on how best to access the information it offers. Many times, key information is offered via special reports and studies that are published on a serial basis (e.g., monthly or annually). In an effort to provide succinct access to this information, navigation tips are offered. The authors make these suggestions with an understanding of the risk associated with providing information that may become quickly outdated. It is likely that after this book's publication, there will be sources listed in Part II where a website's design, content, or address will have been changed, upgraded, or enhanced. To address this issue, the authors are utilizing the Web Added Value (WAV)™ Download Resource Center offered by J. Ross Publishing for this book (www.jrosspub.com/wav). Continuous updates on the resources listed, and new ones of value, will be maintained and presented at the publisher's website.

Last, concerning some entries, for associations and organizations in particular, the authors used language provided in the "About" section of the websites. Links to resource content are provided in every entry.

THE IMPORTANCE OF SOCIAL MEDIA

Practically all of the resources listed in Part II of this book have accompanying blogs that are worth reading and following. Often, they provide detailed summaries and key nuggets of data when introducing new research reports. Blogs not associated with a resource listing that are particularly rich in best practice and/or statistical data are also included in this book. Well-written and maintained blogs have proven to be an important part of supply market research.

Traditionally, in the life cycle of a news event, the most authoritative writing is published during the later phase, when scholars and experts have had time to read, digest, and analyze the event and its subsequent ramifications. The format is usually an annual report, scholarly journal, or book. The first phase of a news event may start out with a Twitter feed or other social media channel, and then progresses to the daily news articles of content provider websites, such as newspapers, trade journals, and market analyst firms. Print publications will cover the news event with a one-week or one-month view of the event, with possibly some analysis. Blogs, particularly the ones written by the analysts and experts that follow a certain market, service, or product, combine the news reporting phase of the life cycle with the important later phase of analysis, thus providing enriched intelligence in a compressed timeframe.

Even though specific LinkedIn Groups are not listed in the resources section, it is important to note that LinkedIn is one of the most valuable tools a procurement professional can use to get information on any type of research and in any type of market. The discussion forums are an extremely important feature for inquiring about what resources and solutions are being used by peer professionals in similar situations. When logged into LinkedIn, use the search function to search for groups or to see a full listing of the groups that are available to join. In addition, most of the resource providers listed in this book have groups that you can join to discuss and learn about enhancements and upgrades to their products or services.

YouTube.com is also a wonderful resource for seeing how resources are used. Many large research providers put training videos and tutorials for their products on YouTube, understanding that visual training is more effective than just reading instructions. Mintec is an example of a provider that uses YouTube effectively.

Twitter is a great way to keep up-to-date on research that is released by your favorite news source, analyst, or writer. New research that is published is almost always announced via Twitter. Twitter allows you to build a network of peers that have the same information needs as you. It also provides the opportunity to "listen" to relevant news updates without contributing any of your own.

8

SUPPLIER IDENTIFICATION (NOT MARKET/CATEGORY SPECIFIC)

Identifying potential suppliers, especially for new products or services, can be a time-consuming and frustrating experience for procurement. Searching the "open" web many times produces a large number of results that simply are not relevant. Yet, this component of the sourcing project can arguably be considered the most important. Having the right supplier candidates to select from is critical in ensuring a solid foundation for moving forward in the evaluation process.

The sources listed in this chapter cover multiple categories/industries (see Table 8.1). For sources specific to a market or category of spend, please refer to the supplier identification section in the relevant chapter. Refer to Chapter 30 for industrial distributor identification resources.

Alibaba.com

http://www.alibaba.com

Launched in 1999, Alibaba.com is China's giant e-commerce marketplace. It is a platform for cross-border trade that helps in finding "quality manufacturers, suppliers, exporters, importers, buyers, wholesalers, products, and trade leads." It provides access to more than 2.8 million supplier online storefronts and more than 5,900 product categories.[1] For product searches, tools such as Related Search and category/country/type breakdown options help narrow search results. Assessment tools are also available.

Table 8.1 Resources—supplier identification

RESOURCES—SUPPLIER IDENTIFICATION	Manufacturing Focus	Most/All Industries	Keyword Search Capability	Public Library Access Best Option	Free	International In Scope	North America/ U.S. Only	Asia Focus
Alibaba.com		✓	✓		✓	✓		
AtoZdatabases		✓		✓			✓	
Made-In-China.com		✓	✓		✓			✓
B2BManufacturers.com	✓		✓		✓			✓
Global Sources	✓		✓		✓			✓
Kompass		✓	✓		✓	✓		
MacRAE's Blue Book	✓		✓		✓		✓	
MFG Connect	✓		✓		✓	✓		
NTMA Manufacturing Suppliers Guide	✓		✓		✓		✓	
ReferenceUSA		✓		✓			✓	
Solusource/Global Supplier Directory	✓		✓		✓	✓		
Thomasnet.com	✓		✓		✓		✓	

AtoZdatabases

http://www.atozdatabases.com/home

This source provides access to 30 million businesses, and uses codes such as SIC and NAICS to support searching. It allows a way to narrow search results by selecting different types of criteria, including a specific geography, business size, or ownership model. This is a popular business resource available in public libraries. All industries are covered. Select the option to make lists. There is no keyword search option, which can be limiting.

Made-in-China.com

http://www.made-in-china.com

Made-in-China.com describes itself as a one-stop platform for sourcing Chinese products. There are over 10 million products in the directory, and the products are classified under main categories: Industrial Supplies, Consumer Electronics, and Service, to name a few. Within each of these broad categories, there is detailed categorization. There is also a search feature.

B2BManufacturers.com

http://www.manufacturers.com.tw

This online platform helps buyers locate suppliers through its comprehensive database of manufacturers in Taiwan and China. Supplier listings provide detailed information on company profiles, website links, contacts, product descriptions and photos, and new product information.

Buyers Guides—Industry Associations

There is a professional association for just about every type of industry. Associations often provide buyer guides that are free to members and nonmembers, as well. A good way to find associations for an industry is to use a search engine; type the industry name with the term "association." Another useful source, Gale's *Encyclopedia of Associations*, is the standard reference source for industry associations and is found in all libraries.

Buyers Guides—Trade Journals

Just as there is a professional association for almost every type of industry, there is also a professional or trade journal for every type of industry, many of which are published by professional associations. These publications, more often than not, have companion websites with buyer guides that are almost always free to access. To find journal titles for an industry, use a search engine; enter the industry name with the term "trade journal." The authoritative source for this type of information, found in all libraries, is *Ulrich's Periodicals Directory.*

Global Sources

http://www.globalsources.com

Global Sources is a business-to-business online marketplace that facilitates trade with Greater China. It is used by more than 1 million international buyers to help with sourcing from overseas supply markets. You can do an advanced search where you can enter a keyword, and narrow the search by category and location. There is also a product and supplier Browse feature. You can sort results by relevancy, supplier rank, and new supplier. The Compare feature allows you to view products/suppliers side-by-side. The use of star rankings and verification levels help with identifying quality suppliers.

Kompass

http://us.kompass.com

Kompass is a free worldwide directory of business and commercial companies, representing 55,000 products and services. Kompass uses a unique classification system, which is more detailed than SIC, to help you target specific companies/suppliers more easily. Click on "Kompass Classification" to browse. Categories are comprehensive, and include Agriculture, Business Services, Construction, Chemistry, Energy, IT/Internet, Paper/Printing, Tourism/Leisure, Transport and Lodging, Training, and Textile/Clothing, to name a few. You can enter a search term to begin, and then search by location to narrow results.

MacRAE'S Blue Book

http://www.macraesbluebook.com

MacRAE'S bills itself as "America's Original Industrial Directory Since 1893." Here, you can find free information on more than 1.2 million North American industrial companies with more than 2 million product listings indexed under more than 50,000 product headings.

MFG Connect

http://www.mfg.com/mfgconnect

Offered by MFG.com, this free international supplier discovery service includes unique custom manufacturers in more than 100 disciplines, including assembly,

CNC machining, die casting, forging, injection molding, fabrication, and metal stamping, to name a few. You can use drop-down menus for product and location, combined with a keyword search that aids in narrowing results. It is international in scope.

NTMA Manufacturing Suppliers Guide

http://manufacturingsuppliersguide.com

The National Tooling and Machining Association (NTMA) provides a Manufacturing Suppliers Guide with main categories that include Business Services; Cutting and Forming Tools; Engineering Services; Equipment Sales and Services; Maintenance, Repair and Overhaul (MRO); Raw Materials; and, Software and Technology.

ReferenceUSA

http://www.referenceusa.com

There is a good chance that your local library subscribes to this database portal. The U.S. Businesses database, which contains information on 24 million U.S. businesses, is helpful in finding suppliers by using different criteria, such as SIC/NAICS code, geography, and business size. All industries are covered. There is no free text search option, which can be limiting.

Solusource/Global Supplier Directory

http://www.worldindustrialreporter.com/solusource

Solusource is a free directory of manufacturers and distributors from countries in Asia, Europe, and the Americas. The search box allows you to search by Global Products, Suppliers by Category, or Company Name. All available categories and companies (not products) will display when you begin to type. You can narrow results by country.

Thomasnet.com

http://www.thomasnet.com

Thomasnet.com is a standard reference that has been a favorite of buyers for years. There are now six applications to choose from when using the redesigned platform: Supplier Discovery, Product Sourcing, CAD Models, Custom Quotes, Diversity and Quality, and Industry News. The Supplier Discovery application lets you find industrial and commercial suppliers by product/service category, company name, brand name, and UNSPSC. You can search by keyword and filter according to Mile Radius, Ownership/Diversity, Quality and Other Certifications, Product Detail, Company Type, Locations Served, and then search within results. The comparison tool allows for side-by-side comparisons. The Product Sourcing application has semantic search capabilities based on a classification system specific to engineering. Here you can find components, MRO products, materials and equipment by specification, keyword, part number, or UNSPSC commodity. The Diversity and Quality application helps to find suppliers by ownership, such as female owned, and suppliers that are certified according to quality standards. The platform is free, and the coverage focuses on North America.

REFERENCE

1. Jillian D'onfro, "18 Mind-Blowing Facts About Alibaba, The Chinese E-Commerce Giant on the Verge of a Gigantic IPO," *Business Insider*, March 19, 2014, http://www.businessinsider.com/alibaba-ipo-facts-2014-3.

9

SUPPLIER RESEARCH, DILIGENCE, AND RISK MONITORING

Procurement professionals have always understood the importance of evaluating a potential supplier's financial and operational health, but there is now a more intense focus on the overall practice of supplier risk management. There are multiple reasons why companies are taking increased measures to research and monitor their suppliers for risk. Two of the reasons identified by Deloitte are: 1) the emergence of an "increasingly complex global sourcing landscape," with organizations using a mix of external providers, and at times "multi-sourcing for a single product," and 2) a "growth in new service delivery locations, e.g., China, Brazil, Egypt, and others, each with their own social, economic, demographic, and political risks."[1] In addition, there are times when suppliers use poor and/or unethical practices, which increase the reputational risk for the companies that buy from them. Examples of unethical practices include the Mattel toy recalls due to lead paint in 2007, the Tesco horse meat scandal in 2013, and the horrific factory collapse in Bangladesh in 2013.[2]

Many supplier risk research services and products have emerged over the last decade from providers who previously offered credit risk and rating data and from "traditional" companies that provide company, news and industry research offerings. These firmly rooted companies have expanded into supplier research coverage with the advantage of having deep and comprehensive reservoirs of company and industry data. For example, LexisNexis, a major player in the supplier risk diligence and monitoring information services space has, in its history, connections to the development of a "free-text" search and retrieval system in

Table 9.1 Resources—supplier research

RESOURCES—SUPPLIER RESEARCH	Private Supplier Information	Public Supplier Information	Financial Health and/or Risk Rating	Market/Industry News/Analysis	Supplier/Supply Chain Risk Monitoring	Possible Public Library Access	Purchase Without Subscription
Alacra Store	✓	✓	✓	✓			✓
American City Business Journals	✓	✓		✓			
Bloomberg	✓	✓	✓	✓			
BvD	✓	✓	✓	✓	✓		
ChinaScope Financial	✓	✓	✓	✓			
Cortera	✓	✓	✓	✓	✓		✓
CreditRiskMonitor	✓	✓	✓	✓	✓		
Dow Jones (Factiva, DJX)	✓	✓	✓	✓	✓		
Dun & Bradstreet	✓	✓	✓	✓	✓		✓
EBSCO	✓	✓	✓	✓		✓	
Experian	✓	✓	✓		✓		
Hoover's	✓	✓	✓	✓			✓
Investext		✓	✓	✓			
LexisNexis	✓	✓	✓	✓	✓		
MarketLine	✓	✓	✓	✓		✓	✓
Mergent Online		✓	✓	✓			
Morningstar		✓	✓	✓		✓	
PrivCo	✓		✓	✓			✓
ProQuest	✓	✓	✓	✓		✓	
RAGE Frameworks	✓	✓	✓	✓	✓		
Rapid Ratings	✓	✓	✓	✓	✓		
Regional Business News	✓	✓		✓		✓	
Resilinc	✓	✓	✓	✓	✓		
riskmethods	✓	✓	✓	✓	✓		
SEC Filings (open access)		✓	✓				
SkyMinder	✓	✓	✓	✓			✓

1967 and the first electronic data-search system to retrieve full-text documents in 1966.[3] Credit reporting provider Dun & Bradstreet, according to its website, originally dates back to 1841 as The Mercantile Agency. Its Supplier Risk Manager tool has been around for over ten years. These established companies are facing competition from newer risk credit and financial health providers. For example, Rapid Ratings and Cortera have introduced unique, innovative models. Rapid Ratings technology was created in 1991 and implemented in 1998-2001. Cortera was founded in 1993, and its Pulse product is about five years old. Utilizing advanced technology, providers are now entering the market with visual and data analytics offerings such as Rage Frameworks and riskmethods. Looking forward, analysts predict the growth of geospatial representation of supplier risk data. Spend Matters predicts "that 2014 will be the year in which procurement organizations begin to deploy geospatial views of their spend and supplier data in regular practice."[4]

The resources listed in this chapter, which are shown in Table 9.1, include third-party content providers, but do not address offerings from broader supplier management providers. The procurement service provider directories listed in Chapter 12 are also great resources to use for identifying the complete range of supplier management providers.

As detailed in Chapter 4, finding supplier information depends on many variables, including whether the supplier in question is a publicly or privately held company. The challenge for procurement, including seasoned business researchers, is finding information on private companies, especially regarding their financial health. Creativity in the search process will go a long way and resources such as local and regional news sources and social media should be incorporated for more successful and up-to-date results.

CREDIT REPORTS/RISK MONITORING/FINANCIAL HEALTH

Bureau van Dijk (BvD)

https://www.bvdinfo.com/en-gb/products/bvd-s-vertical-solutions/vertical-solutions/procurement-catalyst

Bureau van Dijk (BvD) is a global business intelligence provider known for its private international company information and detailed ownership data. Procurement Catalyst is a supplier risk platform that combines a company's supplier data and BvD's company and risk data to provide a complete view of current and potential suppliers. The platform is comprised of three parts: dashboard, search, and portfolio. The dashboard is customizable and includes Risk Indicators,

Change of Supplier Risk Indicator, Country, Change of Global Ultimate Owner, Legal, Companies with New Accounts, Company and Market News, and Mergers and Acquisitions views. The portfolio feature allows you to analyze your organization's portfolio, and to get reports on spend distribution and key metrics. BvD's detailed ownership data enables you to make ties to companies that previously looked unrelated. It gives total value of what you have expended to a particular group of related suppliers.

Cortera

http://www.cortera.com

Cortera credit reports are different because they look at a business's health by evaluating each company according to purchase behavior. In addition to payment behavior, Cortera looks at what a business buys and how that changes over time. Cortera Pulse is a monitoring and alerting service. The B2B Insight Reports are information reports, ranging from "Flash" to "Deep Dive" reports. Cortera Pulse monitors for bankruptcies, tax liens, civil judgments, CPR score decline, purchase decline, news alerts, growth clues, and risk rating. The reports are visually appealing and easy to read. Credit reports can be purchased individually and are reasonably priced.

CreditRiskMonitor

http://www.crmz.com

Founded in 1977, CreditRiskMonitor is a public company that offers commercial credit reports for public companies worldwide. The reports feature annual and quarterly financial analysis, financial statements, peer analysis, company background information, Moody's ratings and analysis, and Standard & Poor's ratings. Reports also include trade payment data, and public filing information for public and larger private U.S. companies. Customized portfolios can be set up for monitoring purposes.

Dow Jones

http://new.dowjones.com

DJX is a newer offering from Dow Jones, which unites the content of Factiva, Dow Jones Newswires, private equity and venture capital products, and various Risk and Compliance products. With DJX, for supplier risk, you utilize the Risk and Compliance component to access 160 sanction lists and Factiva, which provides access to more than 34,000 company and industry news sources, for news-based alerts. Alerts can be set up via keyword or pre-set criteria. When DJX launched with a new pricing model, it was met with uniform criticism.[5] At the time of publication, Dow Jones is adjusting the pricing of its DJX subscription product.[6]

Dun & Bradstreet (D&B)

http://www.dnb.com/supply-management/supply-risk-manager

D&B has historically been a main source that researchers look to for private company information. The Supplier Risk Manager 2.0 solution allows you to certify, monitor, and analyze suppliers. A subscription to this service provides access to risk ratings, including the Supplier Evaluation Risk (SER) rating, which uses predictive analytics to assess the likelihood that a company will cease operations within the next 12 months. Recent enhancements to the subscription include a Profile page, which provides an overall risk review of a supplier; a Locator page, which provides specific search criteria for suppliers; a Competitors View, which allows you to see who a supplier is competing against; and Enhanced Corporate Linkage with a family tree feature. The Alert tiles display all suppliers with red flags that indicate risk concerns. The Country Risk add-on provides data from 132 countries.

Experian

http://www.experian.com

Experian is a credit reference agency that competes with Dun & Bradstreet. Experian business credit reports provide background and financial information, credit score and risk factors, banking, trade, collection history, liens, judgments, bankruptcies, and Uniform Commercial Code filings. The Supplier Check Reports include risk ratings, payment histories, rising delinquencies, severe delinquency indicators on key account types, probability of business failure, records of legal judgments, and industry financial statistics. Both types of reports offer monitoring services.

LexisNexis

http://www.lexisnexis.com/en-us/other-business-solutions/procurement-and-supply-chain-management.page

LexisNexis offers two products for supplier health and monitoring: Lexis Diligence and SmartWatch. Lexis Diligence enables you to develop a due-diligence report by accessing many resources at one time with a well-designed interface that allows easy searching and navigation. One of the most powerful resources is the global news archive, which taps into the deep LexisNexis collection of news and trade publications. Other important types of data that can be accessed are sanctions and watchlists, international and national company information, country risk information, legal history and ongoing litigation, public records, and biographies. To ensure due diligence, all searches are date- and time-stamped. The monitoring offering, SmartWatch, accesses its collection of content, including news, industry, and legal publications and scans for recent country, industry, and company events in the environmental, political, economic, societal, technical, and legal areas of concern.

RAGE Frameworks

http://www.rageframeworks.com

The RAGE Frameworks Real Time Intelligence (RTI) for Supplier Risk solution uses Big Data to successfully monitor supplier risk. RTI is able to combine analysis from structured data (financial documents, credit bureau information, subscription providers), and unstructured data (text in media, blogs, social media), in addition to internal sources. RTI trawls the web looking for data, and then interprets and identifies what is relevant and what is the most important. Every article is first tested for relevance, as defined by a customizable ontology, and then assessed for impact. Visual impact scoring is graphically presented in a way that is easy to interpret and use.

Rapid Ratings

http://www.rapidratings.com

Rapid Ratings is best known for its quantitative Financial Health Ratings (FHR). FHR offers financial health analysis for both national and international public and private companies in more than 110 countries. Rapid Ratings solicits private company financial information by building relationships with and educating (prospective) suppliers to ensure that disclosure is exclusive to the client being represented. The reports are written in an easy-to-understand manner, and include an extensive use of color-coding and visuals. There are a variety of reports offered, including individual company and portfolio risk reports that provide both analytics and commentary. The Peer Benchmark report compares an individual company to its industry peer group. Recently launched was the Company Comparison Report, which is a visualization tool that allows you to compare up to five public and private companies side by side.

Resilinc

http://www.resilinc.com

Resilinc enables supply chain visibility by creating supplier multi-tier intelligence and mapping it. It creates a worldwide repository of supplier, part, and multi-tier intelligence with solutions for risk management, event monitoring, conflict minerals, corporate social responsibility and business continuity. Its three basic steps are Plan, Monitor, and Protect, pinpointing vulnerability via financial, location, recovery, and operational risk. The strength of this solution is that it visually maps the interrelationships between the multi-tiers in your supply chain.

riskmethods

http://www.riskmethods.net/

riskmethods is a newer company that is offering a cloud-based supply chain and supplier risk solution. Where riskmethods stands out is through its ability to identify multi-tiers (not just the first tier) of supplier production and transportation sites. It also monitors all types of risk found in the supply chain including supplier, country, and location site. For information capture, different types of sources are integrated, including their own risk research, internal systems, third party information providers—either with a fee or free—and "network share," which allows informal sharing of information via a community of companies. The third-party information providers consist of credit agencies, global organizations, and publishers of company and industry data. On a continuous basis, through screening, news events are captured and ultimately transferred into threat risk data for the relevant risk objects of the supply chains. This data is represented visually via an interactive world map that models the supply chains.

SkyMinder

http://www.skyminder.com

SkyMinder is a resource that provides company information on millions of public and private companies, worldwide. Reports include profile and credit information. SkyMinder acts as a portal for 50 different providers around the world, enabling access to company information on a country-by-country basis.

SUPPLIER FINANCIALS

Mergent Online

http://mergentonline.com

At Mergent Online, you will find international and U.S. company data, including historical financial results and financial ratios. Additional modules cover risk ratings and credit information. The interface allows you to create customized comparison lists and reports of companies and industry subgroups.

U.S. Securities and Exchange Commission (SEC) Filings

http://www.sec.gov/edgar/searchedgar/companysearch.html

Look at SEC filings for current and historical companies, and other filings for publicly-traded companies (e.g., 10-Ks, 10-Qs, 8-Ks) through its Electronic Data Gathering, Analysis and Retrieval System (EDGAR). At the EDGAR Company search page, type in a company name. Click on the correct central index key (CIK) number. You can filter results at this page by filing type and date.

Company Websites

You can find financial statements on a public company's website. Look for the section on investor information by searching on an "About Us" page, if available, or looking at the site map.

Morningstar

http://www.morningstar.com

Morningstar provides comprehensive financial information on stocks. The industry peers information provides comparative data on a number of companies within an industry sector. "Morningstar Investment Research Center" is available through many public libraries. Premium content is subscription-based, but basic company and quote information is free, along with peer comparisons.

PUBLIC AND PRIVATE COMPANY/SUPPLIER INFORMATION

Alacra Store

http://www.alacrastore.com

The Alacra Store allows you to purchase one-off reports from sources such as D&B, Fitch, Moody's, Experian, GlobalData, IDC, PrivCo, EIU, or Freedonia. The value of the Alacra Store is that you can search all the databases at one time, allowing for comprehensive coverage. The report categories include Credit Ratings, Market Research, Company Reports, Country Profiles, and M&A Information. Search results include all relevant categories; for example, for a particular company, you could potentially see results for credit reports, financial reports, and any market research reports in which the company is included. When using AlacraStore.com, there are no invoices, contracts, or access fees.

Hoover's

http://www.hoovers.com

At Hoover's website, you can search more than 85 million companies within 900 industry segments. This source provides company information, company histories, lists of competitors, financials, and news for both public and private companies. Industry reports are from First Research. In addition, this resource makes available Dun & Bradstreet credit information. International in scope, this source is easy to search and a good way to quickly scan company information. Hoover's is a subscription-based service, but Company, Industry, IT Spotlight, Competitive Landscape, and Business Credit reports can be purchased separately.

BvD (Bureau Van Dijk)

http://www.bvdinfo.com

BvD features global, regional, and national coverage for listed and private companies with detailed financials and corporate structures data. Its international private company coverage is its strength.

ChinaScope Financial

http://www.chinascopefinancial.com

ChinaScope Financial's private company database covers 3 million unlisted companies. It also covers China-based companies listed on the Shanghai, Shenzhen, Hong Kong, NASDAQ, and New York Stock exchanges. Other products include economic data and research services, as well as industry statistics.

MarketLine

http://www.marketline.com/overview/company-information

MarketLine (formerly Datamonitor) provides company profiles that are known for their strengths, weaknesses, opportunities, threats (SWOT) analysis section. You can purchase reports separately via the company store. Business Source Elite, a database found in many public libraries, provides access to these reports: select the Company Profiles button.

COMPREHENSIVE RESOURCES WITH BOTH FINANCIALS AND NEWS SOURCES

Bloomberg

http://www.bloomberg.com/professional

For company information, you can find financials, news, and analyst recommendations at Bloomberg. Bloomberg's Supply Chain (SPLC) module is where you can get a holistic view of the supply chain structure for a company. Supply chain data includes customer, supplier, and competitive relationship to track a company's performance against peers. Bloomberg is an excellent source, but expensive. It is best to investigate if the service is already in use in your organization, as opposed to purchasing it just for procurement's use, especially for small to medium teams.

Dow Jones' Factiva

http://www.dowjones.com/factiva

Factiva allows you to access thousands of sources all in one place. You can locate U.S. and international company reports, and read the latest news from top business sources. You can search local and global newspapers, newswires, trade journals, newsletters, magazines, and transcripts, with many options to narrow results.

EBSCO Business Source, Corporate and Elite

http://www.ebscohost.com

EBSCO Business Source offers comprehensive business collections for both academic and corporate environments. The corporate version provides access to full-text general business periodicals and trade publications, such as *Chemical Week* and *American Banker*. There are country economic reports from Business Monitor Unit, Global Insights, and Country Watch, to name a few. You can find company profiles with excellent SWOT analysis reports and full-text industry reports. Business Source Elite is a popular database with an academic focus and is often the business database of choice for public libraries. It provides access to scholarly business and trade journals, in addition to company reports that feature the SWOT analysis section.

LexisNexis

http://lexisnexis.com

Lexis is the legal side, and Nexis is the business side, of LexisNexis. When you land on the home page, select Legal and Professional Solutions. *Nexis.com* is a comprehensive source for finding information on millions of U.S. and international companies, as well as full text for thousands of trade journals, newspapers, and newswires. There are numerous quality company databases that you can tap into, such as Business Monitor International, D&B Market Identifiers, MarketLine, Onesource, and Standard & Poor's Corporate Profiles. LexisNexis's Power Search is a good option if you want to search specific sources, construct precise queries, or use SmartIndexing, which lets you refine your searches by clicking on a list of indexed terms.

ProQuest

http://www.proquest.com

ProQuest competes with EBSCO as an information database and provides access to a vast collection of articles from newspapers, trade, and regional publications, in addition to company, industry, and market research reports. This research subscription service is found in many academic and corporate libraries. ProQuest just completed its acquisition and integration of Dialog, a powerful, pioneering information service used mostly by corporate business and scientific researchers when "there was an 'online' before the Internet."[7] It is worth exploring to see if your organization's library or information center (if you have one) subscribes to any of its services.

PRIVATE SUPPLIER COMPANY INFORMATION

PrivCo

http://www.privco.com

PrivCo is used specifically for researching major privately held U.S. companies. Here, you can find private company financials and revenues; mergers and acquisition deals; firm valuations; venture capital fundings; private equity deals; private and family ownership breakdowns; bankruptcies; and restructurings. You can purchase a report individually.

SUPPLIER INFORMATION—LOCAL AND REGIONAL FOCUS

American City Business Journals

http://www.bizjournals.com

One way to find information on private companies (and public as well) is through local business newspapers, like those found at *bizjournals.com*. This source provides coverage of business news from local, regional, and national perspectives. On the homepage, use the "Visit a local business journal" drop-down feature to see the cities that are covered.

Regional Business News

http://www.ebscohost.com/academic/regional-business-news

Regional Business News provides business publications on a regional level for the U.S. and Canada, containing business journals, newspapers, and newswires. This site is produced by EBSCO, a database with excellent search features. An added bonus is that it is a popular database for public libraries, thus providing a good chance for free access.

ANALYST REPORTS

Investext (Thomson Research)

http://research.thomsonib.com

Investext is a powerful research resource primarily used for investment information, but is also useful for extracting very detailed analysis not found elsewhere, such as strategy and operations. These company, industry, and geographic research reports are written by analysts at more than 1,000 leading investment banks, brokerage houses, and consulting firms, worldwide.

REFERENCES

1. "The New Reality for Managing Supplier Risk: It's Harder Than You Think," *Deloitte*. 2012, http://www.deloitte.com/view/en_US/us/Services/additional-services/Service-Delivery-Transformation/504d24af4c4b9310VgnVCM2000001b56f00aRCRD.htm.
2. Keong Leong, "Supplier Ethics Management" (Presentation), Institute for Supply Management, Las Vegas, NV, July 17, 2013.
3. "About LexisNexis—Historical Milestones," *LexisNexis.com*, Accessed May 8, 2014, http://www.lexisnexis.com/en-us/about-us/about-us.page.
4. Jason Busch, "We Predict That Geospatial Category and Supplier Management Will Go Mainstream in 2014," *Spend Matters*, November 25, 2013, http://spendmatters.com/2013/11/25/predict-geospatial-category-supplier-management-will-go-mainstream-2014-introduction.

5. John McDuling, "Everyone's Talking About Dow Jones's DJX on Wall Street, But for All the Wrong Reasons," *Quartz*, December 16, 2013, http://qz.com/150465/dow-jones-djx-underwhelming-on-wall-street-morgan-stanley.
6. Chris Rouch, "News Corp. CEO: DJX to Get Flexible Pricing," *Talking Biz News*, February 6, 2014, http://www.talkingbiznews.com/1/news-corp-ceo-djx-to-get-flexible-pricing/.
7. http://www.dialog.com/about/history/pioneers1.pdf.

10

INDUSTRY AND MARKET RESEARCH

There are two main types of market research: primary and secondary. *Primary research* is when a researcher, often sponsored by an organization or company, is involved in the actual data-gathering through the use of interviews, telephone surveys, and questionnaires.[1] *Secondary research* involves the use of existing data that has either been created to allow for customization, and/or published in an "off-the-shelf" or packaged format. The resources listed in this chapter are all sources of secondary research.

Market research provides detailed and comprehensive data about what markets are currently doing and what they will be doing in the future.[2] Quality market research tends to be expensive to access. Most publishers offer the flexibility to purchase reports separately without being locked into a subscription. To provide even more economy, look for the feature that allows you to download and pay for only specific sections or pages of reports.

As stated in Chapter 4, procurement may find market research reports useful for the development of a category strategy because of their focus on major industry trends and developments. Those unfamiliar with these types of research reports might be surprised about the amount and quality of data that is offered. Market research information covers everything from economic data, country risk, forecast analysis and pricing, trends outlook, market drivers, market share and segmentation, competitive landscape, and supply chain and distribution channel discussions. The geographic coverage is expansive, and product coverage can get quite detailed. Helpful information can be gleaned just by reading the free overview or summary of the report, where key takeaways are highlighted.

The use of "one-stop shops" allows you to purchase reports individually. These resources are extremely effective tools to use to identify market research providers in your specific supplier market or category of interest. In addition, these resources search multiple reports at one time, ensuring due diligence of comprehensive searching. To evaluate the data and providers of market research reports, read the methodology that is used to gather the information and check to see how often the reports are updated.

Listed in this chapter are industry and market research providers with histories of producing quality research.

MARKET RESEARCH ONE-STOP SHOPS

MarketResearch.com

http://www.marketresearch.com

MarketResearch partners with more than 700 publishers of market research reports and provides them for purchase. Many of the publishers listed in this book are available via *MarketResearch.com*, including, MarketLine, Euromonitor International, Freedonia, Frost & Sullivan, IDC, and IBISWorld, to name a few. You can browse by category or use the keyword search feature. Limiting features include date, price, publisher, and location. Sorting by date ensures that you are viewing the most recent data.

Research and Markets.com

http://www.researchandmarkets.com

The *Research and Markets.com* online market research shop provides access to reports from specialist research firms and niche market analysts, covering all industries. Here, you can find the latest data on international and regional markets, key industries, top companies, and trends. You can browse by industry category or search by specific keyword or phrase. Product filters include country, region, categories, price, data, and product type.

INDUSTRY AND MARKET RESEARCH PROVIDERS

BCC Research

http://www.bccresearch.com

BCC Research's reports, which can be lengthy, are intended for industrial, pharmaceutical, and high-tech organizations. BCC Research covers the following areas: Advanced Materials, Advanced Transportation Technologies, Biotechnology, Chemicals, Energy, Environment, Engineering, Food and Beverages, Fuel Cells and Battery Technologies, Healthcare, Information Technology, Instrumentation and Sensors, Manufacturing, Membrane and Separation Technology, Pharmaceuticals, Plastics, Safety and Security, Semiconductor Manufacturing, and Photonics. Reports can be purchased individually and by chapters.

Bloomberg Industries

http://www.bloomberg.com/professional/news-research/industries

Bloomberg Industries (BI), launched in 2012, is a real-time industry research platform that provides analysis and trends for more than 100 industries across ten major sectors in North America, Europe, and Asia. The BI platform "aggregates information from more than 200 third-party providers." Once you select the industry of interest, menu offerings are: Analysis (overall, Bull & Bear, themes, earnings, valuation); Data Library (macro-level industry factors, market share, and segmentation of geography); and Monitor (real-time company-specific data and news).

Business Monitor International

http://www.businessmonitor.com

Business Monitor International provides information that focuses on operating risks in international markets, covering 195 countries and 24 industry sectors. It offers these products and services: Business Monitor Online, Industry Market Reports, Country Business Forecast Reports, Multinational Companies Database, Regional Risk Monitor, and Regional Industry Insights. Business Monitor Online, as published on the website, is a "data and intelligence tool that connects country risk, industry analysis and financial markets and assesses global, regional, country and company developments and trends worldwide."

Euromonitor International

http://www.euromonitor.com

Euromonitor International is known for its international market information and its high quality. The research reports cover trends in 206 countries and more than 200 categories. The industry reports cover consumer goods, services, and industrial markets. According to the website, the reports provide "analysis and statistics on national markets and include data and analysis of market size, distribution channels, market trends, competitive landscape, legislation, local company profiles, company and brand shares and five-year forecasts." Euromonitor's flagship product is Passport.

Factiva

http://www.dowjones.com/factiva/index.asp

By using Factiva, you will find comprehensive profiles on more than 30 industry and 970 sub-industry categories, which include industry rankings, peer comparisons, expert analysis, and the latest news. You also can search local and global newspapers, newswires, trade journals, newsletters, magazines, and transcripts with many options to narrow results. You will need to purchase a subscription for access.

First Research

http://www.firstresearch.com

First Research is a division of Hoover's, which is a Dun & Bradstreet (D&B) company. The First Research industry reports cover 900 industry segments. Reports provide information on critical issues, industry forecast/indicators/drivers, competitive landscape, products/operations/technology, business challenges, trends and opportunities, financial benchmark information, and web links. You can purchase the reports individually.

Freedonia

http://www.freedoniagroup.com

The Freedonia Group was founded in 1985 and publishes industry research studies that mostly cover the manufacturing sector. The industry analysis includes "product and market forecasts, industry trends, threats and opportunities, competitive strategies, market share determinations and company profiles." Categories of coverage include: Automotive, Chemicals, Coatings and Sealants, Construction Materials, Energy and Power Equipment, Household Goods, Life Sciences, Medical and Pharmaceutical Products, Metals and Minerals, Packaging, Paper and Textiles, Plastic Materials and Processing, and Plastics Markets. Reports can be purchased individually, and some can be purchased by the page or section.

Frost & Sullivan

http://www.frost.com

Lore Frost and Dan Sullivan started Frost & Sullivan in 1961. Detailed and global in coverage, research is offered for these industries: Aerospace and Defense,

Automotive and Transportation, Chemicals, Materials and Food, Electronics and Security, Energy and Power Supplies, Environment and Building Technologies, Healthcare, Industrial Automation and Process Control, Information and Communication Technologies, Measurement and Instrumentation. There is access to complimentary research, and you can purchase reports individually.

Global Industry Analysts

http://www.strategyr.com

Global Industry Analysts is a publisher that started as a research boutique, specializing in the medical industry in 1987. It has expanded its coverage to include 180 major industries. You can purchase complete reports, or sections of the reports individually.

GlobalData

http://www.globaldata.com

GlobalData provides market research for the energy and healthcare industries, including these segments: Medical Devices, Mining, Clean Technology, Alternative Energy, Chemicals, Nuclear Energy, Oil and Gas, Pharmaceuticals and Healthcare, Power and Utilities, and Smart Grid. Intelligence covers segmentation, competitors, valuations, trends, forecasts, news, deals, and emerging markets analysis.

IBISWorld Industry and Procurement Research Reports

http://www.ibisworld.com

Since 1971, IBISWorld has been publishing high-quality industry research reports. The Industry Research Reports provide key statistics/analysis on market characteristics and major industry participants. The Industry Risk Rating Reports determine how much risk an industry will face over the next eighteen months and the Business Environment Reports highlight factors of risk including exchange rate, commodity prices, weather conditions, and government policies.

In 2013, IBISWorld started publishing Procurement Research Reports, which cover a multitude of indirect purchasing lines. These detailed reports cover product/service pricing dynamics, product characteristics that may affect the purchasing decision, supplier benchmarking and supply chain risks, and negotiation questions and tactics. The first page of each report, titled "At a Glance," provides the recent price, forecast price, market characteristics, market risk, benchmark price, key price drivers, major vendors, vendor cost benchmarks, and Buyer Power Score.

IHS

http://www.ihs.com

IHS was founded more than 50 years ago and originated as a product catalog database provider for aerospace engineers. Its information now covers these industries: Automotive, Agriculture, Chemicals, Construction, Consumer and Retail, Technology, Oil and Gas, Financial, Life Sciences, Maritime, Metals and Mining, Military and Security, Power and Utilities, and Renewable Energies. IHS provides services specific to Supply Chain Intelligence in the areas of Commodity, Pricing and Cost, MRO, Defense Logistics and Procurement, Component and Parts, and Technology. The IHS Pricing and Purchasing service covers global price and cost analysis, including ten-year forecasts and historical records for commodity prices and wages.

Industry Associations

There is a professional association for practically every industry category. Industry associations are regular publishers of both scholarly and trade journals, and usually provide excellent state-of-the industry and forecast/trend reports. Sometimes these reports are free, but other times they are available to members only, or for an increased fee charged to nonmembers. A good way to find associations for an industry is to perform an Internet search; type the industry name into the search engine with the term "association." The standard reference source to consult is Gale's *Encyclopedia of Associations*, which can be found in most libraries.

LexisNexis

http://www.lexisnexis.com

As stated in Chapter 9, Supplier Research, Diligence, and Monitoring, Lexis is the legal side and Nexis is the business side of LexisNexis. When you land on the home page, select "Legal and Professional Solutions." Here you can find global and country-specific overviews of more than 1000 industries, including market share information and SWOT analysis. Some of the sources available are Business Monitor International, MarketLine Industry Reports, Hoover's Industry Snapshots, and Standard & Poor's.

Standard & Poor's Industry Surveys

http://www.standardandpoors.com/products-services/industry_surveys/en/us

Standard & Poor's Industry Surveys track more than 50 North American industries and 10 global industries. Each report includes current environment, industry trends, key ratios and statistics, how to analyze a company, a glossary of terms, and a comparative company financial analysis.

Trade Journals

Just as there is a professional association for practically every type of industry category, there is also a professional or trade journal for every type of industry. Trade journals have companion websites, and there is often a special annual issue or feature that is devoted to industry trends and forecasts for the upcoming year. To find journal titles for an industry, use an Internet search engine to enter the industry name with term "trade journals." (You can also use the terms "magazines" or "periodicals," but sometimes the results can be different.) The authoritative source for this type of information, found in most libraries, is *Ulrich's Periodicals Directory*.

U.S. Securities and Exchange Commission (SEC) Filings

Use SEC filings for competitive landscape information. Companies will discuss the state of competition in their industries in the "Business Overview" section (Item 1), or the "Management's Discussion and Analysis of Financial Condition and Results of Operations" (Part II, Item 7) section of a 10-K report. You can search the SEC's EDGAR database, which has free, open access for company filings.

Once you have found a specific company, use your browser's Find command and search for specific terms, such as "competition," within that document. There are fee-based products that make searching and extracting information from SEC filings easy. Mergent Online, Morningstar Document Research, and WordsAnalytics are a few resources to consider. WordAnalytics uses natural language processing, and allows you to easily search and extract information from current and historical (from 2001) SEC filings.

Another way to easily find SEC documentation is to go to a company's website. If it is listed on the U.S. stock exchange, there will be a section on "Investor Relations." Here, there will be listed all the SEC filings for that particular company, including the 10-K, with the most recent first. Many finance websites provide competitor and related-companies listings helpful in determining "top players" in a market or industry. A few of these are CNNMoney.com, Google Finance, Yahoo! Finance, MarketWatch.com, and Morningstar.

REFERENCES

1. Mark Goldstein, "ASLAPR Market Research for Entrepreneurs Presentation," *Slideshare*, May 13, 2014, http://www.slideshare.net/markgirc/aslapr-market-research-for-entrepreneurs-mg-irc-presentation-05-1314.
2. *Ibid.*

11

BEST PRACTICES AND OPERATIONS BENCHMARKING

As Nicholas Bloom, Raffaella Sadun, and John Van Reenen (2012) stated, "At least since Frederick Winslow Taylor published *The Principles of Scientific Management* in 1911, businesses have been trying to follow formalized sets of best practices."[1] The Institute for Supply Management defines *best practice* as "a leading-edge activity, operation, or process that is innovative and successfully implemented and thus provides a more efficient and effective means of conducting business, helping an organization to reduce its costs and improve quality and customer service."[2]

Benchmarking, on the other hand, can be thought of as "a systematic process for identifying and implementing best or better practices."[3] In his book, *Supply Management and Procurement: From the Basics to Best-in-Class,* Robert Turner stated that the reason procurement set benchmarks "is to establish a point of reference that can be used to make improvements over current levels of efficiencies and against which our success can be measured."[4] Robert C. Camp wrote that the essence of benchmarking can be captured in the Japanese word *dantotsu,* which means, "striving to be the best of the best," and that benchmarking is a positive and proactive process.[5]

One of the first known studies to link best practices with quantitative performance achievements specific to supply chain activities is attributed to the consulting firm Pittiglio Rabin Todd and McGrath (PRTM) in the early 1990s. This concept went on to become the basis for Supply Chain Council's SCOR model.[6] While the chapters in Part II of this book are predominantly industry-driven, some disciplines apply across industries. Benchmarking is a topic that procurement professionals will need to leverage as their organizations strive to evaluate them for their ability to impact more than savings. As important as activities such as risk mitigation, efficiency, and innovation are professed to be, few organizations have successfully put the metrics in place that will drive tangible benefits in these areas. The resulting limitations, whether deliberately or unintentionally caused, hampers procurement's ability to expand to their full potential, and to recruit and retain top-performing candidates.

Listed below are organizations that provide benchmarking data and best practices information, and services specific to the supply chain and procurement functions.

APICS/Supply Chain Council

http://www.apics.org

It was announced in April, 2014, that The American Production and Inventory Control Society (APICS) and Supply Chain Council (SCC) were merging. APICS was formed in 1957 and SCC in 1996. APICS is known for its CPIM (Certified in Production and Inventory Management) and CSCP (Certified Supply Chain Professional) certifications. SCC is known for its Supply Chain Operations Reference (SCOR) model, described on the website as a framework that enables organizations to "determine and compare the performance of supply chain and related operations within their own companies or against other organizations."

CAPS Research

http://www.capsresearch.org

CAPS Research is a global research organization jointly sponsored by the W.P. Carey School of Business at Arizona State University, and the Institute for Supply Management. CAPS Research has more than 25 years of experience in the publishing industry and topic-specific benchmarking data that organizations can use to evaluate their own performance against their peers. Research publications can typically be accessed through the CAPS Research library, which consists of over 1,300 research and other documents. The popular Focus Studies cover timely, critical topics with reports like "Building Superior Supply/Value Chain Collaboration" and "Managing Commodity Price Volatility and Risk." Subscriber and Member fees are based on a company's annual revenue. The Participant level is for any company that wants to provide data to get access to the Metric Reports. The Member level, the most comprehensive, provides access to all offerings including Metric Reports, Industry Advisory Group, Survey Collaboration, Best

Practices Reports, Comparative Reports, Breakout Reports, Industry Debrief, Executive Roundtables, Best Practices Workshops, Critical Issue Events, Focus Study Reports, and Full Access to the research database.

American Productivity and Quality Center

http://www.apqc.org

The American Productivity and Quality Center (APQC) is a member-based nonprofit organization that provides business benchmarking, best practices, and knowledge management research. It started in 1977 as the American Productivity Center. The Supply Chain Management (SCM) Membership provides resources to help with reducing costs, improving cycle times, and adding value. APQC supply chain management resources include benchmarks, best practices, and case studies in the following areas: supply chain planning, procurement, manufacturing, logistics, and product development. Other membership types include Financial Management, Human Capital Management, Knowledge Management, All-Inclusive, and Professional Services.

Corporate Executive Board

http://www.executiveboard.com

The Corporate Executive Board (CEB) is a member-based advisory company. CEB offers research and insights, peer benchmarks, executive networking, live and online learning, best practices, decision and diagnostic tools and advisory support. As stated on its website, CEB offers memberships that are aligned to "functional and key industry leadership roles." Support is provided via Leadership Councils, which include Finance, Government, Strategy, Legal, Risk Management, Information Technology, Marketing, Procurement, and Operations, to name a few. The Procurement Leadership Council, in addition to providing guidance, tools, and peer perspectives, focuses on five areas of research: procurement transformation, supplier relationship management, category management, internal relationship management, and supplier risk management. A paid membership is required for research and services.

The Hackett Group

http://www.thehackettgroup.com

Founded in 1991, The Hackett Group is a global firm with a reputation for providing high quality research, providing best practice advisory and business benchmarking services for the Finance, Global Business Services, Human Resources,

Information Technology, Procurement, and Supply Chain functions. The Hackett Group bases a great deal of its research on transformational insights, as opposed to newscast reporting. Recently, Hackett Group expanded its Procurement Advisory Research services to include Category Insight Research reports. These reports cover indirect spend areas and combine category market intelligence with best practices and insights on how best to approach each specific area. Every report includes these elements: overview, key market trends, cost structure, competitive landscape, category tools, capability maturity model (CMM), best practices, channel design and additional resources. Their category coverage is impressive and comprehensive.

U.S. Securities and Exchange Commission Filings

http://www.sec.gov

To research the supply chain practices of specific companies, go to the SEC website and under Filings, select "Company Filings Search." Use the most recent 10-K report (listed by date, most recent first) of the company you are interested in researching. Once the 10-K is pulled up, use your browser's Find command to search for the terms "supply chain," "purchasing," "supplier," "sourcing," or other terms within the text. To search supply chain practices for multiple companies in a particular industry, or those offering competitive products and services, use an SEC research offering such as Morningstar Document Research (http://www.tenkwizard.com) or WordsAnalytics (http://www.wordsanalytics.com), which uses textual analytics and is a search portal to SEC documentation.

REFERENCES

1. Nicholas Bloom, Raffaella Sadun, and John Van Reenen, "Does Management Really Work?," *Harvard Business Review*, November 2012, http://hbr.org/2012/11/does-management-really-work/ar/1.
2. "ISM Glossary of Key Supply Management Terms," *Institute for Supply Management*, Accessed April 30, 2014, https://www.ism.ws/glossary.
3. "What Is Benchmarking?," *BPIR.com*, Accessed May 9, 2014, http://www.bpir.com/benchmarking-what-is-benchmarking-bpir.com.html.
4. Robert W. Turner, *Supply Management and Procurement: From the Basics to Best in Class*, Ft. Lauderdale, FL: J. Ross Publishing, 2011, 49.
5. Robert C. Camp, "Best Practice Benchmarking: The Path to Excellence," *CMA Magazine* 72 (1998), Accessed May 20, 2014. Business Source Premier (1039489).

6. Togar M. Simatupang and Ramaswami Sridharan, "A Benchmarking Scheme for Supply Chain Collaboration," *Benchmarking* 11 (2004). ABI/Inform Global (217394540).

12

PROCUREMENT SERVICE PROVIDER DIRECTORIES

The number and specialization of services and solutions specific to procurement grows just as quickly as the importance of the function itself. Like any other market, there is also constant mergers and acquisitions activity. Procurement professionals strive to approach investments in these solutions with great care as a way of demonstrating that they hold themselves to the same standards regarding good spend management stewardship as the rest of the organization. The directories and guides listed below provide the information needed to take the first steps in identifying and evaluating the varied procurement related services and solutions currently being offered.

Buyers Meeting Point Vendor Directory

http://www.buyersmeetingpoint.com/directories/vendor-directory

The Buyers Meeting Point Vendor Directory provides a list of supply management vendors, covering these categories: Business Continuity, Business Intelligence, Communities, e-Sourcing Suite, Professional Services, Professional/Certification Associations, Spend Analysis, Staffing and Recruiting, Supplier Networks, and Supply Chain Management.

Procurement Leaders Essential Guide

http://www.procurementleaders.com/essential-guides/essential-guides/the-2014-essential-guide

The *Procurement Leaders Essential Guide* provides a current listing of procurement related services by Type (Advisory and Consultancy, Training, BPO, Solutions and Technology, Recruitment), Specialization (e.g., Contract Management, e-Procurement, Purchase-to-Pay, Spend Analytics, Procurement Outsourcing, Risk Management, SRM, Transformation), and Spend Area (e.g., Consulting/Legal/Advisory, Contingent Labor, Fleet, IT, Logistics, MRO, Marketing, Office Supplies, Print, Telecoms, Travel).

Institute for Supply Management (ISM) Purchasing and Supply Sourcing Guide

http://purchasingandsupplysourcingguide.com

The *ISM Purchasing and Supply Sourcing Guide,* provided by the Institute for Supply Management, enables purchasing and supply sourcing in a wide range of categories including: Consulting Services, Human Capital Management, Procurement, Sourcing, Support Products and Services, Technology Solutions, and Transportation/Distribution/Logistics.

Spend Matters Almanac

http://spendmatters.com/almanac

The *Spend Matters Almanac* is a categorized online directory of organizations that serve the procurement and supply chain market. It is curated by Spend Matters editors and analysts. Some of the categories covered are: Consulting, Sourcing and Supplier Management, Sourcing, e-Procurement, Analytics and Market Intelligence, Source-to-Pay, Outsourcing, Procure-to-Pay (P2P), e-Invoicing, Supplier [Lifecycle] Management, Supplier Networks and Platforms, Cost Management, Supply Chain, ERP Suites, Data/Content Management, Contract [Lifecycle] Management, Membership Organization, Services Procurement, Training, and Trade Financing.

13

CONSULTING FIRMS

Consulting firms almost always have thought leadership and/or research and insights sections of their websites. The following consulting firms have released current thought leadership pieces on procurement and sourcing.

A.T. Kearney

http://www.atkearneypas.com/knowledge

The Knowledge Center serves as a central hub for all of A.T. Kearney Procurement and Analytic Solutions thought leadership in the areas of procurement, sourcing, supply management, and advanced analytics. In addition, A.T. Kearney, the Institute for Supply Management, and the Chartered Institute of Purchasing and Supply have launched the ROSMA Performance Check, which is an initiative that helps CPOs and sourcing professionals demonstrate their contributions to shareholder value. A.T. Kearney's Assessment of Excellence in Procurement (AEP) is the longstanding global study of supply management best practices.

Accenture

http://www.accenture.com

Accenture provides a wealth of research and insights on sourcing, procurement, and procurement business process outsourcing (BPO). The main navigation bar on the website provides five options: Strategy, Digital, Technology, Operations, and Industries. The Procurement and Sourcing insights are found by selecting Strategy, then Operations Strategy. Find Procurement BPO by selecting Operations, and find industry insights by selecting Industries. For all options, look for the Research and Insights tab.

Deloitte

http://www.deloitte.com

Deloitte's Sourcing and Procurement page features case studies and featured insights that include topics such as supply chain resilience and spend management. To find the information, search the site using the term "sourcing and procurement." One of the key resources offered is the annual *Deloitte Global CPO Survey*.

Ernst & Young

http://www.ey.com

Ernst & Young sponsors the annual Ardent Partners CPO Rising report, where Chief Procurement Officers provide insights about their current performance and intentions for the future.

KPMG

http://www.kpmg.com

KPMG provides reports and studies including *High Impact Procurement Operating Models: A Survey of Global CEOs* (in partnership with Procurement Leaders) and *FUTUREBUY: The Future of Procurement: 25 in 25—Delivering Procurement Value in a Complex World.*

McKinsey & Co.

http://www.mckinsey.com

Four McKinsey professionals, Peter Spiller, Nicolas Reinecke, Drew Ungerman, and Henrique Teixeira, have authored a book entitled *Procurement 20/20: Supply Entrepreneurship in a Changing World* (2013) that covers best practices and strategies for the future of procurement.

Strategy&

http://www.strategyand.pwc.com/global/home/what_we_do/services/operations/ops_thought_leadership

PricewaterhouseCoopers acquired Booz & Co. in 2014, and renamed it Strategy&. Strategy&'s thought leadership in operations covers sourcing, procurement, and supply chain strategy.

14

PROCUREMENT PROFESSIONAL ASSOCIATIONS AND ORGANIZATIONS

These associations and organizations provide the supply management and procurement community with options for networking, education, and certification. It is worth noting that while some resources are reserved for the members of each organization, each association or organization also makes valuable information and learning opportunities available to nonmembers. This may include news, webinars, and reports.

American Council of Sourcing and Procurement Executives

https://www.linkedin.com/groups/American-Council-Sourcing-Procurement-Executives-5120603/about

The American Council of Sourcing and Procurement Executives (ACSPE) was founded by sourcing and procurement executives to share information, ideas, resources, and best practices between its members. As stated on the website, the ACSPE's intention for the group is to be "a valuable resource for Senior Executives differentiating it from generalized procurement groups or those sponsored by suppliers or service providers."

American Purchasing Society

http://www.american-purchasing.com

The American Purchasing Society is a professional association of buyers and purchasing managers, and was the first organization to establish a certification program for buyers and purchasing professionals. The Society's certification programs are: Certified Purchasing Professional (CPP), Certified Professional Purchasing Manager (CPPM), Certified Green Purchasing Professional (CGPP), and Certified Professional Purchasing Consultant (CPPC). Members receive *Professional Purchasing* monthly, the annual salary report, and the annual benchmarking report of purchasing operations.

Category and Sourcing Managers

http://www.casme.com

Category and Sourcing Managers (CASME) is a global membership of corporate procurement enterprises spread across the Americas, Asia, Australia and Europe, with members that are hands-on category and sourcing managers. CASME RoundTable meetings provide opportunities for members to share ideas and are facilitated by a procurement professional with relevant category expertise.

Chartered Institute of Purchasing & Supply

http://www.cips.org

As an influential professional body, the Chartered Institute of Purchasing & Supply (CIPS) promotes and maintains "high standards of professional skill, ability, and integrity" among procurement and supply chain professionals, as stated on its website, through its professional qualifications programs, associated membership standards, public access training, and comprehensive learning resources. In order to promote excellence in organizations, the CIPS provides staff education and training programs in addition to assessment and accreditation. The CIPS Knowledge includes resources on Procurement Topics and Skills, Commodities and Categories, Tools and Templates, Dictionary and FAQs, in addition to the CIPS TV and the CIPS official magazine, *Supply Management*. CIPS for Business provides Performance offerings, including the CIPS Sustainability Index, the ROSMA Performance Check, and the CIPS Risk Index.

Council of Supply Chain Management Professionals

http://cscmp.org

The Council of Supply Chain Management Professionals (CSCMP) is a professional association dedicated to the advancement and dissemination of research and knowledge on supply chain management. Members receive practical, "how to" solutions on the industry's hot topics via publications, professional education, networking opportunities, and cutting-edge research. Members can access publication offerings such as *Case Studies, Annual State of Logistics Report, Third Party Logistics (3PL) Study, Journal of Business Logistics,* and *Supply Chain Quarterly.* SCPro is the three-level certification program offered by the CSCMP.

Institute for Supply Management

http://www.ism.ws/index.cfm

Founded in 1915, the highly influential and respected Institute for Supply Management (ISM) was the first supply management institute in the world. The ISM executes and extends its mission through education, research, standards of excellence, and information dissemination. Key publications include the *Reports on Business, Inside Supply Management*, and *Journal of Supply Chain Management.* Members have access to an extensive database of information, articles, tools, and resources, including the ROSMA Performance Check. The ISM's newest offering is the Supplier Risk Index, which helps in identifying potential supply disruptions. The ISM offers two certification programs: Certified Professional in Supply Management (CPSM) and Certified Professional in Supplier Diversity (CPSD). In addition to the national association, headquartered in Phoenix, Arizona, there are many active local ISM chapters located in major cities.

International Association for Contract & Commercial Management

http://www.iaccm.com

According to information on its website, the International Association for Contract & Commercial Management (IACCM) "provides advisory, research and benchmarking services, and worldwide training for contracts, commercial and relationship management professionals." Commercial and Contract Management (CCM) Certification, and Supplier Relationship Management (SRM) Certification are offered. The Resource Center provides tools, templates, articles, news, and discussions relating to the entire contract lifecycle. The IACCM news channels provide current, cross-industry news through the *Contracting Excellence* e-zine, the *Commitment Matters* blog, and a news feed.

International Institute for Advanced Purchasing & Supply

http://www.iiaps.org

The International Institute for Advanced Purchasing & Supply (IIAPS) is a not-for-profit organization founded in 2009. As stated on its website, the IIAPS "is dedicated to the raising of international standards in purchasing and supply management." Candidates, to attain full professional membership, must successfully complete the Institute's International Green, Red, and Black Belts in Advanced Purchasing and Supply. The IIAPS provides competence assessment and benchmarking tools, in addition to supporting research and organizing events to share best practices.

National Contract Management Association

http://www.ncmahq.org

The National Contract Management Association (NCMA) is a leading professional resource for those in the field of contract management, both in the private and public sectors, and in the buying and selling worlds. Members have access to *Contract Management* magazine, *Journal of Contract Management, CM News* monthly, the annual salary survey, professional certification programs, webinars, e-courses, and networking opportunities. Certifications awarded by the NCMA are: Certified Professional Contracts Manager (CPCM), Certified Federal Contracts Manager (CFCM), Certified Commercial Contracts Manager (CCCM), Industry Certification in Contract Management–Defense (ICCM–D), and Industry Certification in Contract Management–Federal (ICCM–F).

Next Level Purchasing Association

http://www.nextlevelpurchasing.com

As a global organization, the Next Level Purchasing Association was founded in 2000. This organization helps clients establish and utilize procurement best practices. Organizations from more than 100 countries have enrolled their purchasing professionals in the Senior Professional in Supply Management (SPSM) Program and online procurement training. Next Level Purchasing is the provider of the SPSM, SPSM2, and SPSM3 Certifications. Basic membership is free and available to all procurement professionals. *The Purchasing Certification Blog*, written by Charles Dominick, covers trending procurement topics.

Sourcing Interests Group

http://www.sig.org

The Sourcing Interests Group (SIG) is "a membership organization that serves sourcing and outsourcing professionals from Fortune 500 and Global 1000 companies," according to its website. The SIG "blends practitioners, service providers, and advisory firms in a noncommercial environment," and provides "next practice" networking opportunities, events, webinars, "peer 2 peer" connection services, and the Resource Center. The Resource Center provides a wealth of information, including white papers, tools, and more than 100 templates.

15

PROCUREMENT WEBSITES, NETWORKS, AND COMMUNITIES

The resources listed in this chapter, whether open access or fee-based, provide rich, insightful, and current content that will make any procurement professional smarter and give them an edge.

Buyers Meeting Point

http://www.buyersmeetingpoint.com

Buyers Meeting Point offers open access, online knowledge, and professional development resources for supply management and procurement professionals. The editors and contributors monitor and filter the sources of information available to you. At this website, you can connect with peers, read thought leadership articles written by the editors, and find lists of service providers, publications, websites, and blogs—all geared to help professional buyers. The constantly updated Events calendar keeps professionals up-to-date on relevant webinars and conferences. Kelly Barner, co-author of this book, is Managing Editor.

My Purchasing Center

http://www.mypurchasingcenter.com

My Purchasing Center is a source of news and information for procurement and supply professionals. The website has articles, blogs, white papers, webcasts, videos, podcast interviews, supplier profiles, and a bookstore. Channels include:

Electronics, Logistics, MRO/Indirect, Office Products, Technology, and Commodities. The articles are filled with helpful forecasting and trend data from knowledgeable professionals. This open access site is comprehensive and current. Susan Avery is Chief Editor.

Procurement Leaders Network

http://www.procurementleaders.com

Procurement Leaders Network invites an award-winning network membership that provides intelligence through their three premium content channels: Procurement Strategy, Category Intelligence, and Community and Connect. The Procurement Strategy channel provides strategy insights, executive research, benchmark and trend reports, and practical guides for senior procurement leaders. The Category Intelligence channel provides category expertise in 11 key indirect spend categories: Consulting Services, Energy and Utilities, Facilities, Human Resources, Information Technology, Logistics, Marketing, MRO, Print and Packaging, Telecommunications, and Travel and Fleet. There are 49 subcategories, plus raw materials. The Community and Connect channel provides access to news, featured articles, case studies and interviews, news, blogs, commodity watch, events, webinars, and strategy reports. Some information is free to access.

Purchasing Insight

http://purchasinginsight.com

According to Purchasing Insight's website: "Written by purchase-to-pay (P2P) practitioners, this site offers current e-sources and opinions on P2P best practices as well as insights on vendor solutions and emerging trends." Covered here are many topics relating to purchase-to-pay, including e-invoicing, supply chain finance, accounts payable (AP) automation, and e-procurement. The open access Resources section includes how-to content on e-invoicing, building a business case, and procurement and purchasing processes. There is also a high level Supplier Network Fee Modeler. Pete Loughlin is the founder and Managing Editor.

SCM World

http://www.scmworld.com

SCM World is a global community of senior supply chain professionals, which "accelerates learning for current and future supply chain leaders." Webinars, research reports, and best practice insights are accessed via the innovative Content Navigator, which groups the most critical supply chain enablers by relevancy into content modules. For additional educational events, SCM World hosts annual conferences and regional workshops on specialized topics.

Spend Matters

http://www.spendmattersnet.com

Spend Matters, launched in 2004, was the first blog in the procurement and supply chain sector. It has expanded to become a respected global content community and claims to publish more research than all of the traditional industry analyst firms combined. Spend Matters sites include Spend Matters, Spend Matters UK/Europe, Trade Financing, Healthcare Matters, and MetalMiner, to name a few. Spend Matters publishes free research, as well as Premium content for Spend Matters PRO members. Premium content areas include: Category Management, Invoice and Financing, Procurement, Commodity Management, Procurement Metrics, Procurement Services, Procurement Technology, Procurement Strategy, Risk and Compliance, Sourcing, Supplier Management, Supply Chain, and Vendor Intelligence. There are three membership levels with reasonable pricing. Jason Busch is the founder and Managing Director of Azul Partners, the parent company of Spend Matters.

16

PROCUREMENT ONLINE AND PRINT MAGAZINES AND JOURNALS

Most of the magazines and journals listed in this chapter are offered in print and digital formats, and have accompanying websites that provide access to free content. Due to many of them being updated daily, these resources are key in keeping procurement professionals continuously informed and educated about need-to-know issues and topics.

Contract Management (CM) Magazine

http://www.ncmahq.org/NewsPublications/cmmcurrentissue.cfm

As a magazine published by the National Contract Management Association, members can access current and past articles that focus on contract management issues for both the public and private sectors.

Contracting Excellence

https://www.iaccm.com/news/contractingexcellence

Contracting Excellence is an open access e-zine published by the International Association of Contract & Commercial Management (IACCM), providing current articles on contracting and contract management.

Harvard Business Review

http://hbr.org

Harvard Business Review is the gold standard of business strategy and management publications. It covers topics such as procurement, sourcing, and supply chain, especially in the case studies section. This site contains access to the magazine, the HBR Blog Network, and an index of cases.

IMT Procurement Journal

http://www.thomasnet.com/journals/procurement

The IMT Procurement Journal is published by ThomasNet.com. The journal provides news briefs, "best of the web" content, and thought leadership articles for procurement professionals and buyers of industrial and manufacturing products and services.

Industry Week—Supply Chain

http://www.industryweek.com/supply-chain

In *Industry Week—Supply Chain,* you will find information about the latest trends, technologies, and best practices for subjects ranging from procurement and inventory management to logistics. The articles are open access.

Journal of Contract Management

http://www.ncmahq.org

Published annually by the National Contract Management Association, the *Journal of Contract Management* is a scholarly journal that disseminates research in the field of contract management.

Journal of Operations Management

http://www.journals.elsevier.com/journal-of-operations-management

The *Journal of Operations Management* publishes scholarly research that covers operations management theory, procurement, sourcing, and supplier management.

Journal of Procurement Management

http://www.inderscience.com/jhome.php?jcode=ijpm

According to its website, the *Journal of Procurement Management* addresses "the implications that purchasing and supply management functions have on organizational productivity and competitiveness in the global market."

Outsource Magazine

http://www.outsourcemagazine.co.uk

This magazine, published in Great Britain, is a resource for news, views, analysis, and thought leadership for the global outsourcing community.

Procurement Leaders Magazine

http://www.procurementleaders.com/about-the-magazine

Procurement Leaders Magazine is an award-winning magazine that is published six times a year. It provides coverage of the global procurement and supply chain industry.

Professional Purchasing

http://www.american-purchasing.com/default.asp?t=pubs

Published by the American Purchasing Society for members only, *Professional Purchasing* is a monthly magazine that includes reviews of the economy, price indexes, business related news, and tips on purchasing.

Supply and Demand Chain Executive

http://www.sdcexec.com

For the C-level/line-of-business executive, *Supply and Demand Chain Executive* is an open access source that covers the entire global supply chain. It focuses on return on investment, professional development, and change management.

Supply Business (formerly CPO Agenda)

http://www.supplybusiness.com

Supply Business magazine, published in partnership with the Chartered Institute of Purchasing & Supply (CIPS), is a quarterly review publication with topics that include business/procurement strategy, change management, supplier relationships, and performance measurement.

Supply Chain Standard

http://www.supplychainstandard.com/Home/default.aspx

Supply Chain Standard provides thought leadership articles with insights on global views, and transforming and managing the supply chain.

Supply Chain Digest

http://www.scdigest.com

Supply Chain Digest is an open access newsletter that reviews hundreds of news articles, research reports, and analyst opinions to identify the information and news that is most valuable to you.

Supply Chain Management: An International Journal

http://www.emeraldinsight.com/journals.htm?issn=1359-8546

As stated on its website, the *Supply Chain Management: An International Journal* "covers aspects of marketing, logistics and information technology, economics, management and organizational behavior related to the operation of supply chains in all sectors."

Supply Chain Management Review

http://www.scmr.com

Supply Chain Management Review features contributions from business school professors, supply chain management practitioners, and industry analysts. Topics include sourcing and procurement, software and technology, transportation and logistics, and supply chain education.

Supply Chain Quarterly

http://www.supplychainquarterly.com

Supply Chain Quarterly is the official magazine of the Council of Supply Chain Management Professionals (CSCMP) and provides articles about current supply chain hot topics.

Supply Management

http://www.supplymanagement.com

Supply Management magazine is published by the Chartered Institute of Purchasing & Supply (CIPS), and features the latest news and analysis for those working in the procurement profession.

17

PROCUREMENT BLOGS

There is no shortage of talented, well-informed, and passionate bloggers, who write about the various aspects of the procurement and supply chain disciplines. Although many procurement service and solution providers have blogs, the ones included in this chapter achieve the highest level of objectivity and the lowest levels of marketing content through their inclusion of external guest contributors.

Cottrill Research

http://cottrillresearch.com/blog

The Cottrill Research blog provides news and analysis about the latest research and information resource offerings for procurement professionals. This blog is written by Jeanette Jones, an author of this book.

CPO Rising

http://cporising.com

Written for and about chief procurement officers and other supply management executives, the *CPO Rising* blog is updated daily. It is published by noted analyst Andrew Bartolini, the Chief Research Officer at Ardent Partners.

eSourcing Forum

http://www.esourcingforum.com

The *eSourcing Forum* is sponsored and managed by Iasta, a sourcing and spend management solutions provider that was acquired by Selectica effective July 2,

2014. The Blog Squad, which is a group of Iasta procurement professionals and regular guest contributors, includes posts that cover industry news and best practices.

Kinaxis

http://blog.kinaxis.com

Featuring various Kinaxis team members and occasional guests, this blog provides insights on supply chain trends and issues. It was featured in a *Business2Community.com* blog post about creating engaging content for any industry—even "boring" ones. The Kinaxis Supply Chain Expert Community is where professionals can share content.

The Point

http://www.buyersmeetingpoint.com/blogs/bmps-qthe-pointq

The Point is a blog maintained by Buyers Meeting Point. The blog helps professionals stay on top of the major themes and trends in procurement and supply chain management through a regular rotation of notes on webinars, articles, and other blogs, as well as occasional guest contributors. Kelly Barner, an author of this book, is the Managing Editor.

Procurement Insights

http://procureinsights.wordpress.com

Procurement Insights is written by Jon W. Hansen and a panel of regular contributors. It combines a traditional blog format with an online talk radio component that covers a number of professional and procurement topics. This blog is updated daily, and there are regular talk radio programs on PI Window on the World.

Robert Handfield's Supply Chain View from the Field

http://scm.ncsu.edu/blog

Rob Handfield is the Bank of America Distinguished Professor of Supply Chain Management at North Carolina State University, and Consulting Editor of the *Journal of Operations Management*. He serves as Co-Director of the Supply Chain Resource Cooperative (SCRC) and writes a blog that provides excellent analysis of current, critical supply chain topics. He is also author of the 2006 book, *Supply Market Intelligence: A Managerial Handbook for Building Sourcing Strategies*.

Procurement Leaders

http://www.procurementleaders.com/blog

The Procurement Leaders blog is part of the Procurement Leaders Network—a global, membership-led community—that focuses exclusively on executive-level procurement, sourcing, and supply chain management professionals.

The Purchasing Certification Blog

http://blog.purchasingcourses.com

Written by Charles Dominick, SPSM, SPSM2, and President of the Next Level Purchasing Association, this blog focuses on education and interaction outside of any particular software provider or industry.

Sourcing Innovation

http://blog.sourcinginnovation.com

Sourcing Innovation is a resource for sourcing, procurement, and supply chain professionals that covers technology, vendor analyses, best practices, reviews, and analysis of important published articles and white papers. Started in 2006, the blog is authored and edited by Michael Lamoureux, also known as "The Doctor."

Spend Matters

http://spendmatters.com

Spend Matters is a highly respected and popular blog that was launched in November, 2004, making it the first blog and social media site in the procurement and supply chain sector. It focuses on spend management issues, including procurement, sourcing, contract management, spend analysis and visibility, category management, low-cost country sourcing, and supply chain. *Spend Matters* has greatly expanded its offerings to include research and analysis.

The Strategic Sourceror

http://www.strategicsourceror.com

An excellent blog that continuously offers posts that are current, relevant, and helpful, *The Strategic Sourceror* covers strategic sourcing, supply chain, procurement, purchasing, and spend management. It is sponsored by procurement services provider Source One.

Supply Chain Matters

http://www.theferrarigroup.com/supply-chain-matters

Bob Ferrari, a supply chain technology executive, is the founder and editor of the *Supply Chain Matters* blog, which provides insights into key topics surrounding global supply chain business processes and technology.

Supply Chain Management Research

http://scmresearch.org

The international supply chain blog, *Supply Chain Management Research*, is written by Dr. Andreas Wieland, Assistant Professor of Supply Chain Management at the Department of Operations Management, Copenhagen Business School. An example of Dr. Wieland's elegant writing, from the website, is: "A supply chain is a peculiar network of organizations. It is neither fully visible, nor controllable by a single organization, but rather an intangible hybrid between the organization and its environment."

Vested Way

http://www.vestedway.com/blog

Vested Way, written predominantly by author, speaker, and consultant Kate Vitasek, is the blog associated with the Vested Outsourcing model for supply relationships. Like the Vested series of books, this blog uses thought leadership and impressive case studies to illustrate how companies can radically change the way they manage outsourcing relationships as well as the results associated with them.

18

PROCUREMENT BASICS—DICTIONARIES AND REFERENCE SOURCES

The use of these reference sources will help in ensuring that correct terminology is being used to research a topic. These resources cover procurement-related topics.

APICS Dictionary

http://www.apics.org/industry-content-research/publications/apics-dictionary

The *APICS Dictionary* contains more than 4,500 supply chain and operations management terms and definitions. You can search for an industry-specific term on the APICS website. The Dictionary is free for members; nonmembers pay a nominal fee.

Chartered Institute of Purchasing & Supply (CIPS) Glossary

http://www.cips.org/Knowledge/procurement-glossary

The terms and definitions found in the CIPS glossary relate to procurement. There is also a link to an index of abbreviations.

Council of Supply Chain Management Professionals Glossary of Terms

http://cscmp.org/resources-research/glossary-terms

The Council of Supply Chain Management Professionals' (CSCMP) "Glossary of Terms" provides a comprehensive listing of current logistics and supply chain management terms.

Institute for Supply Management (ISM) Glossary of Key Supply Management Terms

http://www.ism.ws/glossary

The *ISM Glossary* is a reference tool from the Institute for Supply Management (ISM). It includes information from all disciplines within supply management. Members must log in to access.

The Procurement and Supply Manager's Desk Reference

The Procurement and Supply Manager's Desk Reference (2012) is a comprehensive reference book by Fred Sollish and John Semanik. The book is easy to read and understand. Examples of chapters include: Procurement and Best Business Practices, Solicitation of Bids and Proposals, Supplier Selection Criteria, Contracts/ Legal Aspects of Procurement, Negotiation, Procurement Function's Internal Relationships, and Regulatory Compliance.

Thesaurus.com

http://thesaurus.com

This online thesaurus helps you get a correct match to another term by using color-coding to display synonyms.

Visuwords

http://www.visuwords.com

Visuwords is an online graphical dictionary, where you can look up words to find their associations with other words via a unique visualization tool.

19

COUNTRY AND GEOPOLITICAL RISK

In addressing the global business environment, Margaret J. Wheatly, Ed.D., writes about the sensitive nature of systems that are interconnected and how movements in one part can greatly affect other parts: "The nature of the global business environment guarantees that no matter how hard we work to create a stable and healthy organization, our organization will continue to experience dramatic changes far beyond our control."[1] This quote speaks directly to the concerns of supply chain and procurement professionals in regard to risk, especially those risks associated with large global businesses.

Knowing and understanding the environments where first- and second-tier supply partners source is becoming a key competency. The types of country risk that procurement professionals research and monitor are environmental, political, criminal, economic, technological, and regulatory, in addition to issues related to infrastructure and social responsibility. There is an abundance of resources that provide country risk intelligence, many of which are made available in open access format via the U.S. government and various worldwide organizations. Some of those resources are listed in this chapter.

CIA World Factbook

https://www.cia.gov/library/publications/the-world-factbook

The *World Factbook* is an open access reference source that has been a standard for researchers for years and covers 267 world entities. Detailed information for each country is organized within main content areas that include: Introduction, Geography, Government, People/Society, Energy, Economy, Communications,

Transportation, Military, and Transnational Issues. It is important to note when the facts were last updated. The FAQs and Definitions/Notes sections are helpful.

Coface Country Risks Assessments

http://www.coface.com/Economic-Studies-and-Country-Risks?OpenDocument

Coface, a provider of trade credit insurance, freely provides 160 frequently updated country evaluations based on macroeconomic, financial, and political data.

Global Risk Insights

http://globalriskinsights.com

On *Global Risk Insights'* open access site, political risk analysts provide insights into political developments around the world that companies and investors need to know about. You can browse by region or by topic (Politics, Economics, Security, Natural Resources, Technology, or Finance).

globalEDGE Country Insights

http://globaledge.msu.edu/global-insights/by/country

globalEDGE is maintained by the International Business Center at Michigan State University. The *globalEDGE Country Insights* page shows statistical data for over 200 countries, in addition to historical, economic, and political conditions. The Country Comparator tool and the Country Rankings tool, which has an interactive map, are nice features.

Maplecroft

http://maplecroft.com

Maplecroft is a global risk analytics and research firm that uses extensive mapping technology. They provide over 200 interactive maps that incorporate 1500 risk indices and indicators.

Organization for Economic Co-operation and Development Country Risk Index

http://www.oecd.org/tad/xcred/crc.htm

The Organization for Economic Co-operation and Development (OECD) is an international organization that promotes policies that "will improve the economic and social well-being of people around the world," as its website attests. The index range is 1 to 7, with 1 being the lowest risk class.

Transparency International's Corruption Perceptions Index

http://www.transparency.org/research/cpi/overview

Transparency International is a global coalition that provides the Corruption Perceptions Index, which measures the perceived levels of public sector corruption in 177 countries and territories.

United States Commercial Service Country Commercial Guides

http://www.buyusainfo.net/adsearch.cfm?search_type=int&loadnav=no

To access the U.S. Commercial Service Country Commercial Guides, select the country name and "Country Commercial Guide (CCG)" from the drop-down menu. These are thorough reports on doing business with particular countries.

United States Department of State—Key Publications

http://www.state.gov/r/pa/ei/rls/dos/221.htm

This page provides links to key U.S. State Department publications that include: Bilateral Relations Factsheets, which focus on U.S. relations with each country; and Country Reports on Terrorism, Human Rights, Religious Freedom, and Trafficking in Persons.

World Bank Data

http://data.worldbank.org

The World Bank provides free and open access to data about development in countries around the globe. On the Data page, you can view information via country, topic, or indicators (over 2,000). By selecting indicators, you can do a search or browse the detailed listing. Topic areas of interest are: Economy and Growth, Education, Energy and Mining, Environment, External Debt, Financial Sector, Infrastructure, Social Protection and Labor, and Trade.

The World Bank—Logistics Performance Index

http://lpi.worldbank.org

The Logistics Performance Index (LPI) is an interactive benchmarking tool that ranks 160 countries on six dimensions of trade and looks at the logistics environments in 116 countries. It is based on survey results provided by "on the ground" operators, such as global freight forwarders and express carriers.

IHS Country Risk

http://www.ihs.com/products/global-insight/country-risk/index.aspx

Market information provider IHS offers country risk coverage that includes political and violent risk forecasts, risk scores for war, terrorism, civil unrest and overall political violence, and banking, sovereign and global risk services.

Euromoney Country Risk

http://www.euromoneycountryrisk.com

The Euromoney Country Risk (ECR) is a measure that evaluates the investment risk of 186 countries, based on their political and economic stability. Data is measured via an online community of economic and political experts.

The Economist Intelligence Unit Country Analysis

http://www.eiu.com

The Economist Intelligence Unit Country Analysis service provides country analysis and forecasts. You can subscribe to various services or purchase reports, and sections of reports, separately. The Premium Country Access service has key sections that include: Economic and Political Outlook, Credit Risk, Business Environment and Market Opportunities, Regulatory Environment, and Financial Services.

MarketLine Country Analysis Profiles

http://www.marketline.com/overview/country-information

From market research provider MarketLine, these Country Analysis Profiles provide business landscape information for more than 150 countries, using the PESTLE framework (Political, Economic, Social, Technological, Legal, and Environmental).

REFERENCE

1. "Writings," *Margaret J. Wheatly*, Accessed June 8, 2014, http://www.margaretwheatley.com/articles/thepaceoflife.html.

20

COMMODITIES PRICING—ALL COMMODITY INCLUSIVE

A *commodity* can be defined as "a reasonably homogeneous good or material, bought and sold freely as an article of commerce. Commodities include agricultural products, fuels, and metals and are traded in bulk on a commodity exchange or spot market."[1] Many times, a buyer will have responsibility for a product or service that is tied to a commodity, although they have the same value, no matter where they are from or who supplies them.[2]

The top-traded commodities are cotton, wheat, soybeans, corn, sugar, silver, copper, gold, natural gas, coffee, and crude oil. One of the main challenges for procurement professionals managing commodity-based categories is dealing with price volatility in contracts and agreements. Price fluctuations can have a major impact on the final price of a product. Therefore, it is crucial for buyers to understand the market and any factors that drive prices up or down. For quick analysis, the resources covered in this chapter are shown in Table 20.1.

An additional challenge facing procurement with regard to commodities is that they are often at the second tier of the supply chain. In other words, they do not buy the corn, sugar, or gold themselves, but their suppliers do. These situations provide an excellent opportunity for buyers to collaborate with their suppliers to manage cost through efficiency or demand, as the commodity portion of the price can be discussed openly. When the portion of an item's price is significantly affected by the cost of a commodity, price escalators and de-escalators may be built into contracts to protect both parties against volatility.

Table 20.1 Resources—commodities pricing

RESOURCES—COMMODITIES PRICING	Market News/ Analysis	Forecast Pricing	Current/ Historical Pricing	Open (Free) Access	Mixed Fee and Free Access
ALERTdata Blueprints	✓	✓	✓		
Bloomberg	✓	✓	✓		
CME Group (CME, CBOT, COMEX, NYMEX)	✓	✓	✓		✓
The Gartman Letter	✓	✓	✓		
The Hightower Report	✓	✓	✓		
IndexMundi	✓		✓	✓	
Intercontinental Exchange (ICE)	✓	✓	✓		✓
International Monetary Fund	✓	✓	✓	✓	
Mintec	✓	✓	✓		
My Purchasing Center	✓	✓	✓	✓	
Platts	✓	✓	✓		
Producer Price Index			✓	✓	
ProPurchaser.com	✓	✓	✓		
USGS Minerals - Commodity Statistics	✓		✓	✓	
World Bank Commodities Markets	✓	✓	✓	✓	
World Bank (GEM) Commodities			✓	✓	
YQ Matrix	✓	✓	✓	✓	

There are many strategies involving supply market intelligence that can mitigate the risk factors associated with commodity price volatility. These risk mitigation strategies are: identifying demand (this is key); benchmarking of prices; using historical pricing to determine current and possible future price; understanding the cost structure of the industry; identifying key cost drivers; identifying supplier price components beyond price; and identifying equivalent products that are less vulnerable to price fluctuations.

Fortunately, there are many resources available to help in determining commodity prices, such as price indices, trading data, government data, and data delivered by for-profit market intelligence providers. The resources listed in this chapter cover all or most commodities, and are key resources to use when researching prices. For the purpose of avoiding duplication of resources, they are not included in the commodity-specific information in Chapters 21 through 25.

COMMODITY ORGANIZATIONS AND WEBSITES

IndexMundi

http://www.indexmundi.com/commodities

The goal of *IndexMundi.com* is to "capture statistics that are scattered or otherwise hidden and present them via user-friendly maps, charts, and tables which allow visitors to understand complex information at a glance." This site is easy to navigate. It covers the average monthly prices for a large number of commodities (energy, tea, cocoa, coffee, metals, fertilizers, livestock, dairy, agricultural raw materials, vegetable oils and protein meal, sugar, seafood, meat, barley, wheat, maize, oats, rice, and sorghum), along with daily prices for a few. Production statistics are available for agriculture, minerals, and energy commodities, in addition to country facts and trade statistics.

International Monetary Fund

http://www.imf.org

As stated on its website, "The International Monetary Fund (IMF) is an organization of 188 countries, working to foster global monetary cooperation, secure financial stability, facilitate international trade, promote high employment and sustainable economic growth, and reduce poverty around the world." The IMF reports on primary commodity prices and forecasts. On the homepage, hover over "Research" on the navigation bar and select "Commodity Prices." The Primary Commodity Price data are updated monthly. The *Commodity Price Outlook & Risks* monthly report presents a price outlook and risk assessment for selected commodities, as depicted in futures and options markets. The *Commodity Market Monthly* provides updates on commodity prices worldwide.

My Purchasing Center

http://www.mypurchasingcenter.com/commodities

MyPurchasingCenter.com reports news, tracks trends, and presents proprietary pricing and supply data. You will find free access to pricing forecast reports that glean commentary and data from a number of pricing data providers and experts for key commodities. Susan Avery, formerly with *Purchasing* magazine, is Chief Editor.

World Bank Commodities Markets

http://go.worldbank.org/4ROCCIEQ50

The World Bank monitors metals, precious metals, agriculture, and fertilizers commodity markets. World Bank Commodities Price Data (The Pink Sheet) show annual and monthly prices, by country, which are published at the beginning of each month. Price forecasts for the next 10 years are published on a quarterly basis. A comprehensive review of commodity markets is published four times a year in January, April, July, and October.

World Bank, Global Economic Monitor (GEM) Commodities

http://data.worldbank.org/data-catalog/commodity-price-data

Updated monthly, the World Bank collection of commodities prices and indices, spanning 1960 to the present. Under Data, at the GEM Commodities page, select "Databank." Click on the appropriate letter to browse the commodities list. From this point, select the desired series, time frame, and country. You can view data in chart, table, or map format.

YQ Matrix

http://www.yqmatrix.com

Thierry Decocq, founder of YQ Purchasing, with the support of the University of Maastricht in the Netherlands, initiated the development of the YQ Matrix in 2009. YQ Matrix makes available, at no charge, global prices, indices, and sourcing graphs on almost any product or raw material. Sourcing graphs vary from the simple to the complex. There are existing sourcing and price graphs that you can view, or you can create your own. YQ Matrix tutorial videos are available on *YouTube.com* to help with creating the charts. The "Web prices: Live" section provides an extensive list of links to other websites that publish raw material prices, free of charge.

GOVERNMENT DATA FOR COMMODITIES

Producer Price Index

http://www.bls.gov/ppi

The Producer Price Index (PPI) measures average change over time in the selling prices received by domestic producers for their output. The prices included in the PPI are from the first commercial transactions for many products and some services. To build a customized table, click on PPI Databases. Select the "One Screen Data Search" option for commodity data. Select the appropriate commodity group, and then drill down to the desired commodity. Data goes back 10 years.

United States Geological Survey, Minerals—Commodity Statistics and Information

http://minerals.usgs.gov/minerals/pubs/commodity

The U.S. Geological Survey (USGS) provides statistics and commodity information for minerals. This index of various non-fuel minerals has links that take you to the *Mineral Commodity Summaries*. Here, you can find statistics on imports, exports, domestic and world production, and prices. The events and trends section covers demand.

MARKET INTELLIGENCE PROVIDERS

ALERTdata.com Blueprints

http://www.alertdata.com

The ALERTdata Blueprints provide analysis for procurement, supply chain, and finance professionals to help in understanding the cost drivers behind prices and the value of looking past price alone. Here you can get updated cost intelligence for more than 600 buyer/seller categories. Analysis in the Blueprints cover validating suppliers' statements about cost changes, evaluating the fairness of price requests, deconstructing industry invoices into costs and margins, and anticipating supply disruptions. Each membership option is reasonably priced. A sample report is provided at *http://www.alertdata.com/scm/sample_blue.php.*

Bloomberg Professional

http://www.bloomberg.com/professional/markets/commodities

Bloomberg Professional Service is a financial news service and platform that monitors and analyzes real-time financial market data. Bloomberg provides tools for monitoring various commodity markets (in detail) in addition to analyzing different vehicles for investing in commodities (e.g., futures, options). Bloomberg shows the latest futures prices for major commodities and tracks the current value of various commodity trading indexes, for no fee, at *http://www.bloomberg.com/markets/commodities/futures.*

The Gartman Letter

http://www.thegartmanletter.com

Dennis Gartman has been publishing the *The Gartman Letter* since 1987. It is a daily commentary on the global capital markets that addresses political, economic, and technical trends from both long-term and short-term perspectives. Commodities are heavily covered.

The Hightower Report

http://hightowerreport.com

Since 1990, *The Hightower Report* has been providing research that focuses specifically on commodities and financial futures. The flagship product is the Daily Commentary, which is sold by market segment or as a package. A free trial subscription is available.

Mintec

http://www.mintecglobal.com/uk

Mintec, based in London, is an independent source of global pricing information for commodities and raw materials. Mintec offers a price tracking tool named Datagain, various reports, and procurement training courses. Datagain tracks the factors affecting the costs and availability of not just a product, but of all the components that make up that product. It also can identify the cost elements related to complex manufactured products, which is useful for finding alternative product specifications. For price risk analysis, Datagain looks at current trends in physical costs, futures markets, currency movements, climate, energy, and transportation. In addition to Datagain, Mintec offers these reports: Factsheets, Commodity Reports, Category Outlook Reports, and Price Indication.

Platts

http://www.platts.com

Platts, a division of McGraw Hill Financial, provides benchmark price assessments and information for the energy, petrochemicals, metals, and agriculture commodity markets. According to the Platts website, in 1909 Warren Cumming Platt started a monthly news magazine, *National Petroleum News,* which provided market-based price information. Today, two of the biggest energy price reporting agencies are considered to be Platts and Argus (see Chapter 23). Platts provides oil, natural gas, electric power, and coal benchmark price assessments. For each of these energy categories, a multitude of real-time news and market alerts, price assessments, indices, newsletters, and maps are offered; on the website, each category can be viewed separately for a list of products. For metals, products cover market news and metals price data, and benchmark price assessments, such as: *Metals Alert, Market Data—Metals, Custom Pricing Data, Metals Daily, SBB Steel Markets Daily, Steel Data and Analysis, Daily Briefing* (steel), *Analytics China, Steel Raw Materials Monthly, World Steel Review*, and *The Steel Index*. For agriculture, sources that cover agriculture news and price data, and benchmark price assessment are: *Biofuels, Agriculture Analyzer, Market Data—Biofuels, Market Data—Sugar, Biofuelscan*, and *Kingsman Sugar Product Offering*.

ProPurchaser.com

http://www.propurchaser.com

ProPurchaser is a pricing tool that allows you to follow transaction-price histories for hundreds of commodities across North America, Europe, and China, and build pricing models that are helpful in negotiations. A 30-day free trial membership is available. To find a commodity chart within the tool, choose a location and then select a category: Chemicals, Currencies, Electricity, Energy, Fiber/Textures/Rubber, Food, Metals, Paper, Plastic Scrap, Wood and Wood Products, Canada and United States economic stats, London Metal Exchange inventories, Indexes/Transportation/Mfg., Bureau of Labor Statistics, or Rare Earths. The full chart view is where you can "crunch numbers" and look at historical data. You can compare as many commodities as you wish. The pricing model that you can create will indicate the actual percentage of a commodity price increase or decrease, and if the percentage is reasonable. Also available are forecasting and budgeting tools. The clutter-free interface is simple and easy to use, along with the tools that allow you to change, save, and e-mail the data.

EXCHANGES

Chicago Board of Trade

http://www.cmegroup.com/company/cbot.html

Part of CME Group, the Chicago Board of Trade (CBOT) was founded in 1848. Futures traded on the CBOT include corn, soybeans, soybean oil, soybean meal, wheat, oats, ethanol, rough rice, gold, silver, and currencies.

Chicago Mercantile Exchange

http://www.cmegroup.com/company/cme.html

The Chicago Mercantile Exchange (CME) is part of the CME Group. Products traded on the CME include butter, dry whey, milk, nonfat dry milk, cheese, feeder cattle, live cattle, lumber, wood pulp, lean hogs, and pork bellies.

CME Group

http://www.cmegroup.com

The CME Group's exchanges—CME, CBOT, NYMEX, and COMEX—offer the widest range of global benchmark products across all major asset classes. Hovering over the "Products and Trading" tab on the navigation bar allows you to click on various product categories. Once at the Commodities product page, you can view the product slate. You can also access links to education resources including product basics, market fundamentals, trading strategies, tools and analytics, product highlights, featured products, and reports.

Commodity Exchange, Inc.

http://www.cmegroup.com/company/comex.html

The Commodity Exchange (COMEX) focuses on aluminum, copper, silver, and gold. It is part of the CME Group and a division of the New York Mercantile Exchange (NYMEX).

Intercontinental Exchange

https://www.theice.com/homepage.jhtml

The Intercontinental Exchange (ICE) is a network of regulated exchanges and clearinghouses for financial and commodity markets. In November 2013, the ICE acquired the NYSE Euronext. The ICE trades in barley, canola, cocoa, coffee, cotton, ethanol, orange juice, wheat, pulp, sugar, soybean, coal, crude oil, electricity, and natural gas.

New York Mercantile Exchange

http://www.cmegroup.com/company/nymex.html

Part of the CME Group, the New York Mercantile Exchange (NYMEX) trades in coal, crude oil, electricity, propane, heating oil, natural gas, NYH RBOB gas, sugar, coffee, cotton, copper, gold, palladium, platinum, and silver.

REFERENCES

1. "Commodity," *BusinessDictionary.com*, Accessed April 5, 2014, http://www.businessdictionary.com/definition/commodity.html.
2. Stacey Vanek Smith, "What Is a Commodity, Anyway?" *Marketplace*, Accessed April 5, 2014, http://www.marketplace.org/topics/economy/what-commodity-anyway.

21

AGRICULTURE

In their book, *An Introduction to Agriculture*, A. A. Upham and G. A. Schmidt (1919), stated, "The three great needs of a human being are food, shelter, and clothing."[1] Most food is produced by farmers, wood is used to build most homes, and clothing is made from agricultural products such as cotton, wool, silk, and leather.[2] According to the U.S. Bureau of Labor Statistics, the Agriculture, Forestry, Fishing, and Hunting sectors include establishments that are often described as farms, ranches, dairies, greenhouses, nurseries, orchards, or hatcheries.

The agriculture industry is primarily comprised of companies involved in the production of food or crops. The animals and products subsector includes dairy, livestock, and poultry. The crops subsector is comprised of field crops (e.g. barley, corn, cotton, food grains, wheat, feed grains and hay, soybeans); fruit and tree nuts (e.g., almonds, bananas, coffee, figs, grapes, olives, pineapple); vegetables (e.g., beets, carrots, lettuce), and horticulture.

Today, global food prices and volatility issues are in the forefront. According to Sophie Wenzlau (2013), author of a Worldwatch Institute article, agricultural commodities markets have always been subject to price volatility due to changing weather conditions. Wenzlau (2013) also noted that "climate change, policies promoting the use of biofuels, rising energy and fertilizer prices, poor harvests, national export restrictions, rising global food demand, and low food stocks" are some of the causes of the recent upward trend in price volatility.[3] In addition, in his book entitled, *Agricultural Supply Chains and the Challenge of Price Risk*, John Williams (2014) noted that "uncertainty, risk, and their associated tradeoffs may be the grist for risk psychologists but the biological uncertainty of agricultural products makes it even more so."[4] For quick analysis, the resources covered in this chapter are listed in Table 21.1.

Table 21.1 Resources—agriculture

RESOURCES—AGRICULTURE	Market Analysis/ Trends	Pricing	Daily/ Weekly Market News	Networking/ Industry Education	Supplier Identification	Background Information	Open (Free) Access	Mixed Fee and Free Access
AgWeb	✓	✓	✓				✓	
Agribusiness Supply Chain Management (book)	✓			✓		✓		
Agricultural Market Information System (AMIS)	✓	✓					✓	
Agriculture.com	✓	✓	✓				✓	
American Restaurant Association	✓	✓	✓					
American Soybean Association	✓	✓	✓	✓				✓
Daily Dairy Report	✓	✓						
Dictionary of Agriculture						✓		
DTN/The Progressive Farmer	✓	✓	✓					✓
FAO Food Price Index	✓	✓					✓	
FAO GIEWS Food Price Data and Analysis Tool		✓					✓	
FAOSTAT - Food and Agriculture Org of the U.S.		✓					✓	
Farm World Agricultural Glossary						✓	✓	
Feed and Grain Magazine	✓	✓	✓		✓			✓
Fruit Growers News			✓	✓	✓			✓
Grainnet.com	✓		✓		✓			✓
High Plains/Midwest AG Journal	✓	✓	✓					✓
Hoard's Dairyman	✓	✓	✓					✓
International Cocoa Organization	✓	✓	✓	✓				✓

RESOURCES—AGRICULTURE	Market Analysis/ Trends	Pricing	Daily/ Weekly Market News	Networking/ Industry Education	Supplier Identification	Background Information	Open (Free) Access	Mixed Fee and Free Access
Intern Dairy Foods Assoc Online Buyers Guide					✓		✓	
International Sugar Organization	✓	✓	✓		✓			✓
National Agricultural Statistics Service (NASS)	✓	✓					✓	
National Cattlemen's Beef Association	✓		✓	✓		✓		✓
National Cotton Council of America	✓	✓	✓	✓				✓
National Corn Growers Association	✓	✓	✓	✓				✓
National Grain and Feed Association	✓		✓	✓				✓
National Livestock Producers Association	✓			✓				✓
SeedQuest			✓		✓		✓	
Understanding Dairy Markets	✓	✓					✓	
United Fresh Produce Association	✓		✓	✓				✓
U.S. Dairy Export Council	✓			✓	✓	✓		✓
USDA - United States Department of Agriculture	✓	✓	✓		✓	✓	✓	
USDA Economic Research Service (ERS)	✓	✓	✓				✓	
USDA Livestock, Poultry, and Grain Market News	✓	✓	✓				✓	
U.S. Soybean Export Council	✓		✓	✓		✓		✓
U.S. Wheat Associates	✓	✓	✓	✓				✓
Vegetable Growers News			✓	✓	✓			✓
World Agri Supply and Demand Estimates (USDA)	✓						✓	

Because of the importance of this industry (everyone needs to eat) and the many subsectors involved, there is a wealth of information that is regularly produced by global organizations, such as the Agricultural Market Information System (AMIS), and Food and Agriculture Organization of the United Nations (FAO). The U.S. Department of Agriculture provides an abundance of statistical, historical, and forecast data through the National Agriculture Statistics Service (NASS) and the Economic Research Service (ERS). In addition, there are councils and associations, on state, national, and international levels, specific to each agricultural commodity that provide excellent background information and market data statistics. It would be easy to fill an entire book with the information resources available. This list highlights important resources and represents the key market sectors.

BACKGROUND INFORMATION

Agribusiness Supply Chain Management

N. Chandrasekaran and G. Raghuram
CRC Press, 2014, Boca Raton, Florida
This book covers all aspects of agricultural product supply chain management.

Dictionary of Agriculture, 3rd ed.

Heather Bateman, ed., Steve Curtis, ed., Katy McAdam, ed.
A&C Black, 2006, London

Subjects covered in the *Dictionary of Agriculture* include cultivation, machinery, livestock, crops, pesticides and herbicides, fertilizers, organic farming, and sales and commodities markets.

Farm World Agricultural Glossary

Farm World

http://www.farmworldonline.com/General/Terms.asp

In the *Farm World Agricultural Glossary*, you can find terms related to agriculture and farming, with a focus on livestock and crops.

National Cattlemen's Beef Association Glossary of Terms

National Cattlemen's Beef Association

http://www.beefusa.org/glossaryofterms.aspx

In addition to the terms in the *National Cattlemen's Beef Association Glossary,* resource links are provided on this site, including agriculture industry statistics and research.

ERS/USDA Information, Crops and Animal Products

Economic Research Services (ERS), United States Department of Agriculture (USDA)

http://www.ers.usda.gov

At the Economic Research Services (ERS) website, on the "Topics" tab, select any of the product categories under "Crops" or "Animal Products." Each category's page has links to helpful overview and background information.

United States Department of Agriculture Glossary

U.S. Department of Agriculture

http://agclass.nal.usda.gov/glossary_az.shtml

Developed by the National Agricultural Library (NAL), the *US Department of Agriculture (USDA) Glossary* contains more than 3800 terms, ranging across agriculture and related subjects. You can search the glossary or browse terms in an alphabetical list. The definitions were developed in conjunction with the *NAL Agricultural Thesaurus*, which can be accessed here as well.

U.S. Wheat Associates Buyer's Guide

U.S. Wheat Associates

http://www.uswheat.org/buyerInfo

The Buyer's Guide, at the U.S. Wheat Associates website, contains excellent background information, including a map that shows elements (export terminals, production areas, and sourcing) of the U.S. wheat supply chain. Also provided is information on wheat grades and grade requirements in addition to a glossary.

SUPPLIER IDENTIFICATION

Fruit Growers News Buyers' Guide

Fruit Growers News

http://fruitgrowersnews.com

At the Fruit Growers News website, select the Buyers' Guide tab located on the navigation bar. This guide is organized by category. Another helpful item is the comprehensive listing of state and national fruit growers and associations.

Grainnet Product and Services Directories

Grainnet

http://www.grainnet.com/equipmentdirectory.html

At the Grainnet website, you can access product and services directories for several industry segments: Grain/Feed, Milling, Seed, and Biofuels. You can also select the tab for the Equipment Catalog Online Version, where you can search the entire catalog or jump to sections listed in the Table of Contents.

Feed & Grain Buyers Guide

Feed & Grain

http://www.feedandgrain.com/product

The *Feed & Grain Buyers Guide* is a free resource. The best way to use this guide is to select a category from the drop-down menu. From here, you can select a subcategory that narrows the options. This is a comprehensive list of more than 570 companies with more than 2035 products for the feed and grain industries.

International Dairy Foods Association (IDFA) Online Buyers' Guide

International Dairy Foods Association (IDFA)

http://idfa.officialbuyersguide.net

The *IDFA Online Buyers' Guide* allows you to browse category headings, and hundreds of subcategories, for services and products. There is an advanced search feature that enables you to narrow the results by location.

U.S. Dairy Export Council Supplier Directory

U.S. Dairy Export Council

http://www.usdec.org/Suppliers

To use the *U.S. Dairy Export Council Supplier Directory*, an interactive database, first select a product category. Then, refine your search by selecting products, attributes, and/or certifications.

SeedQuest

http://www.seedquest.com

The tagline for SeedQuest's site is "Global Information Services for Seed Professionals." You can view news, forums (by geographic location), catalogs, directories, suppliers, solutions, markets, and expos. SeedQuest also offers a data management portal with more news and information resources.

Vegetable Growers News Buyers' Guide

http://vegetablegrowersnews.com

At the *Vegetable Growers News* website, select the Buyers' Guide tab. This guide, similar to the *Fruit Growers News Buyers' Guide*, is organized by category. Examples of categories include greenhouse, farm equipment, post harvest, sprayers, and storage control.

PRICING AND MARKET ANALYSIS

AgWeb

http://www.agweb.com

The Markets section of *AgWeb.com* provides a number of helpful resources. For example, the Hedge Position Monitor is a tool that provides you with a snapshot of the average hedge position of two key positions for corn and soybeans. The Marketing outlooks series provides market analysis on cattle, wheat, hogs, soybeans, cotton, and dairy. The Commodities Markets Center allows you to check futures prices for commodities on grains, livestock, oil, and more. The *Market Weekly News* includes a recap of the week's top market news, commentary, and blogs. *AgWeb.com* is part of Farm Journal Media, which includes its 137-year-old *Farm Journal*, along with *Top Producer*, *Beef Today*, *Dairy Today*, and *Implement*

& Tractor. Farm Journal Media includes the televised programs *AgDay* and *U.S. Farm Report*.

Agricultural Market Information System

http://www.amis-outlook.org/home/en

As stated on its website, the Agricultural Market Information System (AMIS) was established at the request of the Agriculture Ministers of the G20 "to enhance food market transparency and encourage coordination of policy action in response to market uncertainty." The initial focus of the AMIS was on wheat, maize, rice, and soybeans. The *Market Monitor* report gives a synopsis of major market developments, and the policies and other market drivers behind them, including global supply-demand outlook, crop monitor, international prices, futures markets, policy developments, and market indicators. Selecting "Indicators" on the navigation bar will direct you to three main sections. The first section is "Prices and Price Volatility," which shows historical prices/volatility for wheat, maize, rice, soybeans, and The FAO Food Price Index (see listing on the next page). The next section, Energy and Other Indicators, includes energy and fertilizer prices, in addition to ocean freight rates and dollar indices. The last section, Stocks and Utilization, covers stocks (global inventories) and utilization indicators. Selecting "Statistics" on the navigation bar offers an interactive world map to view market summaries and forecasts.

Agriculture.com

http://www.agriculture.com

Published by Meredith Agrimedia, the *Agriculture.com* website offers, "market analysis on commodities, including corn, soybeans, wheat, beef, hogs, and cotton, [in addition] to tracking market trends in grains and livestock." Under the Markets tab, the *Markets Newswire* provides commodity prices and summaries, daily market trends, and news from commodity exchanges around the world. You can also find commodity futures prices and option prices for agricultural commodities at key exchanges.

American Restaurant Association

http://www.americanrestaurantassociation.com

The American Restaurant Association "specializes in assisting food and energy commodity buyers to manage the commodity markets." The market reports, forecasts, and data are disseminated via: *The Maloni Report: Daily Commodity*

Commentary and Daily Contracting Recommendations; The Weekly Commodity Report; The Daily Commodity Bulletin; WeeklyCommodityReport.com; and *Quarterly Commodity Outlook Forecast Report*, which provide detailed outlooks for all of the commodity markets. Webinars and seminars are also offered.

Daily Dairy Report

http://www.dailydairyreport.com

The *Daily Dairy Report* provides a one-page summary of the "domestic and global dairy markets, prices, supply and demand fundamentals, and CME cash and futures dairy trading activity." This publication was founded in 2004 by Mary Keough Ledman, former editor of the *CME Daily Dairy Report.*

Food and Agriculture Organization of the United Nations (FAO), Food Price Index

http://www.fao.org/worldfoodsituation/foodpricesindex/en

The FAO Food Price Index is an important measure of the monthly change in international prices. The Food Price Index consists of the average of five commodity group price indices: Meat, Dairy, Cereals, Vegetable Oils, and Sugar.

Food and Agriculture Organization of the United Nations, Global Information and Early Warning System Food Price Data and Analysis Tool

http://www.fao.org/giews/pricetool

The FAO Global Information and Early Warning System (GIEWS) Food Price Data and Analysis Tool is an online database and charting tool that provides international food prices over time. Drop-down menus allow you to customize a chart by selecting countries, commodities, date range, and price type.

Food and Agriculture Organization of the United Nations, Statistics Division

http://faostat3.fao.org/faostat-gateway/go/to/home/E

The FAO Statistical Division (FAOSTAT) offers the FAOSTAT Database, which contains "over three million time-series and cross-sectional data for over 200 countries and territories covering production, trade, and food supply statistics on agriculture, nutrition, fisheries, forestry, food aid, land use, and population."

By selecting the "Prices" icon, you can find historical producer prices or prices received by farmers for primary crops, live animals by weight, and livestock primary products, as collected at the point of initial sale. Also available are indices of agricultural producer prices that measure the average annual change over time in the selling prices received by farmers.

National Agricultural Statistics Service

http://www.nass.usda.gov

The National Agricultural Statistics Service (NASS), sponsored by the U.S. Department of Agriculture, prepares statistical reports covering all aspects of U.S. agriculture, including "production and supplies of food and fiber; prices paid and received by farmers; farm labor and wages; farm finances; chemical use; and changes in the demographics of U.S. producers." On the sidebar, select "Economics and Prices." Then, selecting "Agricultural Prices" under "Prices Reports" allows you to look at prices received by farmers for principal crops; livestock and livestock products; indexes of prices received by farmers; feed price ratios; indexes of prices paid by farmers; and parity prices.

National Agricultural Statistics Service Quick Stats

http://quickstats.nass.usda.gov

Create customized charts using this agricultural statistical database that covers state, county, and national data.

Understanding Dairy Markets

http://future.aae.wisc.edu

This website of the University of Wisconsin Dairy Marketing and Risk Management Program is maintained by Professor Brian W. Gould of the Department of Agriculture and Applied Economics. There is an abundance of statistical information at this site. The Dairy Data section provides comprehensive links to information on prices, production, sales and consumption, stocks, supply and disposition, daily futures and options, trade data, and state summaries, to name a few. The Dairy Situation section features outlook and demand reports. The Dairy Risk Analyzer provides software tools and information for Dairy Risk Management strategies.

United States Department of Agriculture, Economic Research Service

http://www.ers.usda.gov

The Economic Research Service (ERS) is an important source of economic information in the U.S. Department of Agriculture. There is an incredible amount of valuable information at this site. Selecting "Topics" on the navigation bar will help you get a quick overview of what data is available. Selecting "Commodity Outlook," located under Farm Economy, will take you to links for various outlook reports. Short-term outlook commodity reports are available for cotton and wool, feed, fruit and tree nuts, livestock, dairy and poultry, oil, rice, sugars and sweeteners, vegetables and pulses, and wheat. Another "Topics" category, "Food Prices and Markets," has links to food prices, expenditures, and costs, and the Consumer Price Index. Another way to view the data is by clicking on the "Publications" tab on the navigation bar. Here, you can view what has been published by date, title, or series, or by selecting a topic using the menu.

United States Department of Agriculture

http://www.usda.gov

The U.S. Department of Agriculture (USDA) was established in 1862, by President Abraham Lincoln, who later referred to it as "The People's Department." The USDA administers programs related to agriculture, nutrition, rural development, forestry, rural utilities, and research. Through the National Agriculture Statistics Service (NASS) and the Economic Research Service (ERS), the USDA provides historic, current, and forecast statistical information. See separate entries in this chapter for the NASS and the ERS for details of helpful resources.

United States Department of Agriculture, Livestock, Poultry, and Grain Market News

http://www.ams.usda.gov/AMSv1.0/lsmarketnews

In the Livestock, Poultry, and Grain Market News, found at the USDA Agriculture Marketing Service website, you can find current price and sales information for livestock, meat, poultry, eggs, and grains. Coverage is regional, national, and international.

United States Department of Agriculture, World Agriculture Supply and Demand Estimates

http://www.usda.gov/oce/commodity/wasde/index.htm

Found at the USDA Office of the Chief Economist website, the *World Agricultural Supply and Demand Estimates (WASDE)* report is prepared monthly. The *WASDE* includes forecasts for the United States and world supply-use balances of major grains, soybeans and products, and cotton, and the U.S. supply and use of sugar and livestock products.

MARKET RESEARCH PROVIDERS THAT COVER AGRICULTURE MARKETS

Some of the market research providers listed in Chapter 10, Industry and Market Research, which cover segments of the agriculture markets are MarketLine, Business Monitor International, Euromonitor International, Global Industry Analysts, IBISWorld, and First Research. Searching *MarketResearch.com* or *ResearchandMarkets.com* is helpful in identifying agriculture markets research providers and the types of reports they offer.

PUBLICATIONS

DTN/The Progressive Farmer

www.dtnprogressivefarmer.com

The *DTN/The Progressive Farmer* provides real-time agriculture news, market data, and weather information and alerts. Also available is a database of 30,000 daily, real-time local cash bid prices. Access to information varies, depending on your member/subscriber level. There is a great deal of open access (free) information at this site. The *DTN/The Progressive Farmer* subscriber receives a lot of information for a nominal fee: AG news coverage, archive content, blog discussions, webinars, news alerts, commodities futures (ten-minute delay), featured market commentary, limited local cash grain bids, and local weather updates.

Feed & Grain Magazine

http://www.feedandgrain.com

The Magazine portion of *feedandgrain.com* offers many feature articles. The Feed & Grain website offers information on News, Feed, Grain, Safety, Government, and Congress. The Commodity Quotes section takes you to updated information that includes quotes, future markets, market news, charts, options, and DTN headline news.

Fruit Growers News (FGN)

http://fruitgrowersnews.com

The *Fruit Growers News* is an online publication that provides industry news and information for fruit growers. It features grower profiles, crop protection information, fruit variety guides, production tips, research reports, and fruit industry news.

Grainnet.com

http://grainnet.com

Grainnet is the online news service of *Grain Journal, Milling Journal, BioFuels Journal,* and *Seed Today* magazines. This gateway provides a multitude of links to top stories, directories and listings, statistical reports, and news resources.

High Plains/Midwest Ag Journal

http://www.hpj.com

High Plains/Midwest Ag Journal is published by High Plains Publishers, Inc., for farmers and ranchers. The journal provides news and information, covering the major crops of wheat, corn, cotton, soybeans, sorghum, and cattle, and hog breeds. The Markets section provides daily cash bids that can be filtered by location, bid type, and commodity. There are also crop reports on updated conditions.

Hoard's Dairyman

http://www.hoards.com

According to its website, *Hoard's Dairyman*, the magazine began in 1885 with the mission to provide "factual information to dairy farmers to assist in all facets of their dairy businesses." On the magazine's website you can get milk, butter, and cheese prices and production data. The Dairy News section and selected feature articles from the magazine are open access.

Vegetable Growers News

http://vegetablegrowersnews.com

The *Vegetable Growers News (VGN)* provides news and information for vegetable growers and features, much like its sister publication, *Fruit Growers News*. On this website, you can find crop protection information, new seed guides, production tips, research reports, and industry news.

ASSOCIATIONS AND ORGANIZATIONS

American Soybean Association

http://soygrowers.com

The American Soybean Association focuses on policy development. The association represents 21,000 soybean producers in the United States. They publish *American Soybean Magazine* and *SoyStats*, which provides annual statistics including planting data, yield and production, value, and U.S. exports.

International Cocoa Organization

http://www.icco.org

The statistics section on the International Cocoa Organization (ICCO) website shows daily and monthly average prices, going back to 2005. The organization's *Monthly Review* "reports on the latest developments on the international cocoa futures markets as well as on the supply and demand for cocoa beans and other factors influencing the cocoa trade." The *Quarterly Bulletin of Cocoa Statistics*, which is published in February, May, August, and November, provides analysis on the cocoa economy (subscription is required).

International Grains Council

http://www.igc.int

The International Grains Council (IGC) is an intergovernmental organization that promotes international cooperation in the grains trade. The Markets section of the website contains the latest export prices, and supply and demand data for grains, wheat, maize, barley, soybeans, and rice. Publications, available by subscription, are *Grain Market Report* (monthly), *Grain Market Indicators*, *World Grain Statistics*, *Grain Shipments*, and *Ocean Freight Rates*.

International Sugar Organization

http://www.isosugar.org

The International Sugar Organization (ISO) is "devoted to improving conditions in the world's sugar market." Publications offered by ISO, which are available by subscription, are *Sugar Yearbook*, *Statistical Bulletin*, *Quarterly Market Outlook*, *Monthly Market Report*, *World Sugar Balances*, *ISO Studies*, *Proceedings*, and *Ethanol Yearbook*. Daily sugar prices for the current month are available on the website.

National Cattlemen's Beef Association

http://www.beefusa.org

The National Cattlemen's Beef Association represents 1 million cattle farmers and ranchers in the United States. The Cattle Learning Center provides beef cattle information, industry statistics, Cattlemen's College, and research and educational videos. Policy issues covered are Ag/Food, Cattle Health, Cattle Marketing and Trade, Environment, Federal Lands, and Tax and Credit.

National Corn Growers Association

http://www.ncga.com/home

The National Corn Growers Association creates and increases opportunities for corn growers. The Public Policy section of the website includes issue briefs on Biotechnology, Ethanol, Farm Policy, Global Trade, and Pesticides Permits, in addition to The Legislation Action Center, Testimony Documents, and Policy Book. Farmers have access to best practices, Landviewer (assesses crop progress), and farm safety resources. The "World of Corn" section provides charts on U.S. and global corn production; food, seed, and industrial use consumption; biotech acreage; and ethanol production. Daily DTN market data with commentary is provided.

National Cotton Council of America

https://www.cotton.org

The National Cotton Council of America serves "producers, ginners, warehousers, merchants, cottonseed processors/dealers, cooperatives and textile manufacturers." The Economics section of the website provides statistical information on crops, including costs and returns; crop progress; county, state, national, and world databases; supply and demand; and weekly exports. Resources on prices include Cotlook A(FE) Index, market prices (end of day, intra-day, spot quotes), and monthly prices. Also available are the *Monthly Outlook* and *Weekly Cotton Market Report*.

National Grain and Feed Association

http://www.ngfa.org

The National Grain and Feed Association (NGFA) is the national trade association of "grain elevators, feed and feed ingredient manufacturers, grain and oilseed processors, biofuel producers, exporters, livestock and poultry integrators, and firms providing products and services to the industry." The NGFA maintains trade rules on grain, feed, barge, barge freight, and secondary rail freight.

National Livestock Producers Association

http://www.nlpa.org

The National Livestock Producers Association is comprised of marketing associations and credit corporations, representing more than 215,000 farmers in the United States and Canada, and ranchers involved in animal agriculture.

United Fresh Produce Association

http://www.unitedfresh.org

The United Fresh Produce Association is a leading trade association of regional, national, and international produce companies. Policy and regulatory news cover: Agriculture, Food Safety, Labor and Immigration, and Health and Nutrition. Newsletters are available for several market segments: Grower/Shipper, Wholesaler/Distributor, Fresh-Cut/Processor, and Retail/Foodservice.

U.S. Dairy Export Council

http://www.usdec.org

The U.S. Dairy Export Council (USDEC) "represents the global trade interests of U.S. dairy producers, proprietary processors and cooperatives, ingredient suppliers, and export traders." For members, it publishes the *U.S. Dairy Export Guide*, a resource that covers tariffs, import requirements for 90 countries, and product standards. Resources for trade policy agreements and issues are also available. The USDEC library organizes different categories via virtual books on a library shelf, including market research, exporters guide, and strategic studies, to name a few.

U.S. Grains Council

http://www.grains.org

The U.S. Grains Council "develops export markets for U.S. barley, corn, grain, sorghum, and related products" and there is a voluminous amount of information at this site. The Key Issues segment includes these categories: Trade Policy, Biotechnology, Grain Supply and Demand, Value of Trade, and Food Security. The Buying/Selling section contains export and production data, "How To Buy" Importer Manuals, and Notice to Exporters, and lists of suppliers and exporters for the Corn, Sorghum, Barley, DDGS, and Corn Gluten sectors. The Market Data section includes FOB (Freight on Board) Reference Prices, Bulk Freight Indices for HSS (Heavy Grain, Sorghum, and Soybeans), DDGS (Distiller's Dried Grains with Solubles) Price Indicators, FOB Price Comparisons, Top U.S. Export Customers, and CBOT Market Quotes. The weekly *Market Perspectives* provides current coarse grain markets information, including price, weather and freight information for buying U.S. grains.

U.S. Soybean Export Council

http://ussec.org

The U.S. Soybean Export Council (USSEC) represents soybean producers, commodity shippers, merchandisers, allied agribusinesses, and agricultural organizations. Chapter 3 of the *Buyer's Guide,* in the Resources section, focuses on procuring soybeans and products. The entire *Buyer's Guide* is useful and includes chapters on history, quality standards, shipping, and managing risks. Also included are links to organizations associated with soybeans, in addition to a technical library, educational materials, statistical resources, trade rules, and a conversion table.

U.S. Wheat Associates

http://www.uswheat.org

The U.S. Wheat Associates (USW) is the "export market development organization for the U.S. wheat industry." USW promotes all six U.S. wheat classes to "wheat buyers, millers, bakers, food processors, and government officials in more than 100 countries around the world." Selecting the "Market and Crop Information" tab on the navigation bar allows you to view excellent price, supply and demand, commercial sales, harvest, and crop quality reports. Every month, the USW updates the *World Wheat Supply and Demand Situation* report, using USDA source data. The Policy tab takes you to information on trade issues, government programs, biotechnology, policy statements, and study and analysis.

Vegetable Growers News

http://vegetablegrowersnews.com

In the *Vegetable Growers News Buyers' Guide*, there is a comprehensive listing of national and state associations.

REFERENCES

1. A. A. Upham and G. A. Schmidt, *An Introduction to Agriculture*, New York: D. Appleton, 1919, 1, Google Books, http://books.google.com.
2. *Ibid.*
3. Sophie Wenzlau, "Global Food Prices Continue to Rise," *Worldwatch Institute*, April 11, 2013, http://www.worldwatch.org/global-food-prices-continue-rise-0.
4. John Williams, *Agricultural Supply Chains and the Challenge of Price Risk*, New York: Rutledge, 2014.

22

CHEMICALS

According to the American Chemical Council (ACC) website, more than 96 percent of all manufactured goods are directly touched by chemistry. In chemical business literature, industry segmentation is represented in many ways. The chemistry segments identified by the ACC are pharmaceuticals, basic chemicals, specialty chemicals, agricultural chemicals, and consumer products.

This industry's dependence on the global economy and national regulatory concerns are two of the toughest challenges facing chemical producers. These challenges both directly and indirectly affect the companies buying from them. Pricing is highly subject to aggressive price competition, as well as wild fluctuations in raw material and energy costs. For quick analysis, the resources covered in this chapter are listed in Table 22.1.

Unlike other materials that "are what they are" for the purposes of specifications, chemicals are often altered by the intended end use. According to an A.T. Kearney case study (2014) on the chemicals industry, "Externally purchased materials and services represent more than 70 percent of the sale price of finished products. In large, integrated companies, purchasing departments usually have multiple internal customers for a single raw material, each with a different set of needs and priorities."[1] The fact that third-party spend represents a high percentage of sale price not only increases the importance of well-negotiated, well-managed contracts, it elevates the strategic importance of the procurement organizations in those companies.

When searching for chemical product information, either for identification or pricing, familiarize yourself with the compound/product/element, geographic location, and relevant monetary denomination. Researching markets and products in this industry is easier if you have an understanding of commonly used

Table 22.1 Resources—chemicals

RESOURCES—CHEMICALS	Market Analysis/ Trends	Pricing	Daily/Weekly Market News	Networking/ Industry Education	Supplier Identification	Background Information	Open (Free) Access	Mixed Fee and Free Access
American Chemical Society			✓	✓		✓		✓
American Institute of Chemical Engineers			✓	✓				✓
ChemExper Chemical Directory					✓	✓	✓	
Chemical and Engineering News	✓		✓	✓				
Chemical Engineering	✓	✓	✓	✓	✓			✓
ChemicalInfo					✓			
Chemicool.com						✓	✓	
ChemSpider.com					✓	✓	✓	
Hawley's Condensed Chemical Dictionary						✓		
ICIS Chemical Business/News/ Reports	✓	✓	✓					✓
IHS Chemical Week/Market Service	✓	✓	✓		✓			✓
National Assoc. of Chemical Distributors			✓	✓				✓
Perry's Chemical Engineer's Handbook						✓		
Pharma Info Source					✓			✓
Society of Chemical Manufacturers Assoc.			✓	✓	✓			✓
ThomasNet.com Chemicals					✓		✓	
WolphramAlpha.com		✓				✓	✓	

acronyms, numbers, and formats such as InChI, CAS registry number, SKU, commodity number, SIC, NAICS, PPI, trade names, and product names.[2]

BACKGROUND INFORMATION

The Chemistry Dictionary

Chemicool.com

http://www.chemicool.com/dictionary.htm

The *Chemistry Dictionary* provided by Chemicool.com is a helpful online resource for anyone seeking background information on chemicals. It was developed by David D. Hsu of the Massachusetts Institute of Technology. In addition to the dictionary, there are interactive melting and boiling point graphs, density and property graphs, and an interactive periodic table.

ChemSpider

http://www.chemspider.com

ChemSpider, produced by the Royal Society of Chemistry (RSC), provides information for over 29 million chemical structures. You can search by chemical names (systematic, synonyms, and trade) and chemical structure. For the structure search, you can input a structure by drawing it, uploading a file, or converting by name (SMILES, InChI, or ChemSpider ID). Various data elements include names and identifiers; properties; articles from RSC articles and books, PubMed, and Google books; vendors; data sources; Google patents; and description and images.

Hawley's Condensed Chemical Dictionary, 15th ed.

Wiley Online Library, 2014

http://onlinelibrary.wiley.com

Highly recommended for corporations and science libraries, *Hawley's Condensed Chemical Dictionary* is an authoritative reference that provides definitions of terms covering thousands of chemicals, trade name products, processes, and reactions. Compounds are arranged in A-Z order and include subheadings that list properties, derivation, hazard, grade, and use.

Perry's Chemical Engineer's Handbook, 8th ed.

McGraw-Hill Global Education, 2013, New York

http://www.mhprofessional.com

This classic work, first published in 1934, covers all aspects of chemical engineering, "from fundamentals to details." Examples of sections included in the handbook include: Physical and Chemical Data; Thermodynamics; Heat and Mass Transfer; Distillation; Gas-Solid Operations and Equipment; Transport and Storage of Fluids; Heat Transfer Equipment; and Materials of Construction.

Wolfram Alpha

http://www.wolframalpha.com

Wolfram Alpha is a computational knowledge engine that provides fact-based answers to queries. It does not search the web, but uses its own data and algorithms. In the search box on the homepage, click on the "Examples" option to get an idea of how Wolfram Alpha can be used. For chemicals, examples show how to ask about elements, compounds, quantities, solutions, reactions, thermodynamics, formulas, and functional groups. You can also get historical prices on selected chemicals. Even though this resource is listed in this chapter and is especially strong in covering chemicals, it is also useful for the information covered in Chapters 20-25.

SUPPLIER IDENTIFICATION

ChemExper Chemical Directory

http://www.chemexper.com

With the *ChemExper Chemical Directory,* any chemical supplier can share information. The Directory allows for various ways of finding information, including options for Quick, Structure, and Advanced searches. Explanations on how to perform the searches are helpful. There are also chemical tools, such as the Chemical Calculator, Property Explorer, and Chemdoodle (for drawing). The Top Products section lists the most accessed chemicals in the Directory.

Chemical Engineering Buyers' Guide

http://www.che.com/buyersguide/public

The *Chemical Engineering (CE) Buyers' Guide* offers three ways to search. You can do a search by company or product, or browse by category. There are 13 categories, with each category divided into subsections. The company search results provide subsidiary and division identification up front, and both products and trade names are listed.

ChemicalInfo

http://chemicalinfo.com

Chemical Information Services, the publisher of ChemicalInfo, was established in 1972 and began as a publisher of chemical supplier data. Its flagship product, *The Directory of World Chemical Producers (DWCP),* is an extensive database of producers of chemical raw materials. The *DWCP* is searchable by chemical name, CAS number, structure, functional group, manufacturer, country, categories, color index number, or DUNS Number.

IHS Chemical Week Buyers' Guide

http://www.chemweek.com/buyersguide/public

Access to this company and product database, the *IHS Chemical Week Buyers' Guide* is enhanced by the flexible search options available. Separate search fields are provided for companies, products, and trade names. You can also search by state and country. Links to broad categories allow for browsing chemical products and chemical services companies.

Pharma Info Source

http://www.pharmainfosource.com

Pharma Info Source provides sourcing solutions to the pharmaceutical industry, and is a place to find chemical suppliers, surplus materials, and pharma services. The three main sections you can search are API/Raw Materials, Surplus, or Impurities. You can search by CAS number or chemical name.

SOCMA Marketplace and Chemical Services Directory

https://www.socmachemicaldirectory.com/socma-marketplace-directory

The *Society of Chemical Manufacturers and Affiliates (SOCMA) Directory* includes suppliers of specialty and fine chemical products and services. The advanced search option provides a guided search feature. You can provide a keyword or start by clicking on a predetermined term to start searching for information. Terms are categorized by: Equipment, Industries/Markets Served, Capabilities/Services, Company Type, Certifications, Performance Improvement Awards,

Reactions Directories/Types of Chemicals, Consulting Services, Manufacturing/ Toll Capabilities, and Content Type.

ThomasNet.com Chemicals

http://www.thomasnet.com/browse/chemicals-1.html

ThomasNet.com Chemicals is another great source for researching suppliers of chemicals and chemical-related products and services. Listed are manufacturers, distributors, and service companies, representing a wide range of chemicals and chemical compounds, including those used for medical and industrial needs. For browsing, there are 34 "chemicals" categories, which then break down into multiple subcategories (these do not include the related categories, such as equipment, which are in the hundreds). The robust search and limiting features aid in producing highly relevant results.

PRICING AND MARKET ANALYSIS

Chemical Engineering's Plant Cost Index

http://www.che.com/pci

The *Chemical Engineering's* Plant Cost Index (CEPCI) helps chemical engineers improve plant cost estimates by adjusting process plant construction costs from one period to another.

ICIS Price Reports

http://www.icis.com/about/price-reports

Pricing information is available for 120 chemical commodities from ICIS Price Reports. Reports include spot and contract price assessments, and information on price trends. ICIS assessments are based on verified market activity, bids, offers, and deals. Markets covered are the Americas, Europe, Middle East, China, and Asia Pacific. Reports are issued weekly and flexible subscription options are available. ICIS Dashboard is a platform that allows you to select various commodities and locations for a customized view of pricing data, news, and analysis.

IHS Chemicals

http://www.ihs.com/industry/chemical/index.aspx

IHS is a prolific publisher of chemical industry information, and publishes "global chemical data, benchmarking, forecasts, and analyses [in addition] to pricing, standards, engineering, supply chain management and sustainability solutions." For supplier management, IHS provides cost, price, and inventory analysis and product/supplier information. Offerings include IHS Chemical Market Advisory Service, IHS Chemical World Analysis, Chemical Company Handbooks, and Global Insight Pricing and Purchasing.

PUBLICATIONS

Chemical Engineering Magazine

http://www.che.com

Chemical Engineering is a magazine published for chemical engineers in the chemical process industries. The magazine focuses on practical information that aids with decision making. The online site, *www.che.com,* provides an updated news feed and information on webinars and conferences. Content is organized via four channels: Process and Handling; Software, Automation, and Control; Environmental, Health and Safety; and Business and Economics.

Chemical & Engineering News

http://cen.acs.org

Published by the American Chemical Society (ACS), *Chemical & Engineering News* covers all aspects of chemistry, including business and industry, government and policy, science and technology, and education. The online version provides news, research, and back issues of the magazine. Online content is available to ACS members, although nonmembers can access the publication for 30 days for $20.00.

ICIS Chemical Business

http://www.icis.com/v2/magazine/home.aspx

ICIS Chemical Business, formerly *Chemical Market Reporter*, offers key issues, news, and analysis of chemical markets. The Trends section includes the "latest market intelligence and insight into the factors impacting price movements and supply/demand trends." Commodity markets covered are: Petrochemicals, Polymers, Intermediates, Inorganics, Oleochemicals, Green Chemicals, Biofuels and Energy, and Feedstocks. Other sections include News, Plants, Projects, Market Outlook, Chemical Profiles, and Special Reports.

ICIS News Service

http://www.icis.com/about/news

All sectors are covered in this news service, which provides real-time news, 24/7. Market coverage includes the United States, Asia, Europe, Russian Federation, China, India, and Latin America. News is provided for 50 chemical commodities in addition to Properties; Process Technology; Plant and Project Listings; and Market and Price Information.

IHS Chemical Week

http://www.chemweek.com/home

IHS Chemical Week provides global chemical industry news and analysis, covering all sectors and geographies. Insights and analysis are presented in these categories: World News and Views, People and Business, Environtech, Markets, Services, and Economics. This publication once published price reports every week, but no longer provides them. However, articles about pricing and market forecasts and demand for all sectors are published frequently.

MARKET RESEARCH PROVIDERS THAT COVER CHEMICAL MARKETS

There are well over 100 publishers that provide chemical market research reports. Many of the publishers listed in Chapter 10, Industry and Market Research, cover chemical markets, including BCC Research, Euromonitor International, Freedonia, Frost & Sullivan, Global Industry Analysts, IBISWorld, Platts (see Chapter 20), and MarketLine. Searching *MarketResearch.com* or *ResearchandMarkets.com* is helpful in identifying chemical market research providers and the types of reports they offer.

ASSOCIATIONS AND ORGANIZATIONS

American Chemical Society

http://www.acs.org

The American Chemical Society (ACS) was founded in 1876 by 35 chemists. Now, the ACS has more than 160,000 members. The ACS, as stated on its website, "represents professionals at all degree levels and in all fields of chemistry and sciences that involve chemistry." The ACS is a prolific publisher of books, magazines, journals, and reference and research materials. Chemical Abstract Services, a division of the ACS, is the authority for chemical research information. The ACS also publishes a weekly magazine, *Chemical & Engineering News*, described on page 209.

American Institute of Chemical Engineers

http://www.aiche.org

The American Institute of Chemical Engineers (AIChE) represents 45,000 chemical engineering professionals from more than 100 countries. Content offered by the AIChE covers the topics of Chemicals and Materials, Chemical Engineering Practice, Process Safety, Biological Engineering, Sustainability and Environment, Energy, Professional Development, and Outreach. Twenty-two divisions and forums allow for networking.

National Association of Chemical Distributors

http://www.nacd.com

The National Association of Chemical Distributors (NACD) is made up of 400 member companies and affiliates. Established in 1971, the NACD is an international association of chemical distributors and their supply-chain partners. "Member companies process, formulate, blend, re-package, warehouse, transport, and market these chemical products for over 750,000 customers." The NACD publishes *Chemical Distributor Magazine.*

Society of Chemical Manufacturers Association

http://www.socma.com

The Society of Chemical Manufacturers Association (SOCMA) is based in the United States and serves the batch, custom, and specialty chemical industry. Membership is comprised of small to large chemical companies, worldwide. The SOCMA was historically dedicated to the needs of the organic specialty chemical sector, but has expanded its scope to include inorganic producers and biotechnology companies.

REFERENCES

1. "Procurement Transformation for a Major Chemical Company," *A.T. Kearney.com* Accessed June 23, 2014, http://www.atkearney.com/chemicals/case-study/-/asset_publisher/WFwHvp9557jx/content/procurement-transformation-for-a-major-chemical-company/10192.
2. Jan Carver and Patricia Kirkwood, "Untangling the Chemical Information Pricing Web," *American Chemical Society,* Division of Chemical Information, Accessed February 8, 2014.

23

ENERGY

Everything that we do in life is connected to energy in one way or another. Although there are many sources of energy, they can be broken down into one of two types: nonrenewable and renewable. *Nonrenewable energy sources* cannot be replenished once used, and include oil and petroleum products, natural gas, coal, and uranium. *Renewable energy sources*, on the other hand, can be regenerated, and include biomass (from plants and animals), hydropower, geothermal, wind, and solar.[1]

In the United States, there are four major sectors that consume energy at the point of end use: Industrial, Commercial, Transportation, and Residential. In the manufacturing, commercial, and residential sectors, the most common energy sources are natural gas and electricity. The main source of energy for the transportation sector is petroleum. China consumes the most energy, followed by the United States.[2] For quick analysis, the resources covered in this chapter are shown in Table 23.1.

Even though the energy industry includes alternative energy sources, the production of petroleum and natural gas dominates the industry. The petroleum sector can be characterized as being unstable, due to the fact that supply and prices are greatly affected by geopolitical instability in the supplier regions.[3] According to the U.S. Energy Information Administration (EIA), "average annual U.S. natural gas prices have remained relatively low over the past several years as a result of the availability of abundant domestic resources and the application of improved production technologies."[4]

Like almost all modern supply chains, energy companies are affected by the global economy, new and emerging regulations, and issues that "cross borders, continents, and political divides."[5]

Table 23.1 Resources—energy

RESOURCES—ENERGY	Market Analysis/ Trends	Pricing	Daily/Weekly Market News	Networking/ Industry Education	Supplier Identification	Background Information	Open (Free) Access	Mixed Fee and Free Access
Alternative Energy News	✓		✓				✓	
American Coal Council Online Buyers Guide				✓	✓		✓	
American Gas Association (AGA)	✓	✓	✓	✓	✓	✓		✓
American Petroleum Institute	✓		✓	✓		✓		✓
Argus Media	✓	✓	✓					
Association of Energy Engineers	✓		✓	✓				✓
BP Energy Economics	✓	✓					✓	
Dictionary of Energy: Expanded Edition						✓		
Effectively Managing Natural Gas Costs (AEE)	✓			✓		✓		
Energy Industry Today	✓		✓				✓	
Gasworld Gas Reports	✓		✓			✓		
HydroWorld Online Buyers Guide					✓		✓	
ICIS Energy	✓	✓	✓					
IHS Energy and Power	✓	✓	✓					
Independent Petroleum Association of America	✓	✓	✓	✓				✓
International Energy Agency	✓	✓	✓	✓				✓
Natural Gas Market Indicators (AGA)	✓	✓	✓				✓	

RESOURCES—ENERGY	Market Analysis/ Trends	Pricing	Daily/Weekly Market News	Networking/ Industry Education	Supplier Identification	Background Information	Open (Free) Access	Mixed Fee and Free Access
Natural Gas Supply Association	✓	✓	✓	✓				✓
Oil and Gas Journal	✓	✓	✓	✓				✓
Oil and Gas Production Handbook						✓		
Oil, Gas and Petrochem Equipment Buyers Guide					✓		✓	
Oilprice.com	✓	✓	✓					✓
OPEC.org	✓	✓		✓			✓	
Power Engineering International	✓		✓	✓				✓
Public Utilities Fortnightly (magazine)	✓		✓	✓				✓
Renewable Energy World	✓		✓	✓				✓
Solar Energy Industries Association	✓		✓	✓				✓
Solar Industry's Online Buyers Guide					✓		✓	
ThomasNet.com Electrical and Power Generation					✓		✓	
U.S. Energy Information Administration	✓	✓	✓	✓		✓		✓
Understanding Today's Electricity Business				✓		✓		
Understanding Today's Natural Gas Business				✓		✓		
World Energy Council	✓							✓

For this industry sector, the U.S. government, mostly through the U.S. Energy Information Administration (EIA), provides excellent open access market analysis and pricing information, including historical, current, and forecast.

BACKGROUND INFORMATION

American Gas Association Glossary

http://www.aga.org/Kc/glossary/Pages/default.aspx

In the *American Gas Association (AGA) Glossary*, you can browse terms specific to natural gas, alphabetically.

Dictionary of Energy: Expanded Edition

Elsevier, 2009

Written by Cutler Cleveland, the *Dictionary of Energy* has more than 10,000 entries within 40 scientific disciplines. There are scientists' essays, biographical entries, and 100 photos and illustrations.

Oil and Gas Production Handbook: An Introduction to Oil and Gas Production, Transport, Refining and Petrochemical Industry

ABB Oil and Gas, 2013

http://www.abb.com/industries/us/9AAC123932.aspx?country=US

Available to download for free from the ABB website, the *Oil and Gas Production Handbook*, written by Havard Devold, provides basic information on the Upstream, Mainstream, Refining and Petrochemical processes. At the ABB Oil, Gas, and Petroleum Industry Portal, select "Oil and Gas Production Handbook" from the Oil and Gas Brochures section.

U.S. Energy Information Administration (EIA) Energy Explained

http://www.eia.gov/energyexplained/index.cfm

This section of the EIA website is filled with basic, introductory information that covers these energy sources: Oil and Petroleum Products, Gasoline, Natural Gas, Nuclear, Coal, Hydropower, Biomass, Biofuels, Wind, Geothermal, Solar, Electricity, and Hydrogen.

U.S. Energy Information Administration (EIA) Glossary

http://www.eia.gov/tools/glossary/index.cfm

This comprehensive glossary, from the information-rich EIA website, provides a search function and allows you to browse by a term's starting letter or by fuel groups: Alternative Fuels, Coal, Electricity, Natural Gas, Nuclear, Petroleum, and Renewable.

Understanding Today's Natural Gas Business

Enerdynamics Corp., 2011

Understanding Today's Natural Gas Business is authored by Bob Shively and John Ferrare. It is an introductory text that offers a comprehensive overview of the natural gas industry. Also by the same authors is *Understanding Today's Electricity Business.*

SUPPLIER IDENTIFICATION

American Coal Council Online Buyers' Guide

http://www.americancoalonline.com/accdirectory

The *American Coal Council Online Buyers' Guide* is a directory that allows you to search by keyword, specific category, and location. You can browse detailed category listings as well.

American Gas Association Buyer's Guide

http://www.aga.org/Kc/findvendorsuppliers/Pages/buyersguide.aspx

The *American Gas Association Buyer's Guide* is a resource used to locate products and services for the natural gas industry. You can perform a keyword search or a category-specific search.

Gasworld Directory

http://www.gasworld.com/directory

The *Gasworld Directory* houses a comprehensive database, covering the industrial gas sector. You can find details about gas suppliers, equipment manufacturers, and distribution companies.

HydroWorld Online Buyer's Guide

http://buyersguide.hydroworld.com

The *HydroWorld Online Buyer's Guide* covers the hydropower marketplace in more than 250 categories, including: Turbines, Dam Construction, Regulatory Assistance, and Fish Passage.

Oil, Gas and Petrochem Equipment Buyer's Guide

http://buyersguide.ogpe.com

As stated on the website for *Oil, Gas, and Petrochem Equipment,* "Oil, Gas & Petrochem Equipment and OGPE.com serve global buyers, specifiers, and purchasing decision-makers throughout upstream, midstream, and downstream oil and gas operations." In the *Buyer's Guide*, you can use the advanced search filter in addition to browsing by company, product, or category.

Solar Industry's Online Buyer's Guide

http://www.solarindustrymag.com/buyersguide

The *Solar Industry's Online Buyer's Guide* is a comprehensive directory of suppliers of goods and services to the solar industry. You can browse the directory by business category or search by keyword.

ThomasNet.com Electrical and Power Generation

http://www.thomasnet.com/browse/electrical-power-generation-1.html

ThomasNet.com is a classic resource that is a favorite among buyers. There are 14 electrical and power generation categories on the Electrical and Power Generation website. Each category is then divided into subcategories. For example, "Fuel Cells" is broken down into 17 subcategories.

PRICING AND MARKET ANALYSIS

Argus Media

http://www.argusmedia.com

Argus Media publishes market reports that contain price assessments, market commentary, and news for the Global Crude, Oil Products, Natural Gas,

Electricity, Coal, Emissions, Bioenergy, Fertilizer, Petrochemical, Metals, and Transportation industries. In the world of energy benchmarks, Argus and Platts (see Chapter 20, Commodities) are considered to be two of the largest price reporting agencies.

BP Energy Economics

British Petroleum

http://www.bp.com/en/global/corporate/about-bp/energy-economics.html

British Petroleum (BP) publishes two reports that provide historical data and long-term forecasts. The *BP Statistical Review of World Energy* is published every June, and examines historical data on world markets, documenting the changing patterns in the ways that energy is produced and consumed. Spot crude prices are listed from 1975 onward, and crude oil prices from 1861. Natural gas prices are listed from 1985, and coal from 1992. A second publication, *BP Energy Outlook*, identifies long-term energy trends and develops projections for world energy markets to 2035. From the website, you can download country insights and fact sheets for Africa, Brazil, China, European Union, India, Middle East, Russia, United States, and North America.

Gasworld, Gas Reports

http://www.gasworld.com/intelligence/gas-reports

The "Gas Reports" series of country profiles serve the industrial gas industry, and "provide up-to-date information on the market size and supply structure of industrial gases in each country and region analyzed." Reports can be selected according to region or country.

ICIS Energy

Reed Business Information

http://www.icis.com/energy

ICIS provides independent pricing information for the global energy markets. Comprehensive price reporting covers key energy markets, including Gas, Liquefied Natural Gas (LNG), Electricity, Carbon-Emissions, Coal, and Oil. Coverage includes historical pricing data; price assessments for key energy sectors; information and analysis on price drivers and fluctuations; and market commentary on developments.

Energy & Power Insight

IHS

http://www.ihs.com/products/cera/index.aspx

IHS CERA Advisory Research Services provide regional and global analysis of the Oil, Natural Gas, Electric Power, Coal, and Renewables industries. These research services provide price, supply, and demand outlooks for all major energy segments; advance warning of adverse trends and developments; and geopolitical and regulatory information.

International Energy Agency

http://www.iea.org

The International Energy Agency (IEA) is an organization made up of 28 member countries. The IEA's four main areas of focus are: Energy Security, Economic Development, Environmental Awareness, and Worldwide Engagement. As an agency, the IEA gathers and analyzes worldwide statistics. The IEA publishes the annual *World Energy Outlook (WEO)*, an authoritative source of market analysis that looks at trends in energy demand and supply (requires payment). Available for free download is *Key World Energy Statistics*, which contains annual data on the supply, transformation and consumption of all major energy sources. The IEA produces 30 subscription publications and about 70 no-fee publications per year. Popular reports are *Medium Term Oil Market*, *Medium Term Gas Market*, and *Energy Technology Perspectives*.

Natural Gas Market Indicators

http://www.aga.org/Kc/analyses-and-statistics

Free reports like Natural Gas Market Indicators published by the American Gas Association, are made available on or about the fifteenth and thirtieth of each month. The two-page reports summarize recent developments in natural gas pricing, heating and cooling degree days statistics, underground storage, domestic gas production, rig counts, pipeline imports and exports, and international liquefied natural gas issues.

Oilprice.com

http://oilprice.com

OilPrice.com is an energy news site that focuses on oil and gas, alternative energy, and geopolitics. A price chart on the homepage offers detailed information, found by clicking on icons. Pricing is available for crude oil, ethanol, natural gas, gasoline, heating oil, and gold.

U.S. Energy Information Administration

http://www.eia.gov

The U.S. Energy Information Administration (EIA) is the foremost source for comprehensive historical and current energy data. National and international statistics are provided for Petroleum, Natural Gas, Coal, Electricity, Nuclear, and Renewable/Alternative Energy. The *Short Term Energy Outlook* provides pricing and analysis reports for global and U.S. petroleum, as well as other liquids, natural gas, coal, electricity, renewables, CO^2 emissions, and U.S. economic assumptions. Other popular reports are *Annual Energy Outlook*, *International Energy Outlook*, *Weekly Petroleum Status Report*, *Natural Gas Weekly Update*, and *Electric Power Monthly*. Daily wholesale and retail prices for various energy products are shown at *http://www.eia.gov/todayinenergy/prices.cfm*, including spot prices and select futures prices at national or regional levels.

MARKET RESEARCH PROVIDERS THAT COVER ENERGY MARKETS

The publishers listed in Chapter 10, Industry and Market Research, that cover segments of the energy markets are Euromonitor International, Freedonia, BCC, First Research, Global Industry Analysts, IBISWorld, MarketLine, GlobalData, and Business Monitor International. Searching *MarketResearch.com* or *ResearchandMarkets.com* is helpful in identifying the energy market research providers and the types of reports they offer.

One market research firm that specializes in energy market intelligence is Emerging Markets Online (http://www.emerging-markets.com). The firm provides research and consulting services in the areas of Algae, Biofuels, and Energy Infrastructure.

PUBLICATIONS

Alternative Energy News

http://www.alternative-energy-news.info

In *Alternative Energy News*, you can view the latest alternative and renewable energy news headlines from a variety of "clean energy" news sources. News and information can be narrowed by selecting the following categories: Energy, Biofuels, Environment, Hydrogen, Solar, Transportation, and Wind.

American Petroleum Institute

http://www.api.org

The American Petroleum Institute (API) is a national trade association that represents all aspects of the U.S. oil and natural gas industry. The Oil and Natural Gas Overview section focuses on production. The Publications section lets you download and order documents from the API inventory of more than 600 standards and recommended practices. Also in this section is access to statistical information, including the *Monthly Summary Reports,* which provide facts about oil and gas production, imports, and costs. The reports help to explain the supply and demand factors behind energy costs. Other sections on the site detail API's Certification Programs and events dedicated to standards development. Top industry policy issues are also presented.

Energy Industry Today

http://energy.einnews.com

Energy Industry Today is a subscription-based news service for energy professionals. News is distributed among energy/alternative energy topics, or selected by country or state.

Oil & Gas Journal

PennWell Corporation

http://www.ogj.com

The *Oil & Gas Journal* is a petroleum industry publication, which started in 1902 and is widely read and respected. The journal's website is organized in five channels: General Interest, Exploration and Development, Drilling and Production, Processing, and Transportation. Updated news articles are provided for all categories within each channel, with most of them being free to access. The Research option under the Home tab takes you to the PennEnergy Research page, where you can search or browse a comprehensive list of research products, for a fee, that include industry data, surveys, statistical tables, directories, databases, and forecast reports.

Organization of the Petroleum Exporting Countries

http://www.opec.org/opec_web/en/publications/340.htm

From the Organization of the Petroleum Exporting Countries (OPEC) website, you can download the annual *World Oil Outlook*, which shares OPEC's views on the world's energy prospects, providing a detailed analysis by region and sector. Also available for download is the *OPEC Annual Statistical Bulletin (ASB)*, which provides historical data on the global oil and gas industry. The *OPEC Bulletin*, also an open access publication, is OPEC's monthly magazine, featuring news from member countries, articles, a review of the oil market, and topical issues. The OPEC Basket Price chart can be viewed by desired dates. The Market Indicators section of the website provides the latest data on OPEC output levels, oil prices, and supply and demand. The *OPEC Monthly Oil Market Report* "covers major issues affecting the world oil market and provides an outlook for crude oil market developments for the coming year."

Power Engineering International

PennWell Corporation

http://www.powerengineeringint.com

On the home page of Power Engineering International (PEi), you can click on the Business tab, and then select the option for "Market Intelligence." The Energy Market Intelligence News section provides the latest energy market news for the global power industry, covering energy prices, electricity prices, economic indicators, and supply and demand analysis. The print version provides articles on new technologies and installations, as well as market reports, news, commentary, and analysis.

Public Utilities Fortnightly

http://www.fortnightly.com

Public Utilities Fortnightly is a monthly magazine intended for management at utility and energy companies. The magazine focuses on providing information and analysis to the Electric, Natural Gas, Water and Telecom industries. The magazine's website presents information through these channels: T&D Grid, Regulation and Policy, Finance, Generation and Markets, Retail, Management and Leadership, News and Events, Reports and Data, and white papers.

Renewable Energy World

http://www.renewableenergyworld.com

The *Renewable Energy World* website provides news, commentary, featured blogs, in-depth technology, research/reports, videos, and events for the Solar, Wind, Geothermal, Bio, Hydro, and Storage sectors. The online magazine, *Renewable Energy World,* covers industry, policy, finance, and markets for all renewable technologies.

ASSOCIATIONS AND ORGANIZATIONS

American Gas Association

http://www.aga.org

The American Gas Association (AGA), founded in 1918, represents more than 200 local energy companies and advocates in both federal and state regulatory arenas. The AGA website provides many statistics, reports, and analyses about natural gas. The "Our Issues" option, on the navigation bar, lists and provides information on all of the issues the organization represents. A sampling of these issues are: Rates and Regulatory, Energy Efficiency, Environment, Natural Gas Vehicles, Safety, and Supply. AGA also publishes *American Gas* magazine.

Association of Energy Engineers

http://www.aeecenter.org

The Association of Energy Engineers (AEE) offers the Certified Energy Procurement Professional (CEP) program. The AEE publishes the book, *Effectively Managing Natural Gas Costs,* which is intended to serve as a "comprehensive reference which can be used by the natural gas purchaser to sort out both the potential pitfalls that can negatively impact gas costs, and the opportunities for significant savings available to the informed user."

Independent Petroleum Association of America

http://www.ipaa.org

The Independent Petroleum Association of America (IPAA) is a national trade association that represents independent oil and natural gas producers and service companies from across the United States. Its purpose "is advocacy for federal policies that promote the development and use of domestic petroleum and natural gas." The IPPA publishes a weekly newsletter in addition to publishing economic reports and industry statistics.

Natural Gas Supply Association

http://www.ngsa.org

The Natural Gas Supply Association (NGSA) represents suppliers that produce and market natural gas. The association's members produce approximately one-third of the U.S. natural gas supply. White papers and reports are published on issues that include the environmental and economic benefits of natural gas; natural gas supply and infrastructure; financial reform (Dodd-Frank) and related competitive market issues; and, pipeline rates. Analyses and studies include winter and summer outlook reports, and Top 40 producer reports.

Solar Energy Industries Association

http://www.seia.org

The Solar Energy Industries Association (SEIA) advocates for the protection and expansion of the U.S. market for solar technologies at the federal and state levels. The SEIA represents the entire solar industry, advocating issues that are related to distributive solar, finance and tax, power plant development, renewable energy deployment, international trade, health and safety, environment, and solar technology.

World Energy Council

http://www.worldenergy.org

The World Energy Council (WEC) is "comprised of more than 3000 member organizations, located in more than 90 countries, coming from governments, private and state corporations, academia, NGOs, and energy-related stakeholders." Selecting the Data tab makes information available for these four topic areas: Energy Resources, Issues Monitor, Sustainability Index, and Efficiency Indicators. The Energy Resources section presents the key figures for reserves and production from the most recent World Energy Resources report, with the option to search by resource, region, or country. The Issues Monitor looks at the global energy agenda, and analyzes the trends and outlooks in world regions and multiple countries. The Energy Sustainability Index assesses the sustainability of national energy policies, and Efficiency Indicators monitor trends in energy use and CO^2 emissions.

REFERENCES

1. "Energy Explained," *U.S. Energy Information Administration*, Accessed February 26, 2014, http://www.eia.gov/energyexplained.
2. *Ibid.*
3. "Energy: Introduction," *globalEDGE*, Michigan State University, Accessed February 26, 2014, http://globaledge.msu.edu/industries/energy.
4. "Annual Energy Outlook 2014," *U.S. Energy Information Administration,* May 7, 2014, http://www.eia.gov/forecasts/aeo/MT_naturalgas.cfm.
5. "U.S. Energy Oil and Gas Industry Solutions," *IHS*, Accessed February 26, 2014, http://www.ihs.com/industry/oil-gas/us.aspx.

24

METALS

The metals, minerals, and mining industry is defined "as activities involved in locating, excavating, and processing metals, minerals, and other geological resources that are needed in the economy."[1] Metals can be categorized as precious metals (e.g., gold, silver); base metals (e.g., copper, lead, zinc, nickel); ferrous metals, which have a strong chemical affinity with iron; non-ferrous metals, which have no affinity with iron (and include base metals); and specialty metals, such as titanium.[2]

The metals industry is sensitive to broad economic conditions and is capital-intensive. Heavy demand drivers for the mining and metals industry are manufactures of durable goods, such as motor vehicles, machinery, and construction steel.[3] Due to advances in technology, there has recently been an intense focus on rare earth metal mining. China, controlling 97 percent of production, is the top producer of rare earth metals.[4] For quick analysis, the resources covered in this chapter are listed in Table 24.1.

A rising topic in the procurement of metals is that of "conflict minerals," which commonly include tungsten, tantalum, gold, and tin. One of the challenges with sourcing conflict minerals is that it is often done at the second or third tier of the supply chain. In other words, even companies that do not buy tungsten, tantalum, gold, and tin directly are now subject to regulatory and reporting scrutiny. These companies must work with their suppliers, and their suppliers' suppliers, to ensure that they abide by the industry standards they set. Conflict minerals are involved in the supply chains of many industries, including consumer electronics, aerospace, medical devices, and information technology. Procurement professionals in these industries need to be informed about conflict minerals in order to clearly outline expectations for their suppliers and to monitor their adherence.

Table 24.1 Resources—metals

RESOURCES—METALS	Market Analysis/ Trends	Pricing	Daily/Weekly Market News	Networking/ Industry Education	Supplier Identification	Background Information	Open (Free) Access	Mixed Fee and Free Access
AIST Steel Glossary						✓	✓	
Aluminum Industry Buyers Guide					✓		✓	
American Iron and Steel Institute	✓		✓	✓				✓
AMM (American Metal Market)	✓	✓	✓	✓	✓	✓		✓
Association for Iron and Steel Technology	✓		✓	✓				✓
American Society of Metals International	✓		✓	✓				✓
CommodityMine (InfoMine)	✓	✓	✓			✓	✓	
Critical Metals Handbook						✓		
CRU Indices	✓	✓						
Dictionary of Metals						✓		
Engineering and Mining Journal	✓		✓	✓				✓
Kitco Metals	✓	✓	✓				✓	
London Metal Exchanger (LME)	✓	✓				✓		
Metal Bulletin	✓	✓	✓	✓		✓		✓
Metal Center News	✓		✓		✓			✓
MetalMiner	✓	✓	✓	✓		✓		✓
MetalMiner IndX	✓	✓						✓
MetalPrices.com	✓	✓	✓	✓				✓
Metals Service Center Institute	✓		✓	✓				✓

RESOURCES—METALS	Market Analysis/ Trends	Pricing	Daily/Weekly Market News	Networking/ Industry Education	Supplier Identification	Background Information	Open (Free) Access	Mixed Fee and Free Access
Mining Engineering	✓		✓	✓				✓
Mining Journal	✓		✓	✓		✓		✓
Minor Metals Trade Association	✓		✓	✓				✓
Platts Steel Glossary						✓	✓	
Steel Market Update Resource Page						✓	✓	
SupplyMine					✓		✓	
USGS Metal Prices in US Through 1998		✓					✓	
World Steel Association	✓		✓	✓				✓

The bulk of the resources to consider for metals market intelligence are found in the Pricing and Market Analysis section. Among these resources, MetalMiner, AMM, and Metal Bulletin are the most comprehensive, and provide tailored offerings for procurement professionals who must follow, analyze, and anticipate activity in the metals markets and the conditions that greatly affect supply and prices.

BACKGROUND INFORMATION

Association for Iron and Steel Technology Glossary

http://apps.aist.org/asp/glossary

From the Association for Iron and Steel Technology (AIST), this online glossary of steel-related terms is comprehensive and technically oriented. You can browse for information by using the beginning letter of a term, or search for a term.

American Metal Market Glossary

http://www.amm.com/Glossary.html

The *American Metal Market (AMM) Glossary* contains: "All the metal industry terms you didn't know and are too afraid to ask."

Critical Metals Handbook

The *Critical Metals Handbook*, published in 2014, is edited by Gus Gunn, a principal research scientist at the British Geological Survey. The *Handbook* is timely, as growing economic demand for critical metals and the possibility of future scarcity is a concern. It covers all aspects of critical metals, including geology, deposits, processing, applications, recycling, environmental issues, and markets.

Dictionary of Metals

http://www.asminternational.org/materials-resources

Published by ASM International, the *Dictionary of Metals* is an authoritative reference work for terms and definitions of metals, and terminology related to metals.

London Metal Exchange (LME) Glossary

http://www.lme.com/glossary

Published by the London Metal Exchange (LME), you can search the *LME Glossary* for a term or use the browse feature.

Metal Bulletin Glossary

http://www.metalbulletin.com/Glossary.html

The *Metal Bulletin Glossary* is a free online glossary that covers the metals commodity market and metals industry terms.

Mining Journal Online Knowledge Page

http://www.mining-journal.com/knowledge

The sections of the Mining Journal Online Knowledge Page are helpful in learning the basics of the mining industry. See especially Mining Explained, Mining 101, and the Mining Glossary. Mining 101 divides the mining industry into six sections: Metals and Minerals, Exploration, Geology, Mining, Processing, and the Marketplace.

Platts Steel Glossary

https://www.steelbb.com/steelglossary

Published by Platts, this glossary has long entries with in-depth explanations of terms. A generous amount of links to related terms are provided throughout the glossary.

Steel Market Update Resource Page

https://www.steelmarketupdate.com/resources

The Steel Market Update Resource Page is beneficial to understanding the flat rolled steel industry. Look for common calculations, terminology, thickness tolerances, and steel buyer basics. Click on "Steel Buyers Basics" for brief articles that discuss the basics of steel pricing, and the art of negotiation, from a steel buyer's perspective.

SUPPLIER IDENTIFCATION

American Metal Market (AMM) Buyers Guide

http://servicecentersguide.amm.com

From American Metal Market, this online resource is for anyone sourcing metal materials. You can search by company and keyword, or browse by region, materials, or services.

Aluminum Industry Buyers Guide

http://buyersguide.aluminum.org

You can search the *Aluminum Industry Buyers Guide* by using the advanced search option, which allows you to designate location by state, city, or zip code. The main categories for browsing are Business Services, Casting/Foundries, Distribution Services, Products/Resources, Ingot Products, Mill Products, Equipment Services, Supplier Products, and Excursion. Each category has multiple subcategories.

SupplyMine

http://www.infomine.com/suppliers

SupplyMine is a directory that allows you to browse or search more than 20,000 companies, covering the entire range of products and services used by the mining industry. The browse categories include: Consulting Services, Contracting, Equipment, Supplies and Consumables, and Support Services. You can search by supplier, product, or catalog.

PRICING AND MARKET ANALYSIS

American Metal Market

http://www.amm.com

First published in 1882, the American Metal Market (AMM) is considered an industry standard. Through its website and print publication, the AMM provides pricing and information covering steel, non-ferrous, and scrap markets with a focus on North America and world markets, where applicable. The Custom Price Reports tool allows you to search steel, stainless steel, scrap, and non-ferrous metals in their historic database, going back 50 years, in some cases. In the Pricing section, you can access latest prices, LME at a glance, monthly averages, weekly charts, and current exchange rates. The weekly charts appearing in the daily AMM include *AMM Ingot Indicator/Scrap Aluminum Price Comparison, Weekly Shredded Scrap Price Composite, Weekly Steel Scrap Price Comparison*, and *Weekly Tonnage Raw Steel Production Chart*. Full and basic subscription levels to AMM reports are available, with the print magazine being included in all options.

CommodityMine

InfoMine, Inc.

http://www.infomine.com/commodities

InfoMine is an extremely comprehensive resource that was developed in 1989 with the purpose of providing mining information electronically. CommodityMine, one of the InfoMine websites, is where you can find one-year commodity price charts, along with news and access to the Chart Builder feature. There is a link to the "All Charts" section, where you can compare price changes for gold, silver, copper, and other commodities over a variety of time periods. Clicking on a particular commodity takes you to a page that provides the following information: links to top producing countries, companies, and mines; publications; associations; and upcoming events. InfoMine's Company/Property database is available via a paid subscription, and provides detailed information on thousands of mining companies and mineral properties. Other subsections provided by InfoMine are NewsMine, InvestmentMine, MapMine, CountryMine, CostMine, CareerMine, EduMine, EventsMine, TechnoMine, and ConferenceMine.

CRU Indices

CRU Group

http://www.cruindices.com

CRU, established in 1968, publishes over 200 steel price indices. Most of these are published monthly and cover steelmaking raw materials, and semi-finished and finished products, in all the major regions of the world. Weekly price indices include: United States, Italian, German, and Chinese Hot-Rolled, Cold-Rolled, Hot-Dipped Galvanized, and Plate. Data providers include producers, traders, service centers, distributors, and end users. CRU prides itself as being the first commodity index provider to carry out a third party audit of its data providers.

Kitco Metals

http://www.kitco.com

Kitco is a retailer of precious metals and maintains an information-rich website. You can find real-time spot prices, precious metal charts, recent news reports, and expert commentary. According to Kitco, the website gets nearly 1 million visits every day.

London Metal Exchange

http://www.lme.com

The Welcome page on LME's (London Metal Exchange) website indicates that it "is the world centre for industrial metals trading and price-risk management" and that "more than 80% of global non-ferrous business is conducted here and the prices discovered on our three trading platforms are used as the global benchmark." The LME Free Data Service (*https://secure.lme.com/data)* makes available official prices, opening stocks, daily index value, monthly averages, and price graphs for non-ferrous metals, steel, and minor metals. You must register for this service. Also offered through a subscription service are published prices and reports (*http://www.lme.com/pricing-and-data*). Coverage includes all contracts traded on the LME. The data is available through various licensed third party market data distributors and directly from LME.

Metal Bulletin

http://www.metalbulletin.com

Metal Bulletin is a service that provides pricing information, expert market commentary, and statistics for all global metals and steel markets. Information is organized around these channels: Base Metals, Ores and Alloys, Raw Materials, Exchange News and Prices, Minor and Precious Metals, Carbon Steel, Stainless and Special Steel, Scrap and Secondary, Capital Markets, Events, and Jobs. Metal Bulletin's weekly magazine has been replaced with two products: *Metal Bulletin Daily* and *Metal Bulletin Magazine* (monthly). The *Daily* provides news from the last 24 hours, plus all Metal Bulletin prices. The monthly *Magazine* publishes feature articles, market analysis, and high-profile interviews. The subscription package includes breaking news e-mail alerts, latest metal bulletin prices, 30-minute delayed LME feed, news and price archive (one year), daily newsletter, and monthly magazine. The full archive subscription allows you to go back 15 years for news and pricing. The Company Database provides detailed information on 11,500 companies worldwide, including expansion plans, ship loading facilities, plants capacity, mine reserves, annual output, and executive and financial information.

MetalMiner

http://agmetalminer.com

MetalMiner, a sister site of Spend Matters, is "a digital multimedia resource for metal-buying organizations [and] identifies metal market trends and price direction, provides daily metal market analysis and commentary, and offers insight and strategies to mitigate risk and reduce costs." In addition to market analysis and pricing, you can get industry news; articles on metal appreciation; reports on metal sourcing strategies and commodity risk management; and resources and articles on conflict minerals. The MetalMiner monthly price forecasts include: HRC, CRC, HDG, steel plate, aluminum, copper, nickel, tin, lead, and zinc.

MetalMiner IndX

http://agmetalminer.com/metals-price-index

This index is produced by MetalMiner and features more than 650 price points for a wide range of products that include steel, stainless steel, non-ferrous metals, ferro alloys, precious metals, rare earth metals, and minor metals, in addition to scrap metal. The index is easy to use and features four pull down menus: Metal, Type, Country, and Currency. You can view and create reports using historical data for as many metals as you choose. Alerts can be set up, based on customized price thresholds. Subscription levels are based on type of site user. The current *Monthly Report: Metal Price Index Trends* can be downloaded for free.

MetalPrices.com

http://www.metalprices.com

MetalPrices.com is a market intelligence service that provides raw material pricing for international metal products. The main focus according to the website is "price discovery for 'open market' or over-the-counter (OTC) metal products—reporting the prices of metals that are not listed on the major exchanges, but essential to global trade." The navigation bar has options to select Live Feeds, Daily Exchange Data, Metals, Energy, Currency, News, Reports (e.g. Aurubis, BNP Paribus), Historical Data, and Daily Snapshots. Subscription levels vary, based on LME and COMEX feed delivery times. Free metal price charts for different time ranges can be found at *http://www.metalprices.com/p/FreeCharts.*

USGS Metal Prices in the United States, 1959 Through 1998

http://minerals.usgs.gov/minerals/pubs/metal_prices

Thanks to USGS Metal Prices in the United States, you can view extended price histories for a wide range of metals in a single document. The chapter for each mineral commodity includes a graph of annual current and constant dollar prices for 1959 through 1998, where available; a list of significant events that affected prices; a brief discussion of each metal and its history; and one or more tables that list current dollar prices for metals.

MARKET RESEARCH PROVIDERS THAT COVER METALS MARKETS

There are many market research publishers that provide coverage of the markets for metals. The publishers listed in Chapter 10, Industry and Market Research, which cover segments of the metal markets, are Euromonitor International, Freedonia, Global Industry Analysts, IBISWorld, IHS, and MarketLine. Searching *MarketResearch.com* or *ResearchandMarkets.com* is helpful in identifying metals markets research providers and the types of reports they offer.

PUBLICATIONS

Engineering and Mining Journal

http://www.e-mj.com

The *Engineering and Mining Journal (E&MJ)* covers the copper, gold, nickel, ore, lead/zinc, PGM, and diamonds markets, and focuses on operating processes. Regional news is provided from the United States, Canada, Latin America, Africa, Asia, and Australia. The World Mining Equipment sections deal with operating strategies, supplier reports, processing solutions, and the latest technology issues for mine operators.

Mining Engineering

http://me.smenet.org

Mining Engineering is the official publication of the Society for Mining, Metallurgy and Exploration. *Mining Engineering* covers the global minerals industry and provides feature and peer-reviewed (highly) technical articles, news, and regular columns by industry experts.

Metal Center News

http://www.metalcenternews.com

Metal Center News is the trade magazine of the metals distribution industry: "the service centers that warehouse, process and distribute carbon and stainless steels, aluminum and copper and brass."

Mining Journal

Aspermont Media

http://www.mining-journal.com

Founded in 1835, *Mining Journal* covers all aspects of the mining industry, including exploration, financing, development, production, and marketing. The journal provides news, in-depth interviews, surveys, opinions from industry experts, and market trend data.

ASSOCIATIONS AND ORGANIZATIONS

Association and Society Directories

There is a large number of professional associations and societies that represent all segments and categories of the metals industry, with missions to provide information and support. Publishing directories is one way to support the metals industry. Two directories that provide comprehensive lists of metals industry associations are the AMM Association List (*http://www.amm.com/UsefulLinks.html*) and the Metal Center News Directory of Associations (*http://www.metalcenternews.com; click on Directories and then, Metal Distribution*).

American Iron and Steel Institute

http://www.steel.org

The American Iron and Steel Institute (AISI) represents the North American steel industry and advances the case for steel in the marketplace as the preferred material of choice. The AISI also plays a lead role in the development and application of new steel and steelmaking technology. The AISI is comprised of 23 member companies, including integrated and electric furnace steelmakers, and approximately 125 associate members who are suppliers to or customers of the steel industry.

American Society of Metals International

http://www.asminternational.org

As indicated on the website, "ASM International is a materials science and engineering society for materials users, producers, and manufacturers." ASM International has 30,000 members worldwide. The ASM is a prolific publisher of journals, magazines, books, handbooks, and data sheets. Also made available are databases of peer-reviewed material, including the ASM Alloy Center Database. The ASM Handbooks Online, considered an industry standard, is a comprehensive source of information on ferrous metals, non-ferrous metals, and materials technology with over 25,000 pages of articles, illustrations, tables, graphs, specifications, and practical examples.

Association for Iron and Steel Technology

http://www.aist.org

The Association for Iron and Steel Technology (AIST) is a non-profit organization with 16,000 members from more than 70 countries. *Iron & Steel Technology*, the AIST's monthly publication, provides information on breakthroughs in equipment, processes, and operating practices in the international iron and steelmaking industry. The AIST's Digital Library is a comprehensive source for iron and steel research for members.

Metals Service Center Institute

https://www.msci.org

The Metals Service Center Institute (MSCI) is a metals trade association that offers networking opportunities, education, advocacy, and research. There are five types of research offered: Metals Activity Reports, Metal Tendencies, Executive Chart Book, Compensation Surveys, and Safety Surveys. The *Metal Activity Report* is a monthly report on metals service shipments and inventories and can be used to manage multiple product categories in carbon steel, stainless, copper and brass, and aluminum.

Minor Metals Trade Association

http://www.mmta.co.uk

As stated on the website, "The Minor Metals Trade Association (MMTA) is a not-for-profit organization, with membership comprised of companies actively involved in all aspects of the international minor metals sector." The MMTA Resource Center provides information about the minor metals, and there are sections covering warehouse and arbitration procedures.

World Steel Association

http://www.worldsteel.org

The World Steel Association, formerly the International Iron and Steel Institute, represents "approximately 170 steel producers, national and regional steel industry associations, and steel-research institutes." Worldsteel members represent about 85 percent of world steel production. The association's website is a wealth of information about the industry, including statistics on production. Steel topic pages cover: Safety and Health, Economics, Sustainability, Automotive Steel, Technology, and Construction, to name a few.

REFERENCES

1. "Mining, Minerals, Metals: Background," *globalEDGE*, Michigan State University, Accessed April 4, 2014, http://globaledge.msu.edu/industries/mining--minerals--metals/background.
2. "Mining 101," *Mining Journal*, Accessed April 4, 2014, http://www.mining-journal.com/knowledge/Mining-101.
3. "Mining, Minerals, Metals: Background."
4. *Ibid.*

25

PLASTICS

A *plastic* is "a type of synthetic or man-made polymer; similar in many ways to natural resins found in trees and other plants."[1] The plastics industry is the third largest manufacturing industry in the United States.[2] Because polymer manufacturing is a sector of the petrochemical and chemical industries, a polymer producer is likely to be the division of a bigger petrochemical or chemical company.[3]

Due to an increase in the production of shale oil and gas as a result of the fracking boom, the plastics industry is anticipating growth after the 2008 economic downturn. "Resin manufacturers are taking advantage of increased oil and gas output to boost their production capacity for ethane and ethylene, a crucial component for polyethylene and PVC plastics.... oil and gas production will help the plastics industry grow through an increase in materials, processing and finished goods exports."[4] For quick analysis, the resources covered in this chapter are listed in Table 25.1.

BACKGROUND INFORMATION

IAPD Introduction to Plastics, 11th ed.

http://www.iapd.org

The International Association of Plastics Distribution (IAPD) publishes *Introduction to Plastics,* which is a reference book intended for both novice and experienced industry professionals. IAPD publishes many helpful resources including a Buyer's Guide and *IAPD Magazine.* The websites' Resource Center is an excellent gateway to articles, books, webinars, and certification information.

Table 25.1 Resources—plastics

RESOURCES—PLASTICS	Market Analysis/ Trends	Pricing	Daily/Weekly Market News	Networking/ Industry Education	Supplier Identification	Background Information	Open (Free) Access	Mixed Fee and Free Access
American Chemistry Council - Plastics Division	✓			✓		✓		✓
IAPD	✓			✓	✓	✓		✓
ICIS Plastics Resources	✓	✓						
IHS Plastics and Polymers	✓	✓						
Manufacturers Association for Plastics Processors	✓	✓		✓				✓
Mel Ettenson's Global Plastics Letter	✓	✓						
ThePlasticsExchange.com	✓	✓						✓
Plastics News	✓	✓	✓		✓			✓
Plastics Technology	✓	✓	✓		✓		✓	
Plastics Today	✓	✓	✓		✓			✓
SPI: The Plastics Industry Trade Association	✓	✓	✓	✓	✓	✓		✓
Strategic Management for the Plastics Industry	✓					✓		
ThomasNet.com Plastics					✓		✓	

SPI: The Plastics Industry Trade Association Glossary

http://www.plasticsindustry.org/AboutPlastics

The option for access to the *SPI: Plastics Industry Trade Association Glossary* is on the "About Plastics" page of the SPI: Plastics Industry Trade Association's website. This glossary provides encyclopedic-type entries for more than 30 resins.

Strategic Management for the Plastics Industry: Dealing with Globalization and Sustainability, 2nd ed.

Roger F. Jones
Boca Raton, FL: Taylor & Francis Group/CRC Press, 2013

Even though this book is focused on exploring the management of segments of the plastics industry, it provides excellent background information in an easy to read format. The author, Roger F. Jones, has more than 55 years of experience in the plastics industry.

"Plastics 101"

Plastics Division, American Chemistry Council

http://plastics.americanchemistry.com/Education-Resources/Plastics-101

The "Plastics 101" section of the website educates about plastics basics, its many uses, and how plastics are made.

SUPPLIER IDENTIFICATION

Plastics News Directory

http://www.plasticsnewsdirectory.com

The *Plastics News Directory* allows you to search or browse for Plastics Processors, Plastics Equipment, and Materials. Start your search by browsing these subcategories: Auxiliary Equipment Suppliers, Blow Molding, Extruders, Injection Molding, Materials Suppliers Plastics Industry Services, Plastics Processors, and Primary Equipment Suppliers.

Plastics Today SourceBook

http://www.plasticstoday.com/supplierdirectory/sourcebook

At the *Plastics Today SourceBook* website, you can search by company, state, country, and/or product keyword, or browse via these categories: Auxiliary

Equipment and Computer, Compound Ingredients, Mold and Die, Primary Processing Machinery, Resins and Compounds, Semi-finished Material/Services, and Supplies.

Plastics Technology Suppliers

http://www.ptonline.com/suppliers

This supplier directory allows you to search by company name or product category, or browse within the following main categories: Auxiliary Equipment, Components and Supplies, Chemicals and Additives, Major Processing Equipment, Materials, and Specialized Services.

SPI Plastics365 Suppliers Directory

http://plasticssuppliersdirectory.com

Search or browse the *SPI Plastics365 Suppliers Directory* by using its category options, such as: Auxiliary Equipment, Chemicals/Additives/Masterbatches, Components, Decorating/Finishing, Molds/Dies/Tooling, Primary Processing Equipment, and Resins/Compounds—Thermoplastics and Thermosets.

ThomasNet.com—Plastics

http://www.thomasnet.com/browse/plastics-rubber-1.html

In this *ThomasNet.com* directory, there are 14 main categories listed for Plastics and Rubber: Elastomers, Fibre, Latex, Plastic Materials, Plastics, Rubber, and Rubber Goods. Each category is then divided into subcategories.

PRICING AND MARKET ANALYSIS

ICIS Plastics Resources

http://www.icis.com/resources/chemicals/plastics

A division of Reed Business Information, ICIS is a petrochemical market information provider that offers pricing data, news, analysis, and consulting. Resources specific to plastics are highlighted on this website, and include the latest featured content. ICIS is also covered in Chapter 22, Chemicals, and Chapter 23, Energy.

IHS Plastics and Polymers

http://www.ihs.com/products/chemical/market/plastics-polymers/index.aspx

IHS Chemical provides market advisory services covering plastics and polymers. Weekly and/or monthly reports contain near-term market pricing and other analysis. IHS is also covered in Chapter 22, Chemicals, and Chapter 23, Energy.

Plastics News Resins Pricing

http://www.plasticsnews.com/resin

Current Plastics Resins pricing is available for Commodity TPs, High-Temp TPs, Thermosets, and Recycled Plastics. Historical prices are also available, but a subscription is required for access.

ThePlasticsExchange.com

http://www.theplasticsexchange.com

The Plastics Exchange is a marketplace for buying and selling domestic and international commodity grade resin. The weekly Market Update reports can be accessed on the Research tab.

The Resin Review and Resin Reports

http://www.americanchemistry.com/Jobs/EconomicStatistics/Plastics-Statistics

The Resin Review, published annually by the American Chemistry Council provides statistical measurements of the North American plastic resins industry. Other resin reports, available via subscription include: *Monthly Production and Sales, Monthly Preliminary Production and Sales, Capacity Reports, Inventory Reports,* and *Major Markets.*

Mel Ettenson's *Global Plastics Letter*

http://www.globalplasticsletter.com

This monthly newsletter by author Mel Ettenson, provides pricing trends, news, and insights on plastics, sheet, rod, tube, and film, based on consolidated information from 88 plastics resources.

MARKET RESEARCH PROVIDERS THAT COVER PLASTICS INDUSTRY MARKETS

Market research providers are listed in Chapter 10, Industry and Market Research. The market research providers which best cover the plastics industry are Euromonitor International, BCC Research, and IBISWorld.

PUBLICATIONS

Plastics News

http://www.plasticsnews.com

Plastics News is a weekly newspaper that serves the global plastics industry. The website provides free industry rankings. The Data Store lists available reports and they are comprehensive and current. Market View, Outlook, and Full Ranking reports are available for: Automotive/Transportation, Blow Molding, Compounding, Construction, Extrusion, Film and Sheet, Injection Molding, Medical, Molds/Tooling, Packaging, Rotomolding, Recycling, Thermoforming, and other Resin Reports.

Plastics Today

http://www.plasticstoday.com

Plastics Today is a global community for plastics processing professionals with editorial, vendor-supplied, and user-generated articles and information.

Plastics Technology

http://www.ptonline.com

This publication and website for *Plastics Technology* focuses on plastics processing and covers problem solving, tips and techniques, best practices, and new technology. There is a wealth of open access information via the "Zones" or the Knowledge Centers. The *Resin Prices*, *Market Watch*, and *Processor's Business Index* reports are updated monthly. Gardner Business Media, the publisher of *Plastics Technology*, provides many other high-quality manufacturing publications.

ASSOCIATIONS AND ORGANIZATIONS

Manufacturers Association for Plastics Processors

http://www.mappinc.com

For members, the Manufacturers Association for Plastics Processors (MAPP) provides plastics processing training, networking opportunities, cost reduction programs, and benchmarking statistics, in addition to annual industry reports. *State of the Plastics Industry ... the Processors' Perspective,* and the *Plastics Industry Economic Study,* are two of the reports available.

SPI: The Plastics Industry Trade Association

http://www.plasticsindustry.org

SPI: The Plastics Industry Trade Association delivers advocacy and market research to all professionals in the plastics industry. The e-Store is where you can purchase published reports, such as *Size Impact of Plastics Industry on US Economy* and SPI's *Annual Global Trends* study.

The Plastics Division of the American Chemistry Council

http://plastics.americanchemistry.com

The Plastics Division of the American Chemistry Council (ACC) represents leading manufacturers of plastic resins. Sections of interest on the website include: Product Groups, Product Teams, Sustainability and Recycling, Education and Resources, and Plastics Statistics.

REFERENCES

1. "Life Cycle of a Plastic Product," *American Chemistry Council,* Accessed June 11, 2014, http://plastics.americanchemistry.com/Life-Cycle.
2. "Fast Facts," *SPI: The Plastics Industry Trade Association,* Accessed June 10, 2014, http://www.plasticsindustry.org/aboutplastics.
3. Roger F. Jones, *Strategic Management for the Plastics Industry: Dealing with Globalization and Sustainability,* Boca Raton, FL: CRC, 2013, Accessed June 10, 2014, http://books.google.com.
4. "Plastics Industry Expects Drop in Raw Materials Costs with Shale Production Boom," *The Strategic Sourceror,* November 18, 2013, http://www.strategicsourceror.com/2013/11/plastics-industry-expects-drop-in-raw.html.

26

CONTINGENT LABOR AND PROFESSIONAL SERVICES

The use of contingent labor is a growing trend that is projected to continue to grow in response to shifting staffing requirements and the overhead costs of full hire benefits. Many times, especially in technology-driven organizations, hiring needs are immediate and short term, as opposed to long term and full time.[1] Temporary and/or contingent staffing is used mostly in the areas of Office/clerical, Industrial, Information Technology, Healthcare, Engineering, and Finance and Accounting.[2]

The major challenges for managing this category are tracking spend and large numbers of contingent workers, in addition to finding workers with the correct skills and certifications to meet the needs of appropriate projects and jobs. Tools and services to help with these challenges include the use of vendor management systems (VMS) and managed service providers (MSP). Seventy-three percent of large companies have a VMS, and 58 percent have an MSP in place.[3] For quick analysis, the resources covered in this chapter are shown in Table 26.1.

Although the contingent workforce is a growing area of spend managed by procurement, services may also be acquired from consultants or through outsourcing arrangements. The pricing structure will be different in each case. Contingent workforce agreements are usually based on an hourly "cost plus" arrangement per position. Consulting engagements are often based on an overall fee associated with a specific set of deliverables or milestone accomplishments.

Outsourcing agreements may include elements of both contingent workforce and consulting, but because the responsibility for the associated function is being handed off to a third party, procurement must be careful to ensure that the key performance indicators and basis for compensation motivate the right outcomes,

Table 26.1 Resources—contingent labor/professional services

RESOURCES—CONTINGENT LABOR/PROF SER	Market Analysis/ Trends	Fees/ Rates	Daily/Weekly Market News	Networking/ Industry Education	Supplier Identification	Background Information	Open (Free) Access	Mixed Fee and Free Access
American Staffing Association	✓	✓	✓	✓	✓	✓		✓
Bureau of Labor Statistics	✓	✓					✓	
CompTIA	✓			✓				✓
Consulting Magazine	✓		✓		✓		✓	
Contingent Workforce Index (CWI)	✓	✓					✓	
Contingent Workforce Professionals	✓		✓	✓			✓	
HRO Today	✓		✓		✓			✓
Kennedy Consulting Research and Advisory	✓	✓			✓			✓
Plunkett Research - Consulting Introduction	✓					✓		
Society for Human Resource Management	✓	✓	✓	✓				✓
Staffing Industry Analysts	✓	✓	✓		✓	✓		✓
Towers Watson Data Services	✓	✓						
WageWatch	✓	✓						
Workforce.com	✓						✓	

rather than inadvertently rewarding an inefficiently high number of transactions or cycles.

BACKGROUND INFORMATION

Contingent Workforce Lexicon of Terms

http://www.staffingindustry.com/Research-Publications/Resources

The *Contingent Workforce Lexicon of Terms* is provided by Staffing Industry Analysts (SIA) to ensure that a common language is used among professionals in the industry. As stated on SIA's website, "A lack of common definitions can cause severe communication problems between program managers and suppliers or when benchmarking contingent workforce programs across organizations."

Plunkett's Introduction to the Consulting Industry

http://www.plunkettresearch.com/consulting-market-research/industry-and-business-data

The Introduction to the Consulting Industry is the landing page for Plunkett's Consulting Industry Market Research, providing an excellent introduction to the consulting industry.

SUPPLIER IDENTIFICATION

Supplier identification information can be located in various reports and directories from the American Staffing Association, *Consulting* magazine, *HRO Today* magazine, Kennedy Consulting, and Staffing Industry Analysts. Details for these resources are given below.

FEES, RATES, AND MARKET ANALYSIS

American Staffing Association (ASA) Staffing Index

http://www.americanstaffing.net/statistics/staffing_index.cfm

As described on its website, "The ASA Staffing Index tracks weekly changes in temporary and contract employment and provides a near real-time gauge of staffing industry employment and overall economic activity."

Bureau of Labor Statistics (BLS)—Current Employment Statistics

http://www.bls.gov/ces

Located on the Current Employment Statistics (CES) website are monthly statistics on employment, hours, and earnings of workers on non-farm payrolls. To get updated earnings information, search the "Employment, Hours, and Earnings—National" database. Select the data search option, which is in the CES Databases section.

Bureau of Labor Statistics—Employer Costs for Employee Compensation

http://www.bls.gov/ncs/ect

At the Bureau of Labor Statistic website, select the "Employer Costs for Employee Compensation" option. Here, you can find employer costs per hour worked for employee compensation, and costs as a percent of total compensation. Note the various tables available, for example, "Private industry workers, by occupational group and full-time and part-time status."

Bureau of Labor Statistics—Wage Data by Area and Occupation

http://www.bls.gov/bls/blswage.htm

At the Bureau of Labor Statistics website, you can get national hourly and annual wage data for more than 800 occupations and 400 industries, in addition to regional, state, and metropolitan area data.

Contingent Workforce Index Global Analysis

http://tapfin.com/tapfin-en/Home/Thought+Leadership/White+Papers

The Contingent Workforce Index (CWI), by TAPFIN/ManpowerGroup, compares local labor markets around the globe, and measures the likelihood of identifying and accessing contingent workers. Countries are ranked in descending order by availability, cost, regulation, and productivity of contingent workers.

Kennedy Consulting Research and Advisory

http://www.kennedyinfo.com/consulting

Kennedy Consulting Research and Advisory is a market intelligence provider for buyers and sellers of management and IT consulting services. Research covers market trends, demand drivers and inhibitors, spending projections, and market share. The *Fees & Utilization Rates in Consulting* is a series that provides current and forecasted book rates, realized rates, utilization rates, and engagement size data on various size consulting firms. The *Kennedy Consulting Research & Advisory Wire* is a free e-newsletter on the latest market trends.

Other Salary and Wage Resources

http://www.staffingindustry.com/Research-Publications/Blogs/Subadhra-Sriram-s-Blog/Are-You-Paying-Right

Are You Paying Right?

Subadhra Sriram, Editorial Director of Staffing Industry Analysts (SIA), reviews various free salary and wage information sources, and reports the ones that provide reliable information. The data is based on W-2 workers and can be used as a "starting point for estimating the right contingent pay."[4]

Staffing Industry Analysts

http://www.staffingindustry.com

Staffing Industry Analysts (SIA) is a global research firm that serves buyers of staffing services and those responsible for managing their company's contingent workforce program. The research coverage is detailed and comprehensive. Research topics include: Growth, Market Sizes, and Forecasts; Margins, Pay and Bill Rates, and Fees; Operational Metrics and Best Practices; Staffing—Healthcare, Commercial, and Information Technology; and Legal, Legislative, and Regulatory, to name a few. The *Staffing Industry Report* is now part of the monthly Staffing Industry Report Webinars, which cover economic and market trends. Free newsletters offered are *CWS Global Daily News* and *CWS 3.0. Contingent Workforce Strategies. IT Staffing Report,* also free to access, is published monthly for suppliers of staffing services. Staffing Industry Analysts Certified Contingent Workforce Professional (CCWP) is an accreditation program designed for HR, procurement, solution providers, and others who manage corporate contingent/temporary staffing. A corporate membership is required for the webinars, proprietary tools and research, and access to advisory services and the peer network.

Towers Watson Data Services

https://www.twdataservices.com

Towers Watson Data Services provides data that allows you to analyze compensation trends via different countries, industry sectors and employee groups. Sectors covered are: General Industry, Energy, Financial Services, High Tech, Media, Pharmaceutical/Heath Services, and Retail.

WageWatch

http://www.wagewatch.com

WageWatch provides compensation, wage, and salary surveys for multiple industries with data from employers in more than 108 markets. As stated on the website, "Over 4,500 associations, businesses, companies, franchises, non-profits, organizations, locations and management companies provide compensation, salary and wage data for over one million employees in hourly and salaried positions each year."

PUBLICATIONS

Consulting Magazine

http://www.consultingmag.com

Consulting is a monthly digital publication that provides news, thought leadership, and industry intelligence. Annual features of interest include: "Best Firms to Work For," "Top 25 Consultants," and "Women in Consulting Awards." Articles are organized by service line and client industry.

HRO Today Magazine

http://www.hrotoday.com

HRO Today is an online magazine that focuses on HR operations and outsourcing. It provides news, analysis, and the Baker's Dozen customer satisfaction ratings, which are based solely on feedback from buyers of the rated services. There is an annual ranking for Contingent Labor/Managed Service Providers (MSP). On the website, there is a Contingent Labor/MSP page that provides news and research. The magazine is subscription based, but the Baker's Dozen lists are free to access.

Workforce.com

http://www.workforce.com/topics/105-contingent-staffing

At *Workforce.com*, you can read articles specifically about contingent labor.

ASSOCIATIONS AND ORGANIZATIONS

American Staffing Association

http://www.americanstaffing.net

The American Staffing Association (ASA) represents the U.S. staffing, recruiting, and workforce solutions industry, and publishes research reports that are filled with statistics. Data and research reports provided by the ASA are: *ASA Annual Economic Analysis of the Industry, ASA Staffing Index Weekly Report, ASA Staffing Employee Survey, Staffing Industry Compensation Survey, ASA Sector Benchmarking Survey*, and Fact Sheets. The directory helps in finding a staffing company partner.

CompTIA

http://www.comptia.org

CompTIA is an Information Technology (IT) trade association that offers certifications, business credentials, and research resources. CompTIA has four IT certification series, ranging from beginner to expert: Mastery, Professional, Specialty, and Basic. These certifications are often recommended or required by leading technology companies.

Contingent Workforce Professionals

http://cwprofessionals.org

Contingent Workforce Professionals (CWP) is a national membership association for high-level professionals working in Human Resources, Procurement, and Risk/Compliance fields, related to Contingent Workforce. CWP operates across all industry segments, and offers networking opportunities for sharing best practices and emerging trends. Membership is free.

Society for Human Resource Management

https://www.shrm.org

The Society for Human Resource Management (SHRM) is the world's largest HR membership organization and is devoted to human resource management. The Contingent Staffing page is found under Staffing Management, once you click on the "HR Topics and Strategy" tab. The society publishes *HR Magazine*. The SHRM Compensation Data Center offers customized salary information for multiple jobs. Also offered is the SHRM *Leading Indicators of National Employment* monthly report, in addition to various workplace trends and forecasting reports.

REFERENCES

1. Joslyn Faust, "Surveying the New World of Work," *Tower Lane Consulting*, 2013, https://www.elance.com/q/sites/default/files/docs/ptc/Tower-Lane-Elance.pdf.
2. "Setting Sail for Contingent Workforce Growth," *Staffing Industry Analysts*, January 14, 2014, http://www.staffingindustry.com/Research-Publications/Publications/CWS-3.0/January-22-2014/CW-Growth-2014.
3. *Ibid.*
4. Sriram, Subadhra, "Are You Paying Right?" *Staffing Industry Analysts*, January 7, 2014. http://www.staffingindustry.com/Research-Publications/Blogs/Subadhra-Sriram-s-Blog/Are-You-Paying-Right.

27

INFORMATION TECHNOLOGY

"Technology—information or otherwise—has always been a tough subject to discuss, to explain, to comprehend, to predict, and most important, to buy. Why is that? One reason is that it is very difficult to predict its usefulness, longevity, or value over time."[1] IT procurement can be described in one word: *complex*. Buyers struggle with commodity price volatility, complicated and lengthy contracts, and the challenge of keeping up with new advances in technology. Add this to a sometimes contentious relationship between procurement and IT, and the complexity only rises.

The fear of investing in the wrong technology or service is very real because the consequences can be dire for the organization, both strategically and financially. The importance of the IT spend category, which includes software, hardware, services, and telecommunications, cannot be overstated, as it plays a crucial role in implementing the strategy for building a competitive advantage. With this category of spend being so critical, research of resources needs to be analyzed and conducted carefully for content that is independent, current, and authoritative.

BACKGROUND INFORMATION

Gartner IT Glossary

http://www.gartner.com/it-glossary

In the *Gartner IT Glossary,* you can explore IT technology terms and definitions by using the search bar or browsing terms that are listed alphabetically.

Safari Books Online

http://www.safaribooksonline.com

Safari Books Online is a "digital IT-focused library providing on-demand subscription access to thousands of learning resources." You can access current, high-quality books provided by well-known publishers, and video courses on the latest technology topics. To find needed information, you can search across all books in the library. Individual and enterprise subscriptions are available. Many university and public libraries provide this resource as well.

ANALYST AND RESEARCH FIRMS

451 Research

https://451research.com

The name of this company, 451 Research, is inspired by the Ray Bradbury novel, *Fahrenheit 451*.[2] 451 Research "focuses on the business of enterprise IT innovation." Current 451 Research practice areas include: CloudScape, Datacenter Technologies, Eco-Efficient IT, Enterprise Security, Internet Infrastructure Services, Infrastructure Computing for Enterprise, Information Management, and Multi-Tenant Datacenter. The parent company, 451 Group, purchased well-known global connectivity and mobile research provider Yankee Group in 2013.

Aberdeen Group

http://www.aberdeen.com

Aberdeen Group's research covers 16 different B2B technology disciplines. Membership and content is open access. Research categories include: Analytics and Business Intelligence, Business Planning and Execution, Enterprise Mobility and Collaboration, Financial Management and GRC, Global Supply Management, Information Technology, Manufacturing, Marketing Effectiveness and Strategy, and Supply Chain Management, to name a few.

Computer Economics

http://www.computereconomics.com

Computer Economics provides metrics, research, and advisory services for IT management. The annual *IT Spending and Staffing Benchmarks* study is an important source of IT spending data, IT staffing benchmarks, and related metrics across multiple industries and government sectors. The IT valuations database provides data on vendor pricing and discounting practices, current fair market values, and residual value forecasts for computer hardware. Computer Economics publishes *Computer Economics Report*, which is a monthly journal, and also offers consulting services. Research can be accessed through subscription, or reports can be purchased separately. There is some free research available on the website.

Everest Group

http://www.everestgrp.com

Everest Group specializes in global services and provides information on BPO (Business Process Outsourcing), ITO (Information Technology Outsourcing), locations, and Global In-house Centers (GICs). Research areas include: Market Vista; Banking, Financial Services, and Insurance Outsourcing—BPO and ITO; Healthcare; Information Technology; Finance and Accounting; Procurement; Human Resources; Contact Center; and Recruitment Process Outsourcing. Other research includes Service Provider Intelligence, Global Sourcing, Cloud Vista; and PricePoint, which identifies trends in the pricing of ITO (ADM and Infrastructure) and BPO (voice and non-voice).

Forrester

http://www.forrester.com

Forrester is a big player in the IT industry analyst world. It was founded in 1983 and is a global research and advisory firm focused on servicing clients based on their professional role. Professional roles fall under three main categories: Technology Management, Marketing and Strategy, and Technology Industry. Sourcing and Vendor Management is a role in the Technology Management Professional category. The research Playbooks are integrated reports, tools, and guidance organized in a framework, specific to professional role, to help with critical initiatives. Forrester is known for "The Forrester Wave," which is a graphic that illustrates competing products and suppliers. Forrester also provides access to subject-matter expert analysts, custom consulting, events, online communities, and peer-to-peer executive programs. Forrester is subscription-based, but you can purchase reports separately.

Frost & Sullivan

www.frost.com

Frost & Sullivan refers to itself as a growth partnership company and covers multiple industries (also described in Chapter 10, Industry and Market Research). The company was founded in 1961, and initially analyzed emerging technologies. Its

Information & Communication Technologies practice provides analysis, strategy consulting, market forecasts, and insights that cover the areas of enterprise communications, communication services, conferencing and collaboration, mobile and wireless, space and communications, IT applications and services, network security, contact centers, and kiosks and retail systems markets. The service is subscription-based, and their reports can be purchased separately.

Gartner

https://www.gartner.com

Gartner is the most dominant analyst firm in the IT space. Gideon Gartner founded the company in 1979 with the idea "to go way beyond market research and to really help people in [the] decision making."[3] Gartner is famous for its "Magic Quadrant," a visual graphic that positions competing players in the major technology markets. Gartner's IT spending forecasts are popular, as are their heavily attended technology events and symposiums, where analysts present their research and predictions. Gartner offers these products and services: analysis and advice research, independent contract review, spending and staffing metrics data, peer networking opportunities, consulting, and access to expert analysts. Gartner does have research services for supply chain leaders and enterprise supply chain leaders. Most services and research reports are subscription-based, but free research is offered, and some reports can be purchased on a one-off basis.

Gigaom

http://gigaom.com

Founded in 2006, Gigaom focuses on emerging technologies, and helps clients "better understand major technology disruptions and the new business opportunities they create." Gigaom research provides analyst access and analysis, and content, for individual and corporate subscribers. The blog, featured on the homepage, provides comprehensive, frequently updated news and analysis posts, covering the areas of Apple, cleantech, cloud, data, Europe, media, and mobile. "Buyer's Lens" is a research area that focuses on the impact of emerging technology on IT and business technology buyers.

HfS Research

http://www.hfsresearch.com

HfS Research is an analyst firm that covers global business services and the outsourcing industry. The published research can be filtered by Initiative and Topic.

Examples of Initiative categories include Business Process Outsourcing (BPO), Information Technology Services, and Vendor Performance Evaluation. Examples of Topic categories include Application Outsourcing; contracts, negotiations, and pricing; and location analysis. The Vendor Intelligence Services provide research and financial performance data of the leading service providers. PriceIndicator provides short-, long-term, or transitional outsourcing price data for industries and services, including BPO and ADM (Application, Development, and Maintenance). The Provider Capability Blueprint (PCB) is the research methodology used to evaluate service provider marketplaces. HfS also offers advisory services, events, and the excellent "Horses for Sources" blog. Services are mostly fee-based. Research is both free and fee-based.

IDC

https://www.idc.com

IDC is a provider of market intelligence and advisory services for the information technology, telecommunications, and consumer technology markets. IDC covers multiple industries including: Energy, Financial, Government, Health, Manufacturing, and Retail. IT procurement tools specifically offered to aid with purchasing decisions are: SmartFMV, SmartAnalysis, SmartBuy, and SmartIndex. SmartAnalysis provides peer pricing benchmarks and cost management insights; SmartIndex is a customized, third-party, price benchmarking service; SmartFMV (Fair Market Value) service establishes financial terms for used IT hardware acquisitions; and SmartBuy provides a benchmark to chart your price position. IDC is subscription-based, and you can purchase published reports separately.

Ovum

http://ovum.com

Ovum provides technology research and analysis covering these industries: Consumer Impact, Education, Energy and Utilities, Financial Markets, Government, Healthcare, Insurance, Life Sciences, Media, Oil and Gas, Retail Banking, Telco IT, IT Services, and Software. Specific telecom topics include Components, Devices and Platforms, Enterprise, Emerging Markets, Network Infrastructure, and Policy and Regulations, to name a few. The "Trends to Watch" series explains the trends that will have the greatest impact. You can purchase many reports individually.

Spend Matters: Procurement Technology

http://spendmatters.com

Spend Matters covers technology issues, products, and services relevant to procurement professionals with information that is comprehensive and current. Technology provider analysis is done purely from a procurement point of view. The volume and high quality of news and analysis is impressive, and Spend Matters has a knack for having the pulse on what is important at the moment. Membership level pricing is flexible and reasonable.

RESOURCES THAT ANALYZE THE ANALYSTS

Influencer Relations

http://www.analystequity.com

Duncan Chapple helps clients "use thought leadership and competitive analysis to influence customers, channel partners, and third-party advisors, such as analysts, advisors, and consultants." Chapple writes posts for his blog about IT analysts and the influence they carry. Many of his posts provide helpful insights about the firms. Published annually is the *Analyst Value Survey*, which focuses on analyst independence, and shows the opinions of more than 350 users of analyst research.

Institute of Industry Analyst Relations

http://analystrelations.org

The Institute of Industry Analyst Relations (IIAR) is a not-for-profit organization that raises "awareness of analyst relations and the value of industry analysts." The posts are positive in nature, and written with the intent of aiding communication between analysts and vendors. There are informative nuggets to be gleaned about the firms, and the IIAR awards *Analyst of the Year* and *Analyst Firm of the Year* designations.

Outsell

http://www.outsellinc.net

Outsell is an analyst firm that covers the information industry, including the IT industry analyst space. They occasionally write reports that cover the IT research market (size, share, forecast, and trends).

INDUSTRY-SPECIFIC IT PUBLICATIONS

These publications provide valuable IT information on specific industries, for example: *Bank Systems & Technology, Campus Technology, Constructech, Consumer Goods Technology, Government Technology, Hospitality Technology, Healthcare Informatics, Healthcare IT News, Insurance & Technology, Manufacturing & Logistics IT Magazine, Manufacturing Business Technology, Retail Technology Review, Retail Info Systems (RIS) News, Wall Street & Technology Magazine.*

CROWDSOURCED AND OPEN SOURCE COMMUNITIES

"Peer analysis. Crowdsourced knowledge. User-generated content. Community-based research platform." These are some of the terms used to describe a new generation of IT research startups. This generation is introducing a model that goes against the current IT research/analyst model used by Gartner, Forrester, and others. This model centers on the concept of reviews coming from professionals who are currently using the technologies in enterprise environments and have experience with them. The reviews are intended to be unbiased. Some companies and communities to consider as resources are: G2 Crowd, IT Central Station, Ombud, BestVendor, and Wikibon.

GENERAL IT PUBLICATIONS AND WEBSITES

Baseline Magazine

http://www.baselinemag.com

With the tag line, "Driving Business Success with Technology," both *Baseline* magazine and the website focus on providing information that helps business and technology managers and executives achieve business and IT goals, and improve the ROI for technology investments.

CIO

http://www.cio.com

CIO is a critical publication that covers all areas involved with IT decision making. Two focus topics of interest are Supply Chain Management and Outsourcing. For outsourcing, you can find news, best practices, how-tos, and discussions on vendor management, contract negotiation, and service level agreements (SLAs).

Computerworld

http://www.computerworld.com

Computerworld is a technology news and information industry standard that has been around for more than 40 years. *Computerworld's* website and print publication are some of the best sources for news and technology reviews. IT verticals that are featured are: Financial, Government, and Healthcare. Topic areas include Applications, Cloud Computing, Hardware, Management, and Networking, to name a few.

International Computer Negotiations—Do Better Deals

http://www.dobetterdeals.com/index.htm

International Computer Negotiations (ICN) provides best practices in the areas of sourcing, procurement, and vendor management, specific to IT professionals. ICN provides documentation on licensing, user form contracts, templates, checklists, and "Tips and Tactics" articles.

InformationWeek

http://www.informationweek.com

InformationWeek organizes its high-quality information around these sharing communities: Strategic CIO, Software, Cloud, Mobile, Big Data, Security, Infrastructure, Government, and Healthcare. It is geared for IT buyers and decision makers who need to learn about new products and trends.

InfoWorld

http://www.infoworld.com

InfoWorld focuses on emerging enterprise technologies. The InfoWorld Test Center provides enterprise hardware and software reviews. Information is organized around technology channels and topic centers. Additionally, there are white papers, webcasts, and deep dives, which are in-depth reports from editors.

Knowledge@Wharton—Technology

https://knowledge.wharton.upenn.edu/topic/technology

Knowledge@Wharton is the online business journal of the Wharton School of the University of Pennsylvania. This is one of the best business sites on the Internet because it consistently taps into the most important trends and concerns with writing that offers practical and strategic analysis.

Network World

http://www.networkworld.com

Covered in *Network World* is information about enterprise network products, services, and issues and trends for network IT managers and executives. Topics include: Security, LANs/WANs, UC/VoIP, Cloud, Infrastructure, Wireless, Software, and Data Center. There are Cisco, Microsoft, and Open Source communities.

Sloan Management Review—Technology

Massachusetts Institute of Technology (MIT)

http://sloanreview.mit.edu/topic/technology

The Sloan Management Review, published by MIT, is an influential management research publication. It covers organizational, technological, and societal changes, and the opportunities they bring. Technology topic areas are: Digital Business, IT Governance and Leadership, IT Strategy, and IT Implementation. Site membership allows for two free articles per month.

Network Computing

http://www.networkcomputing.com

Network Computing provides analysis on new and emerging infrastructure technologies, advice on implementation and operations, and strategies for improving skills. Its affiliated conference, Interop, offers attendees information on next-generation networks, data centers, storage systems, communications, and cloud architectures.

GENERAL IT BLOGS

In addition to the blogs that accompany the resources listed above, the following blogs are additional ones to consider reading.

Ars Technica

http://arstechnica.com

Ars Technica is a name that is derived from the Latin terms for the "art of technology." It is a source for "technology news, tech policy analysis, breakdowns of the latest scientific advancements, gadget reviews, software, hardware, and nearly everything else found in between layers of silicon."

Enterprise Irregulars

http://www.enterpriseirregulars.com

The Enterprise Irregulars are "a diverse group of practitioners, consultants, investors, journalists, analysts, and full-time bloggers who share a common passion—enterprise technology and its application to business in the 21st century." The Irregulars provide a unique "in the trenches" analysis about topics in which they are experts.

A Passion for Research Blog

http://softwarestrategiesblog.com

Professor and founder of Software Strategies Research, Louis Columbus, writes this excellent blog that focuses on CRM, cloud computing, ERP, and enterprise software. Columbus writes posts that are analytical, and filled with statistics and graphs. His "Roundup" posts on free cloud computing online courses, cloud computing forecasts, and cloud computing and enterprise software predictions are particularly helpful in understanding those topics. The Cloud Learning Center is full of e-books, infographics, presentations, and videos. The Cloud Computing Index tracks various company stock prices over time.

IT ASSOCIATIONS AND ORGANIZATIONS

Association for Computing Machinery

http://www.acm.org

The ACM was established in 1947 and is a widely recognized organization for computing professionals. The ACM serves members with its well-known journals and magazines, conferences, workshops, and electronic forums. The Learning Center provides access to computing e-books (Safari Books Online and Books24/7), Skillsoft online courses, and Tech Packs on Cloud Computing, Enterprise Architecture, Mobility, Security, and Business Intelligence/Data Management.

Association of Information Technology Professionals

http://www.aitp.org

The Association of Information Technology Professionals (AITP) provides a community network for IT business professionals. The association also "provides education programs for advancing technology and business skills, leadership development opportunities, networking, peer mentoring, knowledge sharing, and online resources."

CAUCUS—The Association of Technology Acquisition Professionals

http://www.caucusnet.com

CAUCUS serves "the specialized needs of the technology acquisition professional." Membership is comprised of technology acquisition professionals representing five core competencies: Procurement, Finance, Legal, IT, and Contract Management. CAUCUS offers their members a vendor-free discussion forum, document library, vendor scorecards, an education center, and advisory practice.

CompTIA

http://www.comptia.org

CompTIA is a nonprofit information technology (IT) trade association. CompTIA's membership includes "technology vendors, computer distributors, value-added resellers and solution providers, training organizations, consultants to the IT industry, and technology users." CompTIA provides research and market intelligence, and collects data from tens of thousands of end-users and IT companies on a wide range of issues that cover tech trends, channel dynamics, and the IT workforce. Research topics covered are: Big Data, Business and Economics, Channel Intelligence, Cloud Computing, Healthcare IT, IT Workforce, Managed Services, Mobility, Security, and Unified Communications. In May, 2014, CompTIA acquired TechAmerica.

REFERENCES

1. Steve Gutzman, "The Challenge of Buying Technology," International Computer Negotiations, Accessed April 22, 2014, http://www.dobetterdeals.com/articles/tips-and-tactics/2012/001.php.
2. 451 Research, "About 451 Research," *YouTube.com,* Video, 3:19, November 6, 2103, https://www.youtube.com/watch?v=WQI5YYAEhQw.
3. "Gideon Gartner on the Genesis of Gartner Group," *YouTube*.com, Video, 1:08, May 2007, http://www.youtube.com/watch?v=viRoBiMbvWE.

28

LOGISTICS

According to the American Association of Exporters and Importers (AAEI), "Few people give much thought to how a product is delivered to its final destination, but logisticians and supply chain professionals throughout history have relied on a combination of technology, creativity, and an unyielding desire to beat the competition—even if it took a herd of elephants to do it."[1]

Market intelligence plays an important part in the spend category of logistics, whether it be trade data, transportation intelligence, or warehousing best practices. The regional, national, and global shipment of goods requires understanding of the main transportation modes (air, land, and water), and the specific requirements and conditions associated with each, such as freight rate, transfer of ownership, seasonality, and capacity. Codes, regulations, and agreements are necessary resources when participating in world trade. International transportation and logistics issues are taking a front seat as globalization initiatives are increasing for both manufacturing and services. However, "even though total supply chain costs may be reduced by global sourcing, typically, transportation and logistics costs have been rising as a percentage of the cost-of-goods sold."[2]

According to the recent CSCMP *State of Logistics* report, the three main categories that make up logistics costs are "inventory carrying costs, including the costs of warehousing (33.9% of the total logistics spend), transportation costs (61.5%), and administrative costs (4.6%). Within transportation, trucking-related costs comprise 77.2% of transport costs."[3]

Another component in the complex logistics space is materials handling. The basic function of all external packaging is to identify and carry a product safely to the final user.[4] Factors significantly impacting the materials handling supplier market include industry consolidation, emerging markets, volatility of raw material prices, a desire for green packaging, and regulation escalation.[5]

The logistics spend category is large and multifaceted, and is supported by a voluminous amount of statistical and regulatory data. This information is available from global organizations, national government agencies, professional associations, and trade literature. A single chapter could be dedicated to each area that falls under the logistics umbrella, such as trade, transportation, materials handling, warehousing, and packaging. This chapter lists key representative resources for each area.

BACKGROUND INFORMATION

Glossary of Maritime Terms

American Association of Port Authorities (AAPA)

http://www.aapa-ports.org

The AAPA *Glossary of Maritime Terms* can be located in the Port Industry Information section on the website.

Dictionary of International Trade: Handbook of the Global Trade Community

World Trade Press, Petaluma, 2010

The *Dictionary of International Trade* is an invaluable resource for learning about global trade. The book is actually one-third dictionary and two-thirds encyclopedia. Important new features include: Guide to Outsourcing; Illustrated Guides to Ocean Freight and Air Freight Containers, Truck Trailers, and Railcars; and Supply Chain Security. The Resources section lists books, directories, periodicals, reports, and websites in detail.

The Handbook of Logistics and Distribution Management, 5th ed.

Alan Rushton, Phil Croucher, and Peter Baker
London; Philadelphia: Kogan Page, 2014

The *Handbook of Logistics and Distribution Management* explores the concepts of logistics and distribution, planning and logistics, procurement and inventory decisions, warehousing and storage, freight transport, and operational management.

Official Harmonized Tariff Schedule

United States International Trade Commission (USITC)

http://www.usitc.gov/tata/hts

Using the Official Harmonized Tariff Schedule, you can access the most recent online versions of the Harmonized Tariff Schedule (HTSA). It provides the applicable tariff rates and statistical categories for all merchandise imported into the United States, and is based on the international Harmonized System, the standardized coding of names and numbers for international trade. Nearly 200 countries, representing 98 percent of world trade, use the code.[6] This schedule is important for procurement professionals to use "because improperly classified products are likely to have a very difficult journey through Customs and incur additional costs."[7]

Foreign Trade—Reference Page

U.S. Census Bureau

http://www.census.gov/foreign-trade/reference/index.html

The Foreign Trade website of the U.S. Census Bureau is the official source for U.S. export and import statistics, and for issuing reporting regulations of export shipments from the United States. The Reference page provides links to help, including "how to complete all of those confusing forms."

World Trade Organization (WTO) Glossary

http://www.wto.org/english/thewto_e/glossary_e/glossary_e.htm

According to its website, the *World Trade Organization (WTO) Glossary* "is designed to help in understanding some of the terms used in the WTO and in international trade."

ICC Incoterms 2010—Short Description

http://www.iccwbo.org/products-and-services/trade-facilitation/incoterms-2010/the-incoterms-rules/

Incoterms (an abbreviation for International Commercial Terms) are a set of rules "which define the responsibilities of sellers and buyers for the delivery of goods under sales contracts." They are published by the International Chamber of Commerce (ICC) and are widely used in international commercial transactions. On the ICC Incoterms website are short descriptions of the eleven rules from the Incoterms, 2010 edition (the most recent).

Inbound Logistics Glossary of Supply Chain Terms

http://www.inboundlogistics.com/cms/logistics-glossary

Inbound Logistics Glossary of Supply Chain Terms allows you to browse for transportation, logistics, supply chain, and international trade terms.

Intermodal Glossary

Intermodal Association of North America (IANA)

https://www.intermodal.org/information/glossary.php

The *Intermodal Glossary* is comprised of terms that deal with the transfer of products, involving multiple modes of transportation, such as truck, railroad, and ocean carrier.

Packaging World Playbooks

http://www.packworld.com/playbooks

The *Playbooks* are helpful for managing and implementing packaging projects, and are intended for beginners and experienced professionals. Examples of *Playbooks* that are available: Primary Packaging Line Equipment, End-of-Line Packaging Equipment, Flexible Packaging, and Labeling, Food Safety, and Serialization.

SUPPLIER IDENTIFICATION

RailResource.com

http://www.railresource.com

RailResource.com was formed to give railroads, suppliers, and contractors a source for "critical contact and product information." The website features daily news, blogs, a searchable contact database of North American freight railroads, a buyers guide, and request-for-quote service.

Transport Topics Buyer's Guide

http://transporttopicsbuyersguide.com

You can search this trucking and freight newspaper *Buyer's Guide* by using the advanced search features or browse by category. Sample categories include: Truck

Parts/Components, Business Management Services, Cargo Handling, Information Systems, Truck Vehicles, and Safety and Security.

Buytruckload.com

http://buytruckload.com

With the goal of saving shippers money, transportation executives Sean Devine and John Labrie introduced this automated freight brokerage service. Buytruckload allows shippers to search and find prospective carriers, get instant rate quotes, and book van, flatbed, and refrigerated loads on the spot market. Carriers can be located by equipment, size, location, age, safety, authority, and more.

Inbound Logistics (Web_Cite City)

http://www.inboundlogistics.com

The "Find Solutions" section of the Inbound Logistics website offers a tool where you can designate various characteristics to match specific needs, in addition to helping you find a third-party logistics (3PL) provider, trucking company, technology company, air forwarder, and logistics school. Web_Cite City is an online guide "for an easier way to surf logistics sites without dealing with search engine infoglut." You can search or browse by over 70 categories. The Logistics Planner gives you detailed information on more than 160 logistics leaders, and the RFP/RFIs section will help with preparing your Request for Proposal list. There are also articles and news stories available.

Logistics Management Buyers' Guide

http://www.logisticsmgmt.com/guide

In the *Logistics Management Buyers' Guide,* categories that you can browse for products and services include: Air Courier, Air Freight Forwarder, Airline, Financial Services, Industry Organizations, Integrated Carrier, Intermodal Carriers, Logistics Technology, Maritime Services, Motor Carriers, Multiple Services, North America Ports, Third Party Services, and Warehouse/DC.

Material Handling & Logistics Buyer's Guide

http://directory.mhlnews.com

The *Material Handling & Logistics (MH&L) Buyers' Guide* allows you to locate key material handling and logistic suppliers and products by selecting a category or typing in a keyword.

Transportweb Directory

http://www.transportweb.com/organisations/search

The *Transportweb Directory* is a business directory that lists more than 32,000 organizations, companies, groups, and individuals involved in logistics and transportation. Transportweb members are listed in the directory, and you can search topics by keyword or location.

WERC Logistics Vendor Locator

http://logisticsvendorlocator.com/

The Warehousing Education and Research Council (WERC) offers a *Guide* that allows you to search for suppliers, which include: Business/Consulting Services, Education and Training, Facility Equipment, Warehouse Equipment, Material Handling Equipment, and Software Systems.

PRICING AND MARKET ANALYSIS

AAA Daily Fuel Gauge Report

http://fuelgaugereport.aaa.com

At this website, daily gasoline prices are shown for markets across the United States. In addition, you can get AAA's weekly commentary on fuel price trends and monthly gas price reports.

Airline Fuel Cost and Consumption

Bureau of Transportation Statistics (BTS), U.S. Department of Transportation

http://www.transtats.bts.gov/fuel.asp

Consult this website for monthly international, domestic, and total data on consumption (per million gallons), cost (per million dollars), and cost per gallon (dollars) for total and individual carriers, gathered by the Bureau of Transportation Statistics.

Airlines for America—Jet Fuel Price Volatility

http://www.airlines.org

Airlines for America's (A4A) link to the Argus U.S. Jet Fuel Index provides a composite daily price for Chicago, Houston, Los Angeles, and New York.

American Transportation Research Institute

http://atri-online.org

The American Transportation Research Institute (ATRI) is part of the American Trucking Associations Federation, and is a not-for-profit research organization. Two focus areas of interest, in the website's Research section, are Economic Analysis and Trucking Industry Operations. Popular reports are *An Analysis of the Operational Costs of Trucking: A 2013 Update*, which provides average costs per mile data, average costs per hour, and cost breakouts by industry sector, as well as *Critical Issues in the Trucking Industry*.

Rail Cost Indexes and Traffic Data

Association of American Railroads

https://www.aar.org/StatisticsAndPublications/Rail-Cost-Indexes

The Rail Cost Indexes provided by the Association of American Railroads, include: Railroad Cost Recovery Index (RCR), Rail Cost Adjustment Factor (RCAF), All-Inclusive Index Less Fuel (AII-LF), and Index of Monthly Railroad Fuel Prices. *Rail Time Indicators* is a monthly report that combines rail traffic data with more than 15 key economic indicators, looking at key trends that can reveal where the economy and rail traffic may be going. The *Weekly Rail Traffic* summary reports can be downloaded for free.

Agricultural Transportation

Agriculture Marketing Service, U.S. Department of Agriculture

http://www.ams.usda.gov

At the home page, click on "Agricultural Transportation." As part of the U.S. Department of Agriculture (USDA), the Transportation Services Division (TSD) assists agricultural shippers via market reports, regulatory representation, economic analysis, and transportation disruption reports. Examples of helpful research reports include: *Grain Truck and Ocean Rate Advisory Quarterly Updates, Weekly Ocean Shipping Container Availability Report,* and *Agricultural Refrigerated Truck Quarterly Report* (national and regional truck rates, diesel fuel prices, truck availability, and shipments).

Baltic Indices Lloyd's List Intelligence

http://www.lloydslistintelligence.com/llint/dry-bulk/baltic-dry-index.htm

With the Baltic Indices, you can view Baltic Dry (Dry Bulk Index), Capsize, Panamac, Supramax, and Handysize indices for various time periods, up to five years historical. Click on "Tankers" in the navigation menu for the Baltic Tanker Indices. The Baltic Dry Index, as defined on the NASDAQ website, "tracks the price of transporting dry bulk cargo like cement, coal, iron ore, and grain on bulk freighters."

Drewry Maritime Research

http://www.drewry.co.uk

Using Drewry Maritime Research's website, you can get insight, trends, and analysis for shipping rates and logistics. Annual, Briefing, Forecaster, Insight, and Spotlight reports are available for these specific markets: Chemical, Container, Dry Balk, Gas, Management and Costs, Oil Tankers, Ports and Logistics, Reefer, Shipbuilding and Repair, and Specialized markets. The Annual reports feature the previous year in focus accompanied by five-year predictions. The Forecaster reports offer short-term forecasts with long-term projections.

CSCMP Annual State of Logistics Report

http://cscmp.org/member-benefits/state-of-logistics

The Council of Supply Chain Management Professionals (CSCMP) releases the annual *State of Logistics Report,* which is used by supply chain management and logistics professionals as a benchmark for U.S. logistics activity. The report provides an economic overview, and covers costs associated with moving freight through the United States and key logistics industry trends.

Gasoline and Diesel Fuel Update

http://www.eia.gov/petroleum/gasdiesel

Provided by the U.S. Energy Information Administration, weekly U.S. regular gasoline prices (dollars per gallon), and U.S. on-highway diesel fuel prices (dollars per gallon), broken down by region, are shown. Change data from one year and one week ago are also provided.

Journal of Commerce (JOC) Trans-Pacific Eastbound Market Data

http://www.joc.com/content/trans-pacific-eastbound-market-data

Market data including ocean, air, and rail pricing, port volumes and other data pertaining to the trans-Pacific eastbound (Asia-to-North America) transportation and logistics market can be found here.

Lloyd's List Intelligence

http://www.lloydslistintelligence.com

Lloyd's List Intelligence is founded on the heritage of Lloyd's List, which is a daily shipping newspaper that started in 1734. Intelligence channels include: Tankers, LNG (liquefied natural gas), Dry Balk, Containers, Insurance, Law and Regulation, and Credit. Via these channels you can view analysis, news headlines, and market outlooks, in addition to tracking the world's tankers, global gas fleets, dry bulk fleet with movements, AIS mapping, vessel characteristics, and company details.

Freight Transportation Services Index

http://apps.bts.gov/xml/tsi/src/index.xml

The Transportation Services Index (TSI), created by the U.S. Department of Transportation (U.S. DOT), Bureau of Transportation Statistics (BTS), measures the movement of freight and passengers. "The Freight TSI measures the month-to-month changes in freight shipments by mode of transportation in tons and ton-miles, which are combined into one index. The index measures the output of the for-hire freight transportation industry and consists of data from for-hire trucking, rail, inland waterways, pipelines, and air freight." Selecting the Press Releases option allows you to read a detailed version of the data.

TRADE INTELLIGENCE

Datamyne

http://www.datamyne.com

Datamyne covers the import and export trade activity of more than 50 countries, including U.S. trade with over 200 markets. Their trade (company) profiles incorporate D&B (Dun and Bradstreet) information with their own for a complete view. They are known for their quality of data, cleansing of data, and strong customer support. The Free Report Library offers Maritime Sector Ranking reports,

Commercial Sector Ranking and Tops in Trade reports, Commercial Sector Quick Look reports, and Commercial Sector Opportunity reports.

PIERS

https://www.piers.com

PIERS is the pioneer in trade data and has been the standard go-to source for years. PIERS converts raw records of U.S. imports and exports into data, which lets you see the amount of traffic through ports and the quantity of shipments from suppliers. You can evaluate suppliers based on records that show volumes, product lines, shipment values, and shipping history. Its free library makes available whitepapers that are helpful. A recent title: *United States Agriculture Exports: Opportunities and Challenges for Containerized Shippers.*

Import Genius

http://www.importgenius.com

Import Genius made a splash when it debuted in 2008 by predicting the arrival of the iPhone.[8] Importers use the service to view U.S. shipping history for overseas suppliers, in any industry, by accessing detailed customs records to verify their shipping volumes and customer lists. You can search by company name or product keywords. The visual mapping feature is a plus.

Panjiva

http://Panjiva.com

Founded in 2006, Panjiva's intelligence platform "enables buyers to develop quickly short lists of potential suppliers, conduct background checks on potential suppliers, keep tabs on competitors' sourcing activities and on existing suppliers." Industries covered are: Hardware and Tools, Apparel and Textiles, Food and Beverage, Chemicals, and Maritime Monitor. Panjiva's main source of information comes from import and export data from the Bureau of Customs and Border Protection.

PUBLICATIONS AND WEBSITES

American Shipper Magazine

http://americanshipper.com

American Shipper magazine is intended for shippers and carriers professionals managing international logistics and supply chains. The website offers free, but not premium, content for registered users. Comprehensive, frequently updated information is offered via these topic channels: Supply Chain, Regulatory, Technology, Transportation, Suppliers, Markets, Opinion, Research, and Webinars. Annual research reports available for download include: *Global Trade Management Report, Global Transportation Planning and Procurement Benchmark, Global Transportation Management Benchmark, Global Transportation Settlement and Measurement Benchmark, Import Operations and Compliance Benchmark,* and *Export Operations and Compliance Benchmark.*

DG&A Transportation Consulting Blog

http://www.dantranscon.com/index.php/blog

Dan Goodwill & Associates is a provider of freight management consulting services to shippers, carriers, and third-party logistics (3PL) providers. This blog features helpful posts about freight management best practices.

Export.gov

http://export.gov

Export.gov provides U.S. government resources to assist businesses with their international sales strategies. Topic areas that you can access include: Export Finance, Trade Data, NAFTA Certificate, "Doing Business In" Guides, HS Codes, Tariffs and Taxes, Export Controls and Licenses, and Trade Complaints and Advocacy. The Market Research section starts you off with a step-by-step process for performing market research. The Market Research Library contains overviews on doing business in more than 120 countries and profiles of 110 industry sectors; the latest trade data by country, state, commodity, year, and more; and webinars about new market and industry information.

Heavy Duty Trucking (HDT) and Truckinginfo.com

http://www.truckinginfo.com

Truckinginfo.com offers daily news and information on equipment, operations, regulations, environmental issues, and more. Navigation categories include Equipment, Fleet Management, Safety and Compliance, Drivers, Maintenance, Fuel Smarts, and Aftermarket.

Journal of Commerce (JOC)

www.joc.com

The *Journal of Commerce* provides a wealth of news, data, and analysis for trade, transportation and logistics professionals. The *Annual Review and Outlook* is an analysis of the critical issues for the year ahead. *JOC.com* has channels that include: Maritime, Ports, Rail and Intermodal, Trucking, Air Cargo, Logistics, Regulation and Policy, Economy, Market Data, and Global Trade. You can register to receive five free articles every month.

Logistics Management

http://www.logisticsmgmt.com

The *Logistics Management* website is for logistics and supply chain professionals, and provides helpful news and articles on these topics: Air Freight, Customs Brokers Trade Compliance, Global Trade, Intermodal, Mobile and Wireless, Motor Freight, Ocean Freight, Ports, Software and Technology, Sustainability, Third Party Logistics, Transportation Management Systems (TMS), Warehouse and Distribution, and Warehouse Management Systems (WMS). *Logistics Management* is published by Peerless Media, which also publishes *Modern Materials Handling.*

Material Handling and Logistics

http://mhlnews.com

Material Handling & Logistics (MH&L) is a website for managers who oversee supply chain, logistics, and material handling across the manufacturing, distribution, and retail sectors. News, articles, and product announcements are offered for: Transportation and Distribution, Facilities Management, Warehousing, Global Supply Chain, Technology and Automation, Powered Vehicles, and Labor Management.

Transport Topics

http://www.ttnews.com

The *Transport Topics* publication and website provide a wealth of information, covering trucking and freight transportation. Navigation channels include: News and Analysis, Fuel Prices, Top 100 Rankings, Resources, Interact, Classified, Multimedia, and Events. The Fuel Prices section provides national and regional fuel prices, Comdata and T-Check (fuel card providers) national averages, and updated articles featuring price updates, including diesel. Annual rankings in the Top 100 Rankings section provide an overview of the largest for-hire carriers and private truck fleets in the United States and Canada. There are also rankings for third-party logistics companies in North America, including the largest freight brokerage firms, freight forwarders, warehouse operators, and dedicated contract carriage service providers.

Journal of Business Logistics

http://cscmp.org/member-benefits/journal-business-logistics

The *Journal of Business Logistics* is a peer-reviewed academic journal and is produced by the Council of Supply Chain Management Professionals. It focuses on logistics and supply chain management theory.

Packaging News

http://www.packagingnews.co.uk

Published in the UK, *Packaging News* provides updated news stories that cover these categories: Cartonboard, Contract Packing, Corrugated, Flexible Plastics, Labeling, Glass, and Environment.

Packaging World

http://www.packworld.com

Packaging World is for professionals who use, recommend, and purchase packaging equipment and materials. The website includes these channels: Package Design, Machinery, Videos, Case Studies, Playbooks, and Galleries.

Supply Chain 24/7

http://www.supplychain247.com

Supply Chain 24/7 is an online business resource for Transportation, Distribution, Logistics, and Supply Chain professionals. Peerless Media brings together all the latest news and industry intelligence from their flagship publications *Logistics Management*, *Modern Materials Handling*, *Supply Chain Management Review*, and *Material Handling Product News*.

SupplyChainBrain

http://www.supplychainbrain.com

SupplyChainBrain is a supply chain management information resource that provides content and news in more than 70 categories, organized by Logistics/Freight, Technology, General SCM, Regions, and Industries.

United States Census Bureau, Foreign Trade—U.S. Export and Import Statistics

http://www.census.gov/foreign-trade

Foreign Trade is the official source for U.S. export and import statistics and is responsible for issuing regulations governing the reporting of all export shipments from the United States. You can find import or export statistics, information on export regulations, commodity classifications, and other trade-related topics. The Data section provides Trade Highlights (key and current statistics), Balance by Partner Country, Country/Product Trade, and State Trade by Commodity and Country. Other sections include Regulations, About Foreign Trade, AES (Automated Export System), Reference, Definitions, and Schedule B.

ASSOCIATIONS AND ORGANIZATIONS

American Trucking Association

http://www.truckline.com

The American Trucking Association (ATA) is a leading advocate for the trucking industry, and produces the *ATA American Trucking Trends* annual report and the *US Freight Forecast to 2024*, as well as updates to the ATA Truck Tonnage Index.

Association of American Railroads

https://www.aar.org

The Association of American Railroads (AAR) sets standards for North America's railroads, and members include the major freight railroads in the United States, Canada, and Mexico. Railinc is a resource for tracking rail data.

The Chartered Institute of Logistics and Transport

http://www.ciltinternational.org

The Chartered Institute of Logistics and Transport (CILT) is a worldwide organization, representing the transport and logistics industries. CILT offers a range of professional qualifications, from an introductory level certificate to higher degree programs.

Contract Packaging Association

http://www.contractpackaging.org

The Contract Packaging Association (CPA) publishes the *State of the Contract Packaging Industry Report* and *Contract Packaging* magazine.

International Federation of Warehousing and Logistics Association

http://warehousinglogisticsinternational.com

The International Federation of Warehousing and Logistics Association is an organization that promotes the warehousing and logistics industries. The Knowledge Center provides best practices articles on Handling, Legislation, Warehousing, Technology, and Distribution.

International Warehouse Logistics Association

http://www.iwla.com/help/links.aspx

Links to various associations related to logistics and warehousing are listed by the International Warehouse Logistics Association.

Packaging World—Packaging Association

http://www.packworld.com/packaging-associations

Links to all types of associations, either related directly or indirectly to packaging, are listed at this *Packaging World* website.

American Society of Transportation & Logistics (AST&L)

http://www.astl.org

The AST&L is a professional organization that offers certification in the fields of transportation, logistics, and supply chain management. The Certified in Transportation and Logistics (CTL) Certification Program began in 1948. AST&L also offers the Global Logistics Associate (GLA), Professional Designation in Logistics and Supply Chain Management (PLS), and the Distinguished Logistics Professional (DLP) certifications. AST&L publishes the quarterly *Transportation Journal.*

Institute of Packaging Professionals (IoPP)

http://www.iopp.org

The IoPP offers a Certified Professionals in Training (CPIT) program and the Certified Packaging Professional (CPP) designation. Candidates achieve the CPP designation by demonstrating significant industry expertise and experience.

Intermodal Association of North America (IANA)

http://www.intermodal.org

The IANA is an important industry association that represents the combined interests of the intermodal freight industry. The Industry Information section provides data and statistics in the form of the quarterly *Intermodal Market Trends & Statistics Report.*

Material Handling Industry of America (MHI)

http://www.mhi.org

The MHI is a nonprofit trade association representing the materials handling and logistics industries. The quarterly *Market Forecast* report is a comprehensive 12- to 18-month forecast of materials handling equipment manufacturing (MHEM). In addition, the MHI provides a resource for materials handling and related standards.

SOLE: The International Society of Logistics

http://www.sole.org

SOLE is a nonprofit organization that focuses on logistics technology, education, and management and offers these certification programs: Demonstrated Logistician Program, Certified Master Logistician (CML), and Certified Professional Logistician (CPL).

Warehousing Education and Research Council

http://www.werc.org

The Warehousing Education and Research Council (WERC) is a warehouse management professional organization. The WERC offers knowledge exchange opportunities for distribution professionals in addition to research and performance metrics for benchmarking. The WERC website's Learning Center provides access to online courses and self-study publications. The online Resource Center has industry tools and helpful links to government agencies, associations, trade journals, industry certification, and industry resources.

American Association of Exporters and Importers (AAEI)

http://www.aaei.org

Focusing specifically on trade issues, the AAEI partners with government agencies. The AAEI's Essential Trade Professional Library provides links to recommended essential references "to ensure its members' adherence to the regulatory requirements and operating procedures fundamental to the proper conduct of international trade."

World Trade Organization

http://www.wto.org

The World Trade Organization (WTO) is an international organization that "deals with the global rules of trade between nations." The WTO publishes a great deal of statistics and economic research. Key publications include the annual *World Trade Report*, which covers trends in trade, trade policy issues, and the multilateral trading system; and *International Trade Statistics*, which offers an annual overview of the latest developments in world trade, detailed statistics on trade by region, merchandise trade by product, and trade in commercial services by category.

REFERENCES

1. "Trade History," *American Association of Exporters and Importers (AAEI)*, Accessed May 28, 2014, http://www.aaei.org/Resources/TradeHistory/tabid/132/Default.aspx.
2. "Best Practices in Global Logistics," *Supply Chain 24/7*, Feb. 3, 2014, http://www.supplychain247.com/article/best_practices_in_global_logistics.
3. Dan Gilmore, "State of the Logistics Union 2014," *Supply Chain Digest*, June 17, 2014, http://www.scdigest.com/ASSETS/FIRSTTHOUGHTS/14-06-17.php?cid=8190.
4. Frank A. Paine, ed., *The Packaging User's Handbook*, (Glasgow: Blackie, 1991), 3.
5. "Packaging," GEP, Accessed May 29, 2014, http://www.gep.com/consulting/strategic-sourcing/category-expertise/packaging.

6. Robert L. Thompson, "Understanding the Harmonized TARIFF System Classification of Products for Import-Export," *World Trade Daily*, July 7, 2013, http://worldtradedaily.com/2013/07/07/understanding-harmonized-codes.
7. *Ibid.*
8. Justin Wolfers, "Amazing New Trade Data," *Freakonomics*, June 27, 2008, http://freakonomics.com//2008/06/27/amazing-new-trade-data.

29

MARKETING

There is no question that gaining access to marketing spend can be an uphill battle for procurement. Procurement and marketing have different approaches to reaching their goals and, if we are honest, have extremely different goals. Marketing is top line focused, while procurement traditionally focuses on guarding or growing the bottom line.

According to a recent Association of National Advertisers (ANA) survey, the relationship between marketing and procurement, which historically has been tenuous, is greatly improving and driving measurable results: "There is agreement between marketing and procurement that cost savings and risk mitigation are the top benefits that procurement brings to marketing."[1] However, Donovan Neale May, in an article in the *CMO Council Journal,* reported that the 2014 "State of the Marketing Report" revealed only 15% (of 525 CMO Council members that were surveyed) are "actively forging relationships with CPOs." This was in comparison to 58% "who are cozying up to CFOs and 53% who are seeking tighter alignment with CIOs."[2]

ANA's Bill Duggin wrote that, traditionally, procurement has "handled areas including contracts, RFIs/RFPs, agency evaluations, scope of work development, and supplier diversity. Agency compensation has long been a priority of marketing procurement; production has more recently become a focus."[3] Duggin emphasized that media procurement is a new, developing trend and is where procurement should now focus.[4]

Digital marketing is a growth area that cannot be ignored. In 2013, U.S. agency digital work accounted for 35.3%, more than one-third, of revenue (in 2012, it was 32.5%); and, digital revenue climbed 13.8%.[5] Another trend of importance to note for procurement is programmatic advertising. According to a recent survey by AdExchanger Research, "the use of data-driven software to automate online

Table 29.1 Resources—marketing

RESOURCES—MARKETING	Rates/ Spending Data/Market Analysis	Daily/Weekly Marketing News	Networking/ Industry Education	Supplier (Advertiser/ Agency/Media) Identification	Background Information	Open (Free) Access	Mixed Fee and Free Access
4A's (American Association of Advertising Agencies)	✓	✓	✓	✓			✓
Ad Age (Advertising Age)	✓	✓		✓			✓
Adforum				✓			✓
Adspender/Stradegy - Kantar Media	✓			✓			
Advertising Research Foundation (ARF)	✓	✓	✓				✓
Adweek		✓					✓
American Marketing Association (AMA)	✓	✓	✓	✓	✓		✓
Association of National Advertisers (ANA)	✓	✓	✓				✓
Chief Marketing Officer (CMO) Council	✓	✓	✓				✓
CMO Today (WSJ)	✓	✓				✓	
Dictionary of Marketing (Oxford)					✓		
eMarketer	✓	✓					✓
Interactive Advertising Bureau (IAB)	✓	✓	✓				✓
Know This - What Is Marketing Tutorial					✓	✓	

RESOURCES—MARKETING	Rates/ Spending Data/Market Analysis	Daily/Weekly Marketing News	Networking/ Industry Education	Supplier (Advertiser/ Agency/Media) Identification	Background Information	Open (Free) Access	Mixed Fee and Free Access
Magna Global	✓						
MarketingProfs	✓	✓	✓				✓
The Media Handbook					✓		
REDBOOKS				✓			
SNL Kagan	✓						
SRDS - Kantar Media	✓			✓			
TVB (Television Bureau of Advertising)	✓	✓	✓		✓	✓	✓
VSS (Veronis Suhler Stevenson) Forecast	✓						
Warc	✓	✓		✓			
ZenithOptima	✓						

advertising, already a fast-growing phenomenon known as *programmatic buying*, is on the cusp of taking over the way most digital ad budgets are spent."[6] Both marketers and agencies are planning to increase their programmatic spend significantly.[7]

Regardless of marketing channel or purpose/function, all sides agree that procurement must continue to strive to partner with marketing for success with strategic long-term initiatives, in addition to implementing cost-saving measures. Resources for marketing information and services are shown in Table 29.1.

BACKGROUND INFORMATION

American Marketing Association Dictionary

https://www.ama.org/resources/Pages/Dictionary.aspx

The *American Marketing Association Dictionary* originated from a print version (1995) and is continuously updated with new terms "to keep marketers up-to-date in the ever-evolving marketing profession."

Dictionary of Marketing

Charles Doyle
Oxford; New York: Oxford University Press, 2011

This paperback dictionary provides more than 2,600 alphabetical entries on every aspect of marketing. Entries cover traditional topics in addition to current, Internet-related issues.

Television Bureau of Advertising General and Multiplatform Glossary

http://www.tvb.org/trends

Television Bureau of Advertising (TVB) glossaries are helpful in understanding television media, containing terms such as Cost-Per-Rating Point (CPP) and Alternate Delivery System (ADS).

Know This.com—What Is Marketing?

http://www.knowthis.com/what-is-marketing

This is the first tutorial in the *Principles of Marketing Tutorials* series that looks at marketing's key concepts. There is also a book available, *Know This: Marketing Basics*, 2nd edition.

The Media Handbook: A Complete Guide to Advertising Media Selection, Planning, Research, and Buying, 5th ed.

Helen Katz
New York: Routledge/Taylor & Francis Group, 2014

The *Media Handbook* provides an introduction to advertising, media planning, and buying processes.

AGENCY, ADVERTISER, AND MEDIA SUPPLIER IDENTIFICATION

4A's Agency Search

https://ams.aaaa.org/eweb/content.aspx?webcode=findagency

"4A's" stands for the American Association of Advertising Agencies. To review agency profiles, enter your selection criteria in one or more of the fields on the website. Also on this site is the Agency Search Information Center, with access to a multitude of documents on best practices and guidance for agency search activities.

Adforum

http://www.adforum.com

AdForum's Agency Gallery lists more than 20,000 agencies worldwide, and is used by advertisers in the process of selecting a new agency. You can browse agencies by competencies, activities, or country. The advanced search option lets you search by name, location, and client in addition to specialization, country, competencies, and clients' industries.

Advertising Age's (Ad Age) 2014 Guide to Audience Buying

http://brandedcontent.adage.com/audiencebuyingguide2014

Advertisers who are listed in this *Guide* help marketers choose the best partners for creating and maintaining key consumer relationships. This *Guide* offers a look at Ad Networks, Exchanges, Platforms, and Solution Providers.

Ad Age's Cable Guide

http://brandedcontent.adage.com/cableguide2014

The *Cable Guide* provides a look at the media opportunities of leading cable networks, their programming, and audience.

Ad Age's LookBook

http://lookbook.adage.com

The Ad Age's *LookBook* is a directory that identifies and provides information on ad agencies that are covered in Ad Age. The Advanced Search option offers the flexibility to filter by type of agency, region, specialty, and category.

REDBOOKS

http://www.redbooks.com

REDBOOKS is useful as a supplier discovery tool. It allows for specific targeting in the areas of advertising, marketing, brands, and media. You can do a keyword search or browse by "All Agencies" or "All Advertisers." For agencies, you can filter by Specialty, Location, and Company Size. For advertisers, you can filter by Media Spend, Industry, Location, Company Size, and Revenue.

AMA Marketing Resource Directory

http://marketingresourcedirectory.ama.org

The *AMA Marketing Resource Directory* is a comprehensive guide that lets you browse multiple categories, in addition to searching. Examples of categories include: Advertising Services, Creative Services, Customer Satisfaction, Data Management, Marketing Consultants, Marketing Research, and Marketing Software.

AMA Specialized Directories

https://www.ama.org/resources/Specialized-Directories/Pages/Specialized-Directories.aspx

AMA specialized directories feature leading marketing services firms that offer the latest in technology and ideas. A few examples: *Directory of Focus Group Providers, Directory of Nonprofit Marketing Providers,* and *Directory of Higher Education Marketers.*

RATES, SPENDING DATA, AND MARKET ANALYSIS

Kantar Media Standard Rate & Data Service (SRDS)

http://next.srds.com/for-agencies

The Kantar Media SRDS is a multimedia planning platform containing more than 125,000 media properties categorized by media type, market, and geography. You can search for media and advertising opportunities by Media Type, Keywords, Titles, Geography or DMA (Designated Market Area) and get data points that include rates and audience metrics. The types of media data you can access are: Business Publication, Consumer Magazine, Digital Media and Digital Networks and Tech, Direct Media, and Local (Newspaper, TV, Radio, and Out-of-Home).

American Association of Advertising Agencies (4A's)

https://www.aaaa.org/agency/compensation/surveys/Pages/default.aspx

The 4A's conducts and sponsors surveys on topics relevant to ad agency business, including the state of the industry, agency costs, employee salaries and benefits, and new business trends. Finance Surveys include: *Analysis of Agency Costs; Accounts Receivable; Total Compensation: Highest Paid Individuals; Planned Salary Increase; Hourly Labor Billing Rates;* and *Non-Disclosure and Intellectual Property Rights*. These are for members only. A recent report, for members and nonmembers, is the *4A's Agency Performance Incentive Compensation Survey Reports Findings.*

AdSpender and Stradegy

http://kantarmedia.us/products

Adspender is a tool that allows you to monitor advertising expenditure and occurrence information for millions of brands across 18 media categories. You can view detailed expenditure information by category, parent company, subsidiary, and brand, and rank top spenders by industry, parent, brand, and more. Stradegy reports on advertising spend, placement, occurrences, and creative. You can track ad activity on more than 4 million brands across 21 different types of media, including television, radio, magazines, newspapers, digital, and outdoor channels.

Advertising Age (Ad Age) Advertising Spending

http://adage.com/datacenter/#advertising_spending

The Advertising Spending category in the DataCenter section of *Advertising Age* provides ad spending data for members. For worldwide and United States marketing spending, *100 Leading National Advertisers* (and archive) provides comprehensive ad spending estimates, most-advertised brands, U.S. ad spending totals and more. *Top 200 Megabrands* ranks the biggest-spending brands based on U.S. measured-media spending.

eMarketer

http://www.emarketer.com

eMarketer covers digital marketing, media, and commerce for top brands, agencies, and media, and provides data and insights on how consumers spend time and money. Research topics covered are Big Picture Trends and Benchmarks (key digital trends, media spending, global landscapes, and worldwide benchmarks); Demographics and Consumer Insights; Digital Advertising and Marketing, including forecast ad spending; Mobile; Social Media; Retail and Commerce; Industry Deep Dives, and Total Coverage.

Interactive Advertising Bureau (IAB) Internet Advertising Revenue Report

http://www.iab.net/insights_research/1357

The *IAB Internet Advertising Revenue Report* is a survey conducted by PricewaterhouseCoopers and is released twice a year. It reports measurement of Internet/online advertising revenues, based on information supplied by companies selling advertising online. The report includes data reflecting online advertising revenues from websites, commercial online services, and e-mail providers, as well as other companies selling online advertising. There is a section on pricing models.

Magna Global

http://www.magnaglobal.com

Magna Global research includes *US Advertising Forecasts*, which provides ad revenues for 20 media categories, from 1980 annually and 1990 quarterly, with forecasts through 2017; and *Global Advertising Forecasts* with coverage including net media owners advertising revenues (historical from 2000, forecasts to 2018), in more than 70 countries, 7 media categories, and 12 subcategories, comparable across all countries. Five-year forecasts are based on macroeconomic, econometric modeling. These forecasts are part of a subscription package, which also includes access to Magna Global analysts.

SNL Kagan

http://www.snl.com/sectors/Media/Default.aspx

SNL Kagan covers the electronic media industry, and provides data and analysis for Broadcast, TV Networks, Wireless and Wireline, Multichannel Operations, Global Multichannel, and Filmed Entertainment and TV Programming sectors.

At this website, you can compare forecasts, tabular historical data, and current results for companies and sectors. You can access company profiles with financials, drill down to sector specific operational metrics, sort companies based on rankings and subscriber counts for each metric, and compare key ratios like affiliate revenue/programming expense.

TVB Trends and Adspend

http://www.tvb.org/trends/KantarQ4_summary

The Television Bureau of Advertising (TVB) provides, in the Trends channel, the health of the television medium over the years, changes in consumer behavior, and economic indicators. The Ad Spending section provides data for all media (broken out by medium), by year and quarter.

Veronis Suhler Stevenson (VSS) Forecast

http://www.vssforecast.com

The VSS Forecast provides detailed strategic intelligence and data on emerging growth trends in media, communications, and entertainment. It provides a comprehensive picture of media spending patterns and evaluates changes in media adoption rates across the media landscape.

World Advertising Research Center

http://www.warc.com

The World Advertising Research Center (Warc) is an online provider of secondary research for advertising and media agencies, brands, market researchers, media owners, and universities. Warc partners with 50 different content curators. The database has an elegant design, and the browse, search, and narrowing features can all be used in combination to produce results that are current and relevant. The Data section provides global highlighted aggregated data that is market- and channel-specific. It contains the latest advertising expenditure data from 85 global markets, a comparison of global media costs, and adspend forecasts for 12 key countries.

ZenithOptimedia

http://www.zenithoptimedia.com

ZenithOptimedia bills itself as "The ROI Agency." ZenithOptimedia helps clients improve the effectiveness of marketing spend. It offers a range of guides and forecasts that cover advertising and media. Publications for purchase include *Advertising Expenditure Forecasts, Top Thirty Global Media Owners,* and Market and MediaFact books for the Americas, Asia Pacific, Central and Eastern Europe, Russia, Western Europe, and the United Kingdom. The Marketers Portal is a comprehensive online resource that includes more than 5,000 links to leading corporate and brand sites by category, top media sites, and relevant quotes.

PUBLICATIONS AND WEBSITES

Advertising Age (Ad Age)

http://adage.com

Advertising Age, also known as *Ad Age,* is an important and respected source for news and analysis for the marketing and media community, and a prolific publisher of industry data. The DataCenter section of the website features excellent content offerings, including the *Annual Agency Report* (industry analysis and rankings), *Agency Family Trees, 100 Leading National Advertisers*; *Publishers Information Bureau (PIB) Index page* (rankings of magazine pages and dollars); *Magazine Circulation Rankings Index* (semiannual rankings of magazines by average circulation); *Newspapers Circulation Rankings*; *Marketing Fact Pack: Annual Guide to Marketers, Media, and Agencies* (key stats and rankings); *Prime-time Broadcast TV Pricing Survey, 2013-2014*; and *Mobile Marketing Fast Facts 2014.*

Adweek

http://www.adweek.com

Adweek is a key trade news source for marketing, media, and advertising professionals. The website channels are: The Press, Television, and Advertising and Branding. For each channel, you can narrow the results by selecting the type of content, with choices being articles, blog posts, galleries, or videos. Each channel also has topic categories listed for further narrowing of results.

CMO Today, Wall Street Journal

http://blogs.wsj.com/cmo

CMO Today is *The Wall Street Journal's* vertical section that focuses on marketing, advertising, and media. It is global in scope, and covers the digital space and traditional media, such as television and radio.

MarketingProfs

http://www.marketingprofs.com

MarketingProfs offers education for marketers through training, best practices, and research. The Real Time section of the website includes the most recent articles, podcasts, online seminars, tutorials, guides and reports, smart tools, and opinions. The Topics section allows you to access content via format or by searching more than 250 topics. The Training section describes the solutions available for individuals, and small and large teams.

ASSOCIATIONS AND ORGANIZATIONS

Advertising Research Foundation

http://www.thearf.org

The Advertising Research Foundation (ARF) was founded in 1936 by the Association of National Advertisers and the American Association of Advertising Agencies as "an open-minded, unbiased environment, free of partisan interests." The Knowledge Center is a central resource for materials relating to advertising research. The Research channel is a collection of research and resources that provides access to online archives and personalized guidance. The forums cover Big Data, Consumer Segments, Creative/Neuromarketing, Cross Platform, and Research Impact, to name a few.

Interactive Advertising Bureau

http://www.iab.net

Founded in 1996, the Interactive Advertising Bureau (IAB) is comprised of more than 600 leading media and technology companies. The IAB educates about the value of interactive advertising. Working with its member companies, the IAB evaluates and recommends standards and practices, and fields critical research on interactive advertising.

American Marketing Association

https://www.ama.org

The American Marketing Association (AMA) was established in 1937. Recent events, articles, multimedia, and resources (case studies and interactive tools and templates) are provided for the areas of Advertising, Branding, Engagement,

Digital, Global, Marketing Communications, Metrics, Market Research, and Strategy. The AMA publishes *Marketing News* (monthly magazine), *Marketing Insights* (bi-monthly magazine), *Marketing Health Services, Journal of Marketing Research, Journal of International Marketing, Journal of Public Policy and Marketing,* and e-Newsletters. In addition, the AMA offers the Professional Certified Marketer (PCM) program.

Association of National Advertisers

http://www.ana.net

The Association of National Advertisers (ANA) was founded in 1910, and communicates marketing best practices and leading industry initiatives. This is one of the best resources to find current and relevant articles on marketing procurement—from the marketing point of view. The ANA Procurement Task Force mission, as stated on the website, is to "define and elevate the role of marketing procurement, [and] close the 'gaps' on the value of procurement between procurement and internal marketing as well as procurement and external agencies." Topics of interest that can be found in the Research and Insights section are Agency, and Finance and Procurement. Presentations and content on the Agency page are for members only, and cover timely and important issues for procurement professionals. A couple of samples are: "Best Negotiating Practices," and "Agency Search: Best Practices on the RFI and RFO Process." Other key research topics are B2B, Brand, Consumer, Data, Leadership, Measurement, Media Channels, and Organization.

American Association of Advertising Agencies

http://www.aaaa.org

Founded in 1917, the American Association of Advertising Agencies (4A's) represents advertising agencies in the United States. The Business Resources channel, especially the "Matters" section, provides a wealth of information helpful to procurement professionals. The Research Matters section offers access to an extensive collection of trends, best practices, surveys, infographics, and more, on topics that include: Advertising Marketing and Media, Agency Business, Consumers, Digital and Industries. The Research Databases portal is for members only and is a gateway to BUDDY (Business Demographics and Data for You), CREW (Creative Running Everywhere Worldwide), GIG (Global Innovations Gateway), and ProQuest (mega research) databases. The Management Matters section includes guidelines and best practices; surveys on methodology, rates, and client perceptions; and negotiating and intellectual property on management-related topics.

The Media Matters section provides resources related to the planning and buying of media via Communities (areas that range from medium-specific to cross-media to media disciplinary), Forms and Contracts (templates of contracts and forms that members can utilize in their negotiations with clients and interested parties), and Information Exchanges. Also helpful are the Production Matters and Creative Matters sections.

The Chief Marketing Officer (CMO) Council

http://www.cmocouncil.org

The CMO Council's mission is to "Operate as the premier knowledge transfer agent and affinity group for chief marketers worldwide. Act as a catalyst for marketing transformation, best practice development, and functional accountability and improvement in global organizations." The CMO Council offers webinars and events, covering current topics of interest in addition to providing a number of services, such as the Assisted Search Service, Content Performance Audit, and Speakers Bureau. White papers on best practices and case studies are useful reports that are available. Program initiatives include the APAC Digital Marketing Performance Index 2014, Online Advertising Performance Outlook 2014, and Grow from the Right Intro, to name a few.

CMO Council's Organizations List

http://www.cmocouncil.org/organizations.php

In the CMO Council's Organizations List are links to marketing and vertical marketing organizations, such as the Medical Marketing Association and Chain Drug Marketing Association.

Television Bureau of Advertising

http://www.tvb.org

The Television Bureau of Advertising (TVB) is the not-for-profit trade association of the commercial broadcast television industry in America. The TVB provides a number of helpful tools and resources. Main navigation categories include: Markets and Stations, Planning and Buying, Research, Trends, and Political Databank. The Research section provides data on media comparisons and measurement, including various rankings. Three areas of interest in the Planning and Buying section are: Ad Platforms, Buying Station Websites, and Buying Mobile Advertising. The Trends section covers ad spending, the Borrell Benchmarking Report, and TV cost and CPM (cost per thousand) trends.

REFERENCES

1. "ANA Survey Reveals Improved Relationships Between Marketing and Procurement," *Association of National Advertisers*, May 5, 2014, http://www.ana.net/content/show/id/30482.
2. Donovan Neale May, "It's Time for Marketing to Buy into Strategic Sourcing," *Peersphere: The CMO Council Journal* 3 (2014): 5, Accessed May 22, 2014, https://www.cmocouncil.org/peer-sphere.php.
3. Bill Duggan, "The Case for Media Procurement," *Association of National Advertisers*, May 20, 2014, http://www.ana.net/blogs/show/id/30696.
4. *Ibid.*
5. Bradley Johnson, "Revenue, Staffing, Stocks, and Digital Show Growth for Agencies in 2014 Report," *Advertising Age*, April 27, 2014, http://adage.com/article/agency-news/2014-agency-report-revenue-staffing-stocks-digital/292849.
6. Robert Hof, "Programmatic Advertising to Gobble Up Even More Ad Budgets—Report," *Forbes.com*, May 15, 2014, http://www.forbes.com/sites/roberthof/2014/05/15/programmatic-advertising-to-gobble-up-even-more-ad-budgets-report.
7. *Ibid.*

30

MAINTENANCE, REPAIR, AND OPERATIONS, AND FACILITIES MANAGEMENT

It is hard to succinctly define maintenance, repair, and operations (MRO) because it can be interpreted in many different ways. In fact, when thinking how to best tackle identifying MRO research resources, the EDS commercial of cowboys herding cats comes into mind.[1]

In a general sense, MRO encompasses the materials, services, and products required to keep a plant running safely and efficiently.[2] MRO products can be items that workers have no idea they will need until an incident happens. For example, an older pump needs to replaced unexpectedly, and in addition to the pump, there is the need for specific tools and safety gear for installation.[3] Product and service spend areas most likely to be considered part of MRO include power transmission, electrical components, fasteners, hand and power tools, brushes, plumbing, fleet/vehicles, lighting, lubricants, filters, fluid power, safety supplies, and heating, ventilation, and air conditioning (HVAC). Resources for MRO and facilities management are shown in Table 30.1.

Facilities management (FM) is also a loosely-defined area, which is sometimes interchanged or combined with MRO. It can be thought of as a management discipline that involves the use of products, services, and technology to create an efficient work environment. Facilities management encompasses MRO, and includes areas such as cleaning/janitorial, food services, landscaping, office supplies, construction, real estate, moving services, and furniture, to name a few.

Table 30.1 Resources—mro/facilities management

RESOURCES—MRO/ FACILITIES MANAGEMENT	Market Analysis/ Trends	MRO/FM Costs	Daily/Weekly Market News	Networking/ Industry Education	Supplier Identification	Background Information	Open (Free) Access	Mixed Fee and Free Access
Association for Maintenance Professionals				✓				✓
BUILDINGS.com	✓	✓	✓					✓
Facilities Manager's Desk Reference	✓					✓		
FacilitiesNet			✓	✓		✓	✓	
Fastenal		✓			✓		✓	
FMLink	✓		✓		✓			✓
Grainger		✓			✓		✓	
Industrial Supply Magazine	✓		✓		✓			✓
Industrial Supply Association				✓	✓			✓
International Facility Management Association	✓	✓	✓	✓	✓	✓		✓
Machinery & Equipment MRO Buyers Guide					✓		✓	
Maintenance World	✓					✓	✓	
Modern Distribution Management	✓	✓	✓		✓			✓
MRO Zone	✓			✓				

RESOURCES—MRO/ FACILITIES MANAGEMENT	Market Analysis/ Trends	MRO/FM Costs	Daily/Weekly Market News	Networking/ Industry Education	Supplier Identification	Background Information	Open (Free) Access	Mixed Fee and Free Access
Penton Manufacturing Publications	✓		✓		✓		✓	
Plant Services	✓		✓	✓				✓
Reliable Plant Glossary						✓	✓	
Reliabilityweb.com	✓		✓		✓	✓	✓	
The Society for Maintenance and Reliability Prof	✓	✓		✓				✓
Whitestone Facility Cost References	✓	✓						

One thing that almost all procurement professionals agree on is that MRO/FM spend categories present great opportunities for cost savings. Identifying the various components in this category is one of many challenges.

The spend subcategories are often managed on a distributed or localized level. As a result, a procurement professional should investigate the industry and supplier intelligence coverage in trade journals and professional associations specific to the product or service being researched, before pulling together a project team.

In addition to the resources that we include in category specific Chapters 21-25, and Chapter 8, Supplier Identification, there are general industrial distributors, as well as distributors that specialize in certain industry sectors, such as Electrical, HVAC, Plumbing, and Power Transmission/Bearing. For help in identifying and referencing these sources, the resources appearing in the first part of the chapter provide comprehensive *lists* of what is available. Other resources in this chapter are key MRO and facilities management publications and websites.

COMPREHENSIVE ASSOCIATION AND TRADE PUBLICATION LISTS

Industrial Supply Association Industry Links

http://www.isapartners.org/for-your-business/industry-links

Using the Industry Links, you can find a listing with links to distributor and manufacturer associations, and distributor and manufacturer publications, provided by the Industrial Supply Association (ISA). Examples of items listed are *American Fastener Journal*, Bearings Specialist Association, and American Hardware Manufacturers Association.

Industrial Supply Magazine and Online Resources

http://www.industrialsupplymagazine.com/pages/Resources.php

The *Industrial Supply* website offers resource links pertaining to the industrial supply chain. The areas are: Alliances, Marketing and Buying Groups; Distribution Industry Consultants; Distributor Trade Associations; and Manufacturing Trade Associations. Examples of links include: National Fluid Power Association, International Glove Association, and The Association for Hose and Accessories Distribution.

FMLink Resources and Organizations

http://www.fmlink.com/ProfResources

FMLink provides a multitude of links to organizations and other websites, including American Society of Heating, Refrigerating and Air-Conditioning Engineers, and Worldwide Cleaning Industry Association.

Modern Distribution Management Distributors and Associations

http://www.mdm.com/directories/174-distributor-and-manufacturer-associations

The Modern Distribution Management Distributors and Associations offer a helpful section, "Distributor and Manufacturer Associations," providing links to associations in all industry sectors.

BACKGROUND INFORMATION

FMPedia

http://www.ifma.org/know-base/fm-glossary

FMPedia is a comprehensive, open access glossary for the facilities management community from the International Facility Management Association (IFMA).

Facilities Manager's Desk Reference, 2nd ed.

Jane Wiggins
Chichester, West Sussex: John Wiley & Sons, 2014

The *Facilities Manager's Desk Reference* provides practical information for all of the principal facilities management services. Chapter 13 in this reference book addresses procurement, and covers service contracts, strategic sourcing, supplier selection, specifications, and cost models, among other topics.

Reliable Plant Glossary

http://www.reliableplant.com/Glossary

This glossary is an A-Z listing of MRO key terms and definitions.

SUPPLIER IDENTIFICATION

AmazonSupply

http://www.amazonsupply.com

Amazon aims "to offer Earth's largest selection of essential products for businesses, labs, workshops, and factories." More than 750,000 products are available on this website.

Fastenal

http://www.fastenal.com

Fastenal is a fastener distributor that also carries a full line of industrial products. The website features a product directory that is visual, which is helpful when browsing categories and subcategories of products.

Grainger

http://www.grainger.com

Grainger is a leading industrial distributor. On the Grainger website, you can drill down by product, category, or brand. You can filter results by selecting brand, price, and rating, and then searching within the results, or browse via more detailed subcategories. There are more than 1 million products available. The top sales product categories are Safety and Security, and Material Handling.

International Facility Management Association Buyer's Guide

http://www.ifma.org/marketplace/buyer's-guide

In the *International Facility Management Association (IFMA) Buyer's Guide,* you perform a keyword search or browse within a specific product category. You can narrow by location for categories, for example: Building Components, Business Services, Fire Protection Systems, Flooring, Furniture, Health/Safety/Security, Janitorial Products/Services, Restoration/Maintenance/Recycling, and Transportation/Moving/Travel.

Machinery & Equipment MRO Buyers' Guide

http://www.mromagazine.com/esource

With the *Machinery & Equipment MRO Buyers' Guide,* you can search more than 550,000 companies and 34,000 products in North America, and narrow by location.

Modern Distribution Management Directories

http://www.mdm.com/directories

This resource lists directories that are helpful for finding distributors and buying groups. Comprehensive directories are available for Technology Providers and Buying and Marketing Groups. "Top" lists are provided for distributor categories, such as: Hose and Accessories, Industrial, Electrical, Power Transmission and Bearing, Building Material/Construction, Industrial PVF, HVACR/Plumbing, Electronics, Fasteners, Fluid Power, Gases/Welding, Safety, Pharmaceuticals, San-Jan, Plastics, and Master Distributors/Wholesalers.

Penton Publications Online Buyers Guides

http://directory.foundrymag.com/Main/DirectoryHome.aspx

Penton offers these manufacturing publications with Buyers Guides: *Foundry Management and Technology*, *American Machinist*, *Forging Magazine* and *Welding Design and Fabrication.*

COSTS PRICING AND MARKET ANALYSIS

Modern Distribution Management Distribution Market Research Reports

http://www.mdm.com/research

Modern Distribution Management (MDM) publishes a number of reports. The *MDM Market Leaders* report is an annual report that lists the top distributors in 14 sectors, including industrial and electrical. The *MRO Market Analysis* report provides market size estimates for MRO products in the United States. Also offered are the *MDM Annual Distribution Trends* report, and the *Wholesale Distribution Industry Landscape* report, which shows market size estimates for most sectors, in addition to market share estimates for the combined Top 5 and Top 40 industrial distributors.

Whitestone Facility Cost References

http://www.whitestoneresearch.com/Books

Whitestone Research provides facility cost research products and services. *The Facility Maintenance & Repair Cost Reference* provides detailed maintenance and repair costs for 74 building types in more than 400 North American and international regions. Data is included for over 1,700 building components, more than 30 trades, and more than 4,900 maintenance tasks. The *Facility Operations Cost Reference, 2013-14, North American Version* profiles operations costs for 74 building types in all major North American regions. The *Facility Operations Cost Reference, 2013-14, International Version* provides detailed operating costs for 74 asset types in more than 150 international locations. Whitestone offers CostLab, a cost analytics tool, which forecasts operating and maintenance costs for every asset type in more than 400 locations, worldwide.

PUBLICATIONS AND WEBSITES

BUILDINGS.com

http://www.buildings.com

BUILDINGS.com is for facility managers and building owners responsible for the operation of commercial and public buildings. Available are BNi Costbooks, articles, and facilities management research.

FacilitiesNet

http://www.facilitiesnet.com

FacilitiesNet offers advice via webcasts on issues including LED lighting and HVAC performance. Its magazines include *Building Operating Management* and *Facility Maintenance Decisions.*

Industrial Supply Magazine

http://www.industrialsupplymagazine.com

Industrial Supply is intended for U.S. industrial distributors and independent manufacturer representatives. Website sections include: News, Articles, Resources, and New Products.

FMLink

http://www.fmlink.com

FMLink is a digital facilities management publication that provides its own information in addition to content from other magazines and associations. There is an interesting mix of content at this website.

Maintenance World

http://www.maintenanceworld.com

Maintenance World is an "article source" for reliability and maintenance management professionals. The articles are brief and practical. For example, one entry deals exclusively with the basics of bolts and screws.

Modern Distribution Management

http://www.mdm.com

Modern Distribution Management (MDM) covers the wholesale distribution industry. It provides news in addition to coverage about distribution companies Grainger, HD Supply, Fastenal, MSC, and others. MDM provides top distribution lists, market research, and directories.

Plant Services

http://www.plantservices.com

PlantServices.com is an MRO publication with topic pages that include: Compressors; Fluid Handling; HVAC, and Indoor Air Quality; Motors, Drives, and Power Transmission; Maintenance and Reliability; and Supply Chain and Process Management, to name a few.

Reliabilityweb.com

http://www.reliabilityweb.com

Reliabilityweb.com is intended for maintenance and reliability professionals. There are articles, videos, audio podcasts, case studies, tutorials, online workshops, benchmark data, and tips on this website.

Reliable Plant

http://www.reliableplant.com

The Reliable Plant website is for plant maintenance and reliability leaders. Sample sections include Maintenance Excellence, Lean Manufacturing, Energy Management, and Workplace Safety.

MRO Zone

http://books.mro-zone.com

The MRO Zone Bookstore features *The Maintenance Strategy Series* by Terry Wireman, which is a five-book bundle. Volume 2 by the same author is *MRO Inventory and Purchasing.*

ASSOCIATIONS AND ORGANIZATIONS

Association for Maintenance Professionals

http://www.maintenance.org

The Association for Maintenance Professionals focuses on asset management practices.

Industrial Supply Association

http://www.isapartners.org

The Industrial Supply Association is a trade association for the maintenance, repair, operations, and production (MROP) supply channel. It makes available opportunities for professional development, educational events, articles, guides, reports, and links to resources.

International Facility Management Association (IFMA)

http://www.ifma.org

IFMA has more than 24,000 members in 94 countries. IFMA makes available three credentials, including the "Facility Management Professional." The Facility Management Knowledge Base houses online courses, webinars, surveys, benchmarking reports, and articles. "Purchasing" is one of the categories. IFMA publishes the *Facility Management Journal,* along with Benchmarks Exchange: BEX, which is an online benchmarking portal that allows facility professionals to compare building data.

The Society for Maintenance and Reliability Professionals

http://www.smrp.org

The Society for Maintenance and Reliability Professionals (SMRP) is a non-profit professional society for reliability and physical asset management industry practitioners. SMRP offers three certification programs, including the Certified Maintenance & Reliability Professional (CMRP). The Library of Knowledge provides access to E-Metrics (standardized metrics, guidelines, and definitions) and the benchmarking portal, BenchMaRX.

REFERENCES

1. CBS, "EDS, an HP Company 'Cat Herders,'" *YouTube.com,* Video, 1:00, Jan. 16, 2009, http://www.youtube.com/watch?v=Pk7yqlTMvp8.
2. Joe Payne et al., *Managing Indirect Spend: Enhancing Profitability Through Strategic Sourcing* (Hoboken, NJ: John Wiley & Sons, 2011), 356.
3. Mary K. Pratt, "Maintenance, Repair, and Operations," *Computerworld,* February 26, 2001, http://www.computerworld.com/s/article/57981/Maintenance_Repair_And_Operations.

31

TRAVEL AND MEETINGS

Even in this day of advanced communications technology, professionals still travel to win sales, build relationships, network, participate in on-site problem solving, train, and obtain knowledge. Air, hotel, rental car, entertainment, meetings, and travel management companies are the most common spend categories associated with travel. The U.S. Travel Association reported that "direct spending on business travel by domestic and international travelers, including expenditures on meetings, events, and incentive programs, totaled $266.5 billion in 2013."[1] In an article by Andrew Bartolini, according to research by Ardent Partners, the business travel category is "one of the top five indirect spend categories within the average company."[2] Louis Berard, published by the Aberdeen Group, stated that "the typical company will spend 10 percent (or more) of its total annual budget on expenses related to business travel in 2014."[3]

Over the years, procurement has taken increasing responsibility for corporate travel spend management with the overwhelming priority being reducing costs.[4] Other major challenges for buyers include "rising costs, poor service from suppliers, lack of competition, disappointing technology, lack of traveler compliance, supplier attitudes and ancillary fees."[5] The greatest frustration for procurement professionals is the lack of compliance to a company's travel policy. Better compliance, it is thought, is key in delivering savings and mitigating risk.[6]

Even when procurement does manage travel spend, there are some considerations that do not arise in any other category they manage. Business travel is more personal than most other purchasing activity. Not only does it take professionals away from their homes and families, it may be the only category of spend that has a role in their personal and professional lives. Depending upon the travel policy and processes in place, they may even be booking business travel through the same channels they use to book personal vacations. This is part of what leads

Table 31.1 Resources—travel and meetings

RESOURCES—TRAVEL and MEETINGS	Market Analysis/ Trends	Pricing	Daily/Weekly Market News	Networking/ Industry Education	Supplier Identification	Background Information	Open (Free) Access	Mixed Fee and Free Access
Aberdeen Group	✓						✓	
Association of Corporate Travel Executives (ACTE)	✓		✓	✓				
BCD Travel/Advito Industry Forecast	✓	✓					✓	
Business Travel News (BTN)	✓	✓	✓		✓	✓	✓	
Buying Business Travel	✓	✓	✓				✓	
Corporate and Incentive Travel	✓		✓				✓	
CVENT Glossary of Important Terms (Events)						✓	✓	
CWT (Carlson Wagonlit Travel) Travel Price Forecast	✓	✓					✓	
Essential Guide to Purchasing Bus Travel Serv (CIPS)	✓			✓		✓	✓	
Find A Facility - Meetings and Conventions					✓			
Gillespie's Guide to Travel and Procurement	✓		✓			✓	✓	
Global Business Travel Association (GBTA)	✓	✓	✓	✓				✓
Hotels.com Hotel Price Index (HPI)	✓	✓					✓	

RESOURCES—TRAVEL and MEETINGS	Market Analysis/ Trends	Pricing	Daily/Weekly Market News	Networking/ Industry Education	Supplier Identification	Background Information	Open (Free) Access	Mixed Fee and Free Access
MeetingMagazines.com Industry/Prof. Associations			✓	✓			✓	
Meetings and Conventions	✓		✓				✓	
Meetings Professional International (MPI)	✓		✓	✓			✓	
MeetingsNet	✓		✓				✓	
Successful Meetings	✓		✓				✓	
Supply Management - Business Travel Page	✓	✓	✓				✓	
Travel Procurement	✓		✓				✓	
U.S. Travel Association	✓	✓	✓	✓				✓

to compliance risk. People believe that they can do a better job of making travel spend decisions, and feel justified in straying from policy.

The other unique requirement associated with business travel is the concept of "Duty of Care." This is the expectation, and in some countries the requirement, that a company knows where all of its business travelers are at all points in a trip so that they can help in the case of an emergency, whether a natural disaster or man-made calamity.

Corporate travel market analysis and forecasting information is provided mostly by travel associations, trade publications, travel management companies, and procurement benchmark and thought leadership organizations. Resources for travel and meetings are provided in Table 31.1.

BACKGROUND INFORMATION

Business Travel News Travel Management Handbook

http://www.businesstravelnews.com/Handbook/

This *Handbook* is a comprehensive primer that details how to create a managed travel program. Topics include structuring a program, establishing a travel policy, working with airlines, setting up a hotel program, handling car rental firms, selecting a corporate payment system, selecting a travel management company, and evaluating automation. The first section is a useful Glossary of Terms.

An Essential Guide to Purchasing Business Travel Services

http://www.cips.org/en/Knowledge/Categories-and-Commodities

The *Essential Guide*, from the Chartered Institute of Purchasing and Supply (CIPS), covers key areas, such as travel policy, the travel procurement process, travel management companies, negotiation skills, the travel ordering process, and authorization/charge/purchasing cards.

CVENT Glossary of Important Terms (Events)

http://www.cvent.com/en/event-management-software/glossary.shtml

This Glossary is an A to Z listing of key terms used in event management.

SUPPLIER IDENTIFICATION

Business Travel News Supplier Directory

http://www.businesstravelnews.com/Suppliers/

The *Business Travel News (BTN) Supplier Directory* allows you to find suppliers by name or location, or browse by category. Categories include: Transportation, Travel Services, Conference, Consultants, Technology, Lodging, and Other.

Find a Facility—Meetings and Conventions

http://www.meetings-conventions.com/meeting-facilities/

Find a Facility will help you to find, compare, and source facilities by doing a search, or you can select specific criteria from drop-down boxes. The options allow you to select location, type, meeting room quantity, meeting room/space per square foot, guest rooms, booths, and exhibit space.

PRICING AND MARKET ANALYSIS

Aberdeen Group

http://www.aberdeen.com

Aberdeen Group's Louis Berard frequently writes reports covering Travel and Expense (T&E) management which are available through a free membership. Using the term "travel" in the search box will pull up all relevant reports on T&E Management.

BCD Travel/Advito Industry Forecast

http://www.bcdtravel.com

The annual *Advito Industry Forecast* provides travel price range benchmarks for major markets around the world. Updates are provided quarterly. Global current situation, outlook, and recommendation sections are provided for air, hotel, meetings, car rental, and rail. The data is comprehensive and presented in an easy to read format. The forecast, along with other helpful reports, can be located and downloaded by hovering over the "Information Center" tab, and then selecting "Research, Reports, and White Papers."

Business Travel News Corporate Travel Index

http://www.businesstravelnews.com

The annual Corporate Travel Index, with market analysis, appears in *Business Travel News,* and is based on actual prices paid by corporate clients of BCD Travel, in addition to research by the BTN Group and Mercer, Inc. Look for the Index in the "Research" section of the website. The Index provides free data on per diems in 100 U.S. and 100 non-U.S. cities; hotel costs in 100 U.S. and non-U.S. cities; car rental costs in 100 U.S. cities; food costs in 100 U.S. cities and 100 non-U.S. cities; total per diems in non-U.S. Americas, Asia/Pacific, Europe, the Middle East, and Africa.

Carlson Wagonlit Travel Price Forecast

http://www.carlsonwagonlit.com/en/global/insights

Carlson Wagonlit Travel (CWT) is a business travel management company. They make many excellent reports available free of charge. The annual *Travel Price Forecast* outlines expectations for supplier pricing and reports on trends. Also included in this report are macroeconomic trends influencing travel; air, ground transportation, hotel, and meetings and events price projections; trends impacting travel management; and geographic snapshots. Quarterly reports provided are *CWT Vision* and *CWT ViewPoint,* which provide recommendations on current managed travel topics. There is also an annual in-depth research report.

Global Business Travel Association BTI Outlook Reports

http://www.gbta.org

At the Global Business Travel Association (GBTA) website, under the Resources tab, select "GTBA BTI Outlook Reports." The reports from the GBTA project aggregate business travel trends and track business travel spending. The United States reports are published quarterly and Brazil, China, and Western Europe reports are published semiannually. GBTA members can access the reports for free, while nonmembers need to purchase them.

Hotels.com Hotel Price Index

http://hpi.hotels.com

The Hotel Price Index (HPI) is a report on hotel prices in major destinations across the world, and is, according to the *Hotels.com* website, "based on bookings made on Hotels.com sites and prices shown are those actually paid by customers per room per night, rather than advertised rates."

U.S. Travel Association—Travel Price Index

http://www.ustravel.org/research/economic-research

The Travel Price Index (TPI) measures the one-month change of the cost of travel away from home in the United States on a seasonally adjusted basis, and also on a seasonally unadjusted basis. The TPI is based on U.S. Department of Labor price data collected for the monthly Consumer Price Index (CPI). The TPI components are food and beverage, lodging, transportation (airline, public, and motor fuel), and recreation services. The most current month of access is free, while archived reports are available to members only.

PUBLICATIONS AND WEBSITES

Business Travel News (BTN)

http://www.businesstravelnews.com

BusinessTravelNews.com is a respected resource for corporate travel buyers that delivers news and research for organizations that manage travel. The website provides daily news updates and a searchable archive of the print issues. News topics are categorized by these topics: Distribution, Lodging, Payment, Transportation, Meetings, Management, Multinational, and Procurement. Research publications, all of which are available for free, include the Corporate Travel Index, BTN's Airline Survey, *Vision 2020: Projecting the Future of Business Travel*, and BTN's Hotel Chain Survey.

Buying Business Travel

http://buyingbusinesstravel.com

A London-based publication, *Buying Business Travel* is for travel and meetings buyers and arrangers. You can find top stories, featured articles, latest news, white papers, e-learning courses, and a discussion forum. The Databank section provides access to infographics, depicting current statistics from all travel sectors.

Corporate and Incentive Travel

http://www.themeetingmagazines.com/corporate-incentive-travel

Corporate and Incentive Travel provides the latest industry trends, news on new and expanded venues, technology, and in-depth profiles of popular meeting destinations. Also on the same website: *Association Conventions and Facilities*, and *Insurance and Financial Meetings Management*.

Gillespie's Guide to Travel and Procurement

http://gillespie411.wordpress.com

Since 2009, strategic sourcing consultant Scott Gillespie has been writing a blog that focuses on corporate travel procurement and management. Gillespie includes many tools, tips, articles, and white papers, in addition to a "Travel 101" section for new buyers. Popular posts include "The Future for Travel Management Companies," "KPI Toolkit for Travel Managers," and "Key Principles of Managed Travel 2.0."

Meetings and Conventions

http://www.meetings-conventions.com

Meetings and Conventions is an online resource from Northstar Travel Media Sites, for meeting, trade show, and convention planning professionals. A print version is available for free to qualified requestors. The website features national and international destination guides, news and feature articles, research, white papers, and poll results. The Tools section provides links to helpful resources such as the latest U.S. Department of State travel warnings; metric measurement converters; passport information; and event budget, seating, and annual meeting cost calculators.

MeetingsNet

http://meetingsnet.com

The MeetingsNet website provides "the meeting industry content for market-segmented meeting decision-makers." Under the Event Management section, there is a Negotiations/Contracts subcategory. Other content on the website include Corporate Meetings, Medical Meetings, Association Meetings, and Global Events.

Successful Meetings

http://www.successfulmeetings.com

Successful Meetings is an online source for news and information for meetings, conventions, incentives, and trade show professionals. The Best Practices section covers the topic of negotiations and contracts. Research and white papers can be found in the News section, along with hotel and destination updates.

Supply Management—Business Travel Page

http://www.supplymanagement.com/topics/business-travel

The Supply Management—Business Travel Page features articles on all segments of corporate travel including air, hotel, meetings and events, and travel management.

Travel Procurement

http://www.omeda.com/cgi-win/prome.cgi

Travel Procurement is a free quarterly print publication that provides trends, case studies, market intelligence, analysis, and benchmarks specifically intended to help travel procurement professionals in all areas, from sourcing to reporting.

ASSOCIATIONS AND ORGANIZATIONS

Association of Corporate Travel Executives

https://www.acte.org

The Association of Corporate Travel Executives (ACTE) is a global educational association that advocates for global corporate travel buyers, agencies, and suppliers. Members represent more than 100 countries and are all executive level. The Global Centre for Research and Education, available through ACTE Connect is where members can find industry research, webinars, white papers, and best practices information.

Global Business Travel Association

http://www.gbta.org

The Global Business Travel Association (GBTA) is an organization for business travel and meeting managers, as well as travel service providers. The organization has more than 5,000 members and provides networking events, news, education and professional development, research, and advocacy. The GBTA offers the Global Travel Professional™ (GTP) Certification through the GBTA Academy. Members can browse and access resources by category, where a robust library offers a comprehensive and current collection of documents and webinars.

U.S. Travel Association

http://www.ustravel.org

The mission of the U.S. Travel Association is to increase travel to and within the United States. Research reports and services that are valuable to travel buyers are *US Travel Outlook*, which examines current industry trends; Travel Industry Forecasts; U.S. Travel Tracker; and, the Travel Price Index (TPI). Industry News is also provided under the News tab on the website.

MeetingMagazines.com Industry and Professional Associations

http://www.themeetingmagazines.com/resources/industry-associations

MeetingMagazines.com lists more than 35 associations that are useful to travel and meeting planners and buyers.

Meeting Professionals International (MPI)

http://www.mpiweb.org

Meeting Professionals International (MPI) provides its members with education, networking opportunities, research, and planning tools. The quarterly report, *Meetings Outlook*, identifies new trends and innovations on the horizon to help with budgeting and planning. MPI, along with GBTA, have joined to create the CMM Designation Program, which is described as "The Business Standard of Excellence for Meeting and Travel Professionals."

REFERENCES

1. "U.S. Travel and Answer Sheet," *US Travel Association*, March, 2014, http://www.ustravel.org/sites/default/files/page/2009/09/US_Travel_AnswerSheet_March_2014.pdf.
2. Andrew Bartolini, "Procurement's Evolution, Part II: Convergence with Travel," *CPO Rising*, February 3, 2014, http://cporising.com/2014/02/03/procurements-evolution-part-ii-convergence-with-travel.
3. Louis Berard, "The Travel and Expense Management Guide for 2014: Trends for the Future," *Aberdeen Group*, March 1, 2014, http://www.aberdeen.com/Aberdeen-Library/8849/RA-travel-expense-management.aspx.

4. AirPlus, "Buying Business Travel: Managing Costs and Driving Policy Compliance," *Supply Business*, Accessed September 6, 2014, http://www.supplybusiness.com/white-papers/airplus-buying-business-travel-download/.
5. *Ibid.*
6. Mark O'Brien, "Beginner's Guide to Travel Compliance," *Supply Management*, February 13, 2014, http://www.supplymanagement.com/analysis/features/2014/beginners-guide-to-travel-compliance.

INDEX